The Last Crusade

The Last Crusade

*Martin Luther King, Jr.,
the FBI, and the Poor
People's Campaign*

Gerald D. McKnight

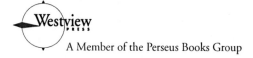

Westview
PRESS

A Member of the Perseus Books Group

Copyright © 1998 by Westview Press, A Member of Perseus Books Group

Published in 1998 in the United States of America by Westview Press, 5500 Central Avenue, Boulder, Colorado 80301–2877, and in the United Kingdom by Westview Press, 12 Hid's Copse Road, Cumnor Hill, Oxford OX2 9JJ

Library of Congress Cataloging-in-Publication Data
McKnight, Gerald.
    The last crusade : Martin Luther King, Jr., the FBI, and the Poor
People's Campaign / Gerald D. McKnight.
        p.   cm.
    Includes bibliographical references and index.
    ISBN 0-8133-3384-9 (hc)
    1. King, Martin Luther, Jr., 1929–1968.   2. United States.
Federal Bureau of Investigation.   3. Hoover, J. Edgar (John Edgar),
1895–1972.   4. Poor People's Campaign.   5. United States—Race
relations.   6. Internal security—United States—History—20th
century.   I. Title.
E185.97.K5M38   1998
364.15'24'092—dc21   97-36992
                                                                                     CIP

The paper used in this publication meets the requirements of the American National Standard for Permanence of Paper for Printed Library Materials Z39.48–1984.

PERSEUS
POD
ON DEMAND   10   9   8   7   6   5   4   3   2   1

Contents

The Last Crusade

Introduction

IN THE FALL OF 1963 senior Federal Bureau of Investigation (FBI) official William C. Sullivan made a career-threatening mistake: He tried to persuade his boss that the civil rights movement was not Communist-controlled. In September 1963 the FBI intelligence chief submitted a 70-page analysis to FBI Director J. Edgar Hoover concluding that efforts by Communists to infiltrate the civil rights movement were remarkably unsuccessful. Sullivan took this action because he regarded the bureau's ongoing marathon probe of the racial justice movement a colossal waste of agency manpower that could be diverted to legitimate and essential investigative purposes. Sullivan hoped the report's findings would convince "The Boss" to reorder his priorities.

Alerted by the announced August 1963 March on Washington, Hoover had authorized Sullivan's Domestic Intelligence Division (DID) to probe for covert subversive elements at the core of the racial movement. Angered over the report's conclusion, the director scornfully rejected it out of hand. Hoover was convinced that the March on Washington was the opening campaign of a social revolution manipulated by Communists and therefore posing a direct threat to the nation's security. The 1963 March on Washington was a defining event for the director. Before the year was over, Hoover decided to use the formidable powers of his agency to destroy the civil rights movement.

Bureau intelligence chief Sullivan, the number-four man in the FBI at the time and the most likely successor to the aging director, felt the sting of his boss's displeasure over the September report's assertion that the Communists had failed to make any impact on the civil rights movement. Hoover taunted and belittled his intelligence chief for ignoring the director's stock maxim that "Communism must be built with non-Communist hands." Fearing a reversal of his own career fortunes, a repentant Sullivan pleaded with Hoover for another chance to flush out all the facts about the alarming extent of Communist penetration of the civil rights movement and influence over the movement's leadership.[1]

1

Hoover relented when Sullivan suggested an aggressive counterintelligence program (COINTELPRO) aimed at Dr. Martin Luther King, Jr., one calculated "to take him off his pedestal" by destroying his reputation and influence within the black community. (COINTELPRO was the FBI's acronym for numerous programs undertaken against individuals and groups targeted by the Hoover Bureau to be discredited, immobilized, and destroyed.) The director approved of Sullivan's recommended course of action and wrote on the memo, "I am glad to see that 'light' has finally, though dismally delayed, come to the Domestic Int. Div. I struggled for months," he went on in his spidery scrawl, "to get over the fact that the Communists were taking over the racial movement but our experts here wouldn't or couldn't see."[2]

Once Sullivan saw the "light," he zealously employed resources and skills of the Domestic Intelligence Division to wage a secret war against King for the next five years in order to destroy his reputation as a national civil rights leader and immobilize his organization, the Southern Christian Leadership Conference (SCLC). With Hoover's approval, Sullivan's division recommended inviting some of the bureau's "highly placed contacts" to meet privately with top FBI officials to discuss ways to ease King from the national scene. Civil rights moderate Roy Wilkins, the prestigious executive director of the National Association for the Advancement of Colored People (NAACP), had several discussions with a senior bureau official, but he later adamantly denied engaging in any plotting to oust King. Sullivan was not discouraged by his apparent failure to recruit Wilkins. This COINTELPRO effort to convince national black leaders that King was, in Sullivan's words, "a fraud, demagogue, and scoundrel" and an unwitting Communist dupe and therefore a clear and present danger to the civil rights movement remained an ongoing high-priority campaign throughout 1964.

Counting on the success of the anti-King campaign, Sullivan proposed to replace King as a national black leader with his own candidate, whom he characterized as "a truly brilliant, honorable and loyal Negro who would steer the 19 million Negroes away from communism." The intelligence chief's choice of a "right-thinking" black leader to replace King was Samuel R. Pierce, Jr., a prominent Manhattan lawyer, a registered Republican, and an African American who, as one newspaper story reported, "was not known as a civil rights activist." Apparently Pierce was never approached and remained unaware at the time of Sullivan's glowing recommendation and the lofty mission envisioned by his admiring FBI sponsor.[3]

Sullivan's agile shifting of his evaluation of the civil rights movement was a common survival strategy for top officials in Hoover's FBI. "Life in the circus," Sullivan's characterization after 30 years in the Hoover Bureau, was possible only if one cardinal operating principle was strictly observed: The director was always correct.[4] However, this is not to imply that Sullivan and the other dozen or so division chiefs and assistant directors were simply placemen devoted only to their careers. These internal security executives were an educated, resourceful, highly motivated, and action-oriented political elite. Their vision of what America should be made no allowances for student rebellions, war dissenters, beatniks, and black protesters at sit-ins and marches. They used their considerable talents, awesome power, and wide-ranging influence to turn back those forces of the 1960s calling for a transformation of national politics, culture, and society. All middle-aged or older white men, they did not question as unbecoming the racist culture that permeated the Hoover-era FBI, even if they did not all share the director's obsessive racism. But as a group they shared the director's near-religious conviction that white over black was the natural order of things in America's racial state. They worked with the director to ensure that the FBI's values would influence the way the federal government would deal with its nonwhite citizens.

In 1967 Hoover and his top internal security chiefs escalated their political warfare against King to a new level of intensity when the SCLC announced its intention to bring an army of the poor to Washington to pressure the government to address the pressing needs of the politically unrepresented and the economically dispossessed. In light of the SCLC's projected Washington campaign, FBI elites decided to single out King for special attention. According to bureau ideological standards, King was now no longer viewed as a troublesome "racial agitator" but as the most dangerous radical in America and a diabolical threat to Hoover's way of life, his bureaucracy, and his vision of a white Christian racial state where blacks knew their place.

That same year King went through an agonizing reappraisal of long-held beliefs and principles. During this last year of his life he suspended his earlier convictions that white racism could be overcome by appealing to the nation's moral conscience with the positive creative force of Christian love. He no longer believed that white America had a moral conscience. More specifically, Vietnam-era America, King believed, was ridden with racism at home and economic exploitation and rampant militarism abroad. Part of the reason for his radical transformation was the realization that the civil rights movement was at an impasse. Despite the civil rights victories since 1954, King was painfully aware that most black Americans had barely moved forward at all. The legislative triumphs embodied in the 1964 Civil Rights Act and the Voting Rights Act of 1965 did precious little to improve the lot of millions of blacks living in the ghettos of the North, a bitter irony recognized by King. To King's mind, America was a sick society that could not be turned around by piecemeal reform. He had reluctantly come to the view that a revolution in values ignited by a profound reorganization of society, including the redistribution of economic and political power, was necessary to redeem the soul of his nation.

In place of the praying and marching tactics of the civil rights movement, the SCLC now opted for more dramatic, militant direct-action programs to shake the foundations of the power structure to make it responsive to the needs of the nation's poor. The SCLC's march on Washington—the so-called Poor People's Campaign—was scheduled for the spring of 1968. The key to King's radical transformation was his shift away from classical civil rights issues to social justice causes involving all the nation's poor: southern rural and northern ghetto blacks, Appalachian whites, Mexican Americans, and Native Americans. King's plan was to bring thousands of poor people to the nation's capital to virtually camp out on the doorsteps of government to arouse a moribund Congress and pressure it into passing an Economic Bill of Rights. King's crusading agenda called for the same sweeping reforms in employment, education, welfare, and housing that President Lyndon B. Johnson's National Advisory Committee of Civil Disorders urged in its 1968 high-priority report to reverse the deepening racial and economic divisions plaguing American society.

Today, when professional historians write about the past, they try to explain it through large impersonal forces and structures. The bureaucratic structure that Hoover created during his five decades as FBI director was strikingly sui generis, an anomaly among other government bureaus and divisions. No other bureau chief ever dominated his subordinates with such an iron hand; the line of command in the Hoover Bureau running from the director's office to all 59 field offices was uncompromisingly rigid, meaning that there was little receptive audience at the top for independent thinking and the views of Hoover's own professional experts and technicians. Hierarchy, not functional status and trust in subordinates, was Hoover's administrative style. During the 1950s and 1960s Hoover could hire, fire, promote, or transfer agents at whim, since there was no external review of his personnel policies and therefore no recourse for appeal by aggrieved employees. No other bureau chief or division head in government had this kind of discretionary power. In addition to being exempt from Civil Service regulations because of the FBI's national security mission, the director's budgetary requests were almost always automatically approved by a deferential and thankful Congress with only pro forma oversight of how Hoover allocated these tax dollars.[5]

According to one student of the FBI, the agency began the 1960s as a "thoroughly rationalized bureaucratic structure" combined with certain "atavistic elements." The primary atavism was the director's authoritarian personality—that impelling, unchecked force that dominated the nation's preeminent law enforcement agency. Structure and personality were virtually inseparable in Hoover's FBI.[6]

Current scholarship making up the body of FBI historiography supports the view that J. Edgar Hoover was a genius at empire building, public relations, and political maneuvering but generally finds little that was admirable in his personality. The general consensus is that he was ruthless, suspicious, willful, petty, vindictive, and a passionate racist.[7]

It is a matter of public record that King's private lifestyle was never respected or off-limits to FBI snooping once he became a subject of Hoover Bureau surveillance. The director on one occasion, with his typical "blue ink" comments on a memo, referred to King as a "tom cat" possessed "with obsessive degenerate sexual urges." It was Sullivan's DID, with Hoover's approval, that manufactured the infamous package containing a tape-recording fabricated in the FBI laboratory of King's alleged sexual activities in the Willard Hotel in Washington, D.C., along with a threatening note calculated to panic King into committing suicide in 1964. The unmarked package was addressed to King at his SCLC headquarters in Atlanta.[8]

King was not, of course, the only black American Hoover detested or had reason to fear because he saw all black Americans as a threat to his white republic. King, however, was a special case because of his prominence and because of the aging director's obsessive and neurotic hatred of him and what he represented. Hoover hated his color, his lifestyle, and his politics. The most revealing evidence of Hoover's obsessive and consuming animus was the FBI's mammoth intelligence file on King.

During the 1970s Congress launched the first systematic investigation into America's intelligence community, including the FBI.[9] The disturbing FBI abuses of power unearthed by these investigations—dubbed the "Hoover horrors" by some of the press—prompted the Justice Department to open its own investigation into the Hoover FBI's private war against King. To conduct its review, Justice asked the FBI for "every single item in your files which relates in any way to Dr. King, his family, friends, associates or SCLC." Assigning the "highest priority" to the review, the attorney general asked for an inventory of all FBI headquarters and field office files in order to expedite the request.[10]

The attorney general's request unleashed an avalanche of bureaucratic paper. The inventories from the 59 FBI field offices alone comprised an impressive 404-page document. FBI Washington headquarters (FBIHQ) failed to create an inventory, but the Justice task force examined over 200,000 pages of King material separately held by FBIHQ. Since the entries in the field office inventories are recorded as "serials" and not pages (each serial is a separate document and is almost always more than one page), an exact page count is impossible. A conservative conversion into pages of the 185,152 field office serials would be at least 500,000 pages.

However, there is good reason to believe that this represents only the tip of the proverbial iceberg. In all likelihood the FBI's intelligence file on King is well over a million pages.[11]

The iceberg metaphor is fitting because at the very start of the review process FBIHQ directed all field offices to limit their inventories to "pertinent main files only." In narrowing the search to only the main King files, FBIHQ conspired to withhold a vast amount of material on King from Justice's task force. For example, by hijacking the review process, bureau elites at FBIHQ contrived to suppress from the public record COINTEL-PROS targeted at King and the SCLC, intelligence gathered from wiretaps and "bugs," and files revealing other illegal and punitive intrusions into King's life and the agency's deliberate campaigns to thwart the efforts of black Americans to achieve equality so long denied them.[12]

Regardless of what still lies hidden below the surface there is one certainty that eliminates all guesswork: The FBI's record in the matter of Martin Luther King, Jr., bears the unmistakable stamp of Hoover's personal influence and his consuming hatred for the civil rights leader. What the public record reveals about the FBI's King file makes it hard to resist the appalling conclusion that this Nobelist and one of the most recognized, respected, and honored Americans of the twentieth century was at the time of his death probably the most harassed, hounded, and investigated citizen in the history of the Republic.

The massive FBI King file was a bonanza of irony. The enormous unrecorded cost in taxpayers' dollars to amass this intelligence record must have been in the millions of dollars. The Hoover Bureau's vendetta against King consumed money and manpower that would have better served society had it been directed to combat serious and unlawful threats—corruption in the public sector, organized criminal conspiracies, domestic terrorism, and white collar crime. While FBI agents piled up tens of thousands of surveillance hours on King and such SCLC-directed movements as the Poor People's Campaign, the Hoover Bureau missed its one certain chance to destroy King.

While a doctoral candidate at Boston University (BU) in the 1950s, the 26-year-old King knowingly pirated the work of a former BU student to complete the dissertation he submitted in fulfillment of his Ph.D. program. His plagiarism was not only the most deep-dyed of academic transgressions; it was a mistake that could have ruined King and seriously impaired the black freedom struggle.[13]

Had the FBI discovered King's plagiarism, Sullivan's DID would have had all it needed to bring King down. Once a case was assigned top priority status, especially one like this with the widest-ranging political implications, the FBI was nothing if not painstakingly thorough. Teams of FBI agents would have pored over King's academic writings at BU and

Crozer Theological Seminary and probably any extant term papers he wrote during his undergraduate days at Morehouse. Time and expense would not have been a concern as the FBI put together an iron-clad case that in his student days King was a chronic plagiarist. For instance, before the FBI identified James Earl Ray as its prime suspect in the King assassination, all it had to work with was the name "Eric Starvo Galt," lifted off the registration card in the suspected getaway car. Alerted by some public-spirited citizens that authors Ayn Rand and Ian Fleming had created characters in their novels named John Galt and Ernest Starvo Blofeld, the bureau assigned teams of agents to index all of their works for other names the fugitive might use to falsify his identity to avoid capture.[14]

Almost certainly the bureau would have gone public with a relentless and hard-hitting campaign of carefully documented charges of intellectual dishonesty, ethical misconduct, and moral wrongdoing. Faced with the evidence that he stole his dissertation, it is hard to see how King could have continued as an effective public figure and have held claim to being a responsible leader and the greatest living American spokesman for racial and social justice. A new national spokesman or coalition of black leaders might have tried to replace King on the civil rights front. But the greater likelihood was that a climate of fear and timidity would have eroded the will and creative energies of America's black leadership as they witnessed the FBI's systematic demolition of the nation's most celebrated race leader.

While Hoover and his bureau elites may have been only one turn of the screw away from destroying King, the agency was still in a unique position in the 1960s to derail the struggle for racial justice and economic equality. Moreover, the FBI's sleeves-rolled-up campaign against King and the poor people's movement enjoyed added firepower because it was encouraged by Capitol Hill lawmakers and responsible government officials. Angered and frustrated that massive southern white resistance failed to smother the civil rights movement, congressional segregationists of every political hue and regional label took every legislative opportunity to rally behind the Hoover Bureau's law-and-order politics of race. The decade's cold war culture of almost-anything-goes-counterinsurgency that touched much official thinking smoothed the way for the acceptance of the FBI's new threat assessment emphasizing the Black Menace over the Red Menace as the nation's number-one internal security problem. The semiautonomous FBI found it expedient to work in tandem with military intelligence in pervasive spying and intelligence gathering on King and the Poor People's Campaign. In fact, it was a COINTELPRO originating from Sullivan's Domestic Intelligence Division that had nothing to do with internal security or proper federal interest of any kind that guaranteed that King would return to Memphis where he was assassinated.

Even Ramsey Clark, the president's liberal attorney general, who did more than any other prominent official in the executive branch to see that the poor people's movement not be turned away from the nation's capital without some victories, was not immune to the Black Menace hysteria. Clark was the founding father of the Johnson administration's so-called community surveillance program, a massive domestic intelligence apparatus targeted at black urban America. It was the president's politically convenient pet thesis that the ghetto rebellions of the 1960s were the work of small cadres of black conspirators. Johnson believed that the community surveillance and intelligence-gathering program coordinated by operatives from the Justice Department, military intelligence, and the FBI would give the government the inside track on when the next ghetto would "blow," allowing the government to take preemptive action. Although the whole concept was spectacularly wrongheaded, it reflected the hold the mystique of counterinsurgency had on official Washington.

By 1968 events had pushed the nation farther and farther away from the "Somedays" of King's well-known dream speech of five years earlier. This was reflected in the way official Washington responded to the Poor People's Campaign. On the whole the Johnson administration reacted as though the campaigners were an invading horde from a strange land intent on the violent disruption of the government rather than fellow Americans, most of whom were underprivileged and powerless nonwhite citizens. Many Kennedy-Johnson government liberals acted no differently than as if they had signed on as outriders in Hoover's private war against King and the poor people's movement. Even though these self-professed racial liberals found the FBI's petty harassment, surveillance, Red-baiting, leaking of derogatory information to the media, and other more disruptive tactics objectionable, still little was done to check the bureau's wide-ranging assaults on citizens who were properly engaged in their constitutional rights of political association and assembly. A cold reality about this decade of Kennedy-Johnson liberalism was that government officials in positions of authority over Hoover and his agency chiefs were men who counseled and approved, at least tacitly and often directly, the sort of secret war for which the Hoover Bureau became notorious.

History, we are told, does not repeat itself but, as Mark Twain observed, it does rhyme. Over the broad sweep of U.S. history democracy has not been in abundant supply where race is concerned. Periods of racial reform marked by suitably moderate political victories that strengthen democracy do occur, but these reforms are usually placed at risk from authoritarian movements that seek to restore the old racial order. The story of America has been in part the story of a racial state historically at odds with its own celebrated creed and professed values and the treatment of its nonwhite citizens. In the challenge posed by King's last crusade, the relationship between government leaders and the Poor People's Campaign was a microcosm of this larger history.

The animating spirit that encouraged many of the poor to come to Washington was the belief that the Poor People's Campaign would end poverty or, at least, prompt the government to take swift action to ameliorate its effects. Civil rights–era America had fostered a consensus among the poor, especially in the South, that all justice resided in Washington. It was federal legislation that had initiated any advances in civil rights against the apartheid politics of the Wallaces and Maddoxes. When they packed their meager belongings into cardboard boxes and boarded the Greyhound buses for the nation's capital, the poor were sustained by the hope that a sympathetic nation would rally around their campaign and force a distracted and uncaring Congress to commit itself to ending poverty instead of ending the Great Society's poverty programs. Going to Washington to air grievances and seek relief was as American as cherry pie. If history is any guide, mass citizen action in the nation's capital is consistent with the character of the American people who have at times expressed their frustration with government by organizing to take charge of events rather than waiting for the government to "get it."

In view of the marathon eulogies pouring forth in the immediate aftermath of King's assassination, it did not seem idle to imagine that the nation might rally to redeem itself. It was not irresponsible to think that King's poor people's movement, his "moral alternative to riots," was a timely and necessary course given the firestorm of violence that shook the nation after his murder. Even though the Poor People's Campaign failed to match the worthiness of its cause, it was discouragingly clear from the outset that a majority of the Congress remained insensitive and unmoved about the plight of the poor. The poor and powerless, especially the majority of the campaigners from the South, learned that official Washington was no more receptive to their call for help than were white lawmakers in Montgomery, Atlanta, Richmond, and Jackson, Mississippi. The campaign's basic demands for decent jobs, housing, and income were in full accord with justice, the promises made by Great Society liberals and the incumbent administration's openly declared war on poverty, and the long-standing government practice of subsidizing the rich and the super-rich. But the poor people's lobby won no significant victories in 1968. The least powerful and unrepresented were sent home to coexist with hunger and hopelessness by a nation awash in superaffluence and distracted by a costly and divisive Asian war.

During project POCAM the FBI marshalled its awesome resources to propagate the thesis that the Poor People's Campaign was instigated by a subversive conspiracy. (POCAM was the code name for the Poor People's Campaign in all internal FBI communications relating to this project, which had initially been identified as the Washington Spring Project. Outside the FBI the Poor People's Campaign was sometimes referred to as PPC.) Hoover and his executive officers used every opportunity to intensify the siege mentality gripping the federal government as it prepared for the army of the poor converging on the nation's capital. The bureau used a massive disinformation operation that cynically manipulated the facts to conform to the director's conspiracy theories and racist law-and-order values to shape the government's perception of the poverty campaigners. In the starkest terms, Hoover and his division chiefs used their considerable influence and power within the federal bureaucracy to set the government and the SCLC's poor people's movement on a collision course. It was a shameful and intolerable fact of American democracy that legitimate and pressing social issues brought to Washington for a fair hearing had to run a gauntlet of FBI wrecking tactics.

one

King, Vietnam, and the Transformation of the Civil Rights Movement

NINETEEN SIXTY SEVEN WAS A YEAR of decision for King. After several false starts, he came out irrevocably against the Johnson administration's war in Vietnam. King had concluded that America was a sick society unable to be reformed by piecemeal measures. The civil rights leader was convinced that a revolution in values, one ignited by a profound societal reorganization resulting in a redistribution of economic and political power, was essential to redeem the soul of America. To accomplish some fundamental change, King and the SCLC planned a new march on Washington to shake the foundations of the power structure and make it responsive to the needs of the nation's dispossessed. Under King's direction the SCLC was planning a radical transformation of the civil rights movement.

By 1965 the U.S. involvement in Vietnam and the civil rights movement were moving along diametrically opposed courses. That year President Lyndon B. Johnson began the buildup of ground forces in the south and the bombing of North Vietnam, code named Rolling Thunder. The administration's domestic energies were focused increasingly on marshalling public opinion behind the White House's crusade to save South Vietnam from Asian communism. That same year King joined with dissenters against Johnson's Asian war, convinced that recent gains on the civil rights front would be jeopardized by new war demands. His role of foreign policy critic was sporadic and tentative, and before the year's end King backed away from the war issue, wary that his opposition might damage the SCLC, the civil rights movement, and his own reputation.[1]

Throughout most of 1966 King tried to avoid taking a public stand on the war. He steadfastly refused to associate himself with the mushrooming peace rallies and held back from any public discussions of Vietnam. His early reluctance to join the antiwar movement was not rooted in uncertainty about the wisdom of U.S. involvement. King was firm in his own mind that the war was a monumental historical mistake, but he was torn between the dictates of conscience and the dynamics of real world politics. As the nation's most prominent civil rights leader, he could not give free rein to his foreign policy views without jeopardizing his relationship with the Johnson administration and alienating a significant segment of his following.

King was especially sensitive about the polarizing effect of the war issue on the black community. Most blacks then regarded Johnson as America's greatest civil rights president. They were not unmindful of the way he cajoled, threatened, and lobbied through Congress the 1964 Civil Rights Act and the Voting Rights Act a year later, landmark legislation that President John F. Kennedy thought politically impossible to pass. "Big Daddy" from the Pedernales had pulled out all the stops to lay the legislative foundation blocks of the civil rights revolution, and to deny him support over a foreign war struck many blacks as towering ingratitude as well as unsound politics. Although more wary of Johnson than most of his movement colleagues, King still held the Texan in a certain esteem. In the 1964 presidential campaign, the SCLC unofficially but actively worked for Johnson against his "law-and-order" opponent Senator Barry Goldwater (R-Ariz.), whom King regarded as a potential American Gauleiter intent on transforming the Republican party into a white man's party.[2]

King had experienced the polarizing effects of Vietnam on the black community. In August 1965 the SCLC failed to endorse a King initiative calling for an end to the war even if it meant negotiating with the National Liberation Front, the political arm of the Vietcong. Linking civil rights with the antiwar movement struck most of the delegates at the SCLC's annual convention as too dangerously radical. Senior movement colleagues and advisers were quick to signal the 39-year-old minister that he had drifted into politically deep and dangerous waters. Bayard Rustin, one of King's erstwhile advisers and the organizational genius behind the 1963 March on Washington, urged the SCLC to dodge the war issue; otherwise, Rustin cautioned, it would be making a grave tactical error that would split the civil rights movement, alienate the White House, and erode prospects for future social reforms. Other black leaders reiterated the same theme of cautiousness. "Johnson needs a consensus," counseled the Urban League's Whitney Young. "If we are not with him on Vietnam, then he is not going to be with us on civil rights."[3]

By 1967 the Vietnam conflict was at full throttle. Mounting American casualties attested to the war's growing ferocity, and home front opinion—both for and against the war—was hardening. For King, the political arguments for avoiding the war issue were no longer compelling. Civil rights no longer commanded presidential interest, Congress had moved hard to the right, and the civil rights movement was at an impasse and was disintegrating. After several months' absence from public attention, King appeared in Los Angeles at a conference organized by *The Nation* magazine as the main speaker on the Vietnam War. His February 25, 1967, address—entitled "The Casualties of the War in Vietnam"—was, in its timing and spirit, King's antiwar commencement address, notifying well-wishers and critics that he had joined the ranks of the dissenters. This time, unlike 1965, he would not draw back; he would not betray his conscience by seeking refuge in silence; he would be heard.[4]

King's public and irrevocable break with Johnson's war was a consummation of more than two years of intense introspection and profound questioning about the state of the nation. King biographer David J. Garrow noted that the recognition of receiving the Nobel Peace Prize in 1964 "signaled the beginning of a fundamental growth in King's own sense of mission and willingness to accept a prophetic role." Like the Old Testament prophets, King broke his silence to speak words that the nation did not want to hear. Increasingly his style took on a controlled and harsh edge in public comments about economic America, the threatening role America played in the world, and the values of most white Americans.[5]

King was becoming more preoccupied with economic justice issues. Economic ideas having a social democratic slant that were foreshadowed in his earlier writings took on sharper programmatic focus as they moved to the top of King's new reform agenda. In a November 1966 address at Howard University in the nation's capital, King reminded his relatively affluent and socially upscale black audience that they had a responsibility to confront "basic issues between the privileged and the underprivileged." A month earlier at an SCLC strategy session, he laid out a three-point program to reanimate his languishing organization. One of the proposed initiatives was the mobilization of the nation's poor in a "crusade to reform society in order to realize economic and social justice." That same year King adopted the idea of a guaranteed annual wage put forward by Bayard Rustin and A. Philip Randolph in their 1966 "Freedom Budget," even if it meant mass protests to create the necessary political will in an increasingly unresponsive Congress.[6]

King's emergent radicalism was fostered by his mounting despair over the callous and reactionary political climate in Washington. The White House's earlier boastful assurances of "guns and butter" was proving a cruel hoax. Johnson's 1966 civil rights bill containing the strong open housing title died in the Senate, largely because the White House, distracted by the Vietnam War, never bothered to lobby the leaders of the political opposition in the upper house. Before the year ended the Congress slashed the budget of the Office of Economic Opportunity, reducing the War on Poverty funds by half a billion dollars and slicing dollars available for "community action" programs by a third. A distracted, uncaring President Johnson and spiraling war costs had turned the Great Society's war against poverty into a war against the poor; a war Republicans would later wage even more fiercely.[7]

By 1967 King had changed his earlier convictions that white racism could be overcome by appealing to the nation's moral conscience with the positive and creative force of Christian love. He was no longer certain that Vietnam War–era America had a moral conscience. In concluding his testimony before a Senate committee at year's end, King voiced his somber perspective on the country's racial dilemma when he said that "America as a nation has never committed itself to solving the problems of its Negro citizens."[8]

King had already crossed his Rubicon on Vietnam before he delivered his most powerful and well-known statement against the war at the Riverside Church in New York City on April 4, 1967. The congregation of about 3,000 heard King explain, in his best cultivated pastoral style, why a civil rights leader and man of the cloth felt compelled to oppose his government's Vietnam policy.

The message of "Beyond Vietnam" was not tailored, however, simply to give King full scope to his rhetorical prowess. The main body of his text was a radical critique of America's foreign policy and the counterinsurgency role U.S. policy was playing in the international arena. King stunned many of his followers when he expressed sympathy for the Vietcong and the emergent revolutionary movements shaping the politics of the Third World. Under the shibboleth of anticommunism the United States had become, King charged, "the greatest purveyor of violence in the world today." Going well beyond the liberal critique of Vietnam, he saw the war not as an aberration of U.S. policy but as "a symptom of a far deeper malady within the American spirit, and if we ignore that sobering reality," he admonished his audience, "[we] will find ourselves organizing clergy-and-laymen committees for the next generation." King urged that America cease being the bastion of reaction and "get on the right side of the world revolution." He went on to call for a five-point policy, including the immediate halt to the bombing of North Vietnam, the recognition of the National Liberation Front, and a unilateral cease-fire. "To atone for our sins and errors" in Vietnam, King proposed reparations "for the damage we have done."[9]

The historic Riverside Church speech ignited a firestorm of criticism through the black community, the media, and the federal government. Prominent black leaders rushed to distance themselves and the civil rights movement from King's ringing denunciation of the government's

Vietnam policy. The NAACP and the Urban League rejected King's dissent on the war out of hand. Senator Edward Brooke (R-Mass.), the only black lawmaker in the upper house, and United Nations Under-Secretary-General Ralph Bunche joined the list of eminent blacks who publicly registered shock and disapproval of the April 4, 1967, speech. They criticized King for the grave tactical error of linking racial reform with the peace movement, thereby risking future civil rights advances, and for poor judgment in publicly attacking Johnson's war policy. Bunche was so incensed with King's merging of the two movements that he insisted publicly that King "give up one role or the other. The two efforts," Bunche contended, "have too little in common." Privately, some, like arch-rival Roy Wilkins, the NAACP's executive secretary, took delight in needling King, accusing him of self-indulgent grandstanding to attract media attention.[10]

"Beyond Vietnam" drew a sharp rebuke from those bastions of eastern journalistic liberalism, the *New York Times* and the *Washington Post*. Like most of the national media at the time, these newspapers interpreted the war within the rigid framework of cold war geopolitics that made fundamental questioning of U.S. policy unthinkable. The *Washington Post*, for example, a steady and vigorous supporter of King and the civil rights movement, attacked the Riverside Church address as "a great tragedy." "Many who have listened to him with respect," an editorial opined, "will never again accord him the same confidence. He has diminished his usefulness to the cause, to his country and his people." Although equally condemning, an editorial in the *New York Times*, entitled "Dr. King's Error," was also laced with patronizing elitism and subtle racism. The editorial berated King for merging the war with civil rights reform. Even though King may have been well intentioned, the *Times* allowed, he was misled and out of his depth in plunging into a complex issue like Vietnam. King would do best, the editorial concluded, if he confined his energies to civil rights matters and left the more recondite questions of geopolitics to the experts.[11]

The FBI pounced on the Riverside Church speech to draw renewed momentum for its ongoing campaign to destroy King's effectiveness as a civil rights leader. Six days after the New York address, Hoover approved an updating of the so-called King monograph and ordered the DID to send copies to the White House and highly placed Washington officials. The document included allegations about Communist influence over King and materials described by Burke Marshall, a civil rights troubleshooter in the Kennedy Justice Department, as a "personal diatribe . . . a personal attack without evidentiary support." In addition to the copy sent to the White House, the revised monograph was circulated to the secretary of state, the secretary of defense, the director of the Secret Service, and the attorney general. A copy subsequently was forwarded to the commandant of the Marine Corps, a variation on the usual dissemination pattern, because the nation's top leatherneck was troubled about possible subversive influences prompting King to link civil rights with the anti–Vietnam War movement.[12]

It is only possible to guess at the impact of the FBI campaign within the higher reaches of the federal government. Some officials, like Burke Marshall, discounted the campaign as "the old Hoover stuff," wanton character assassination pure and simple. Most officials probably were taken in by the copious flow of FBI reports like the monograph, letters, phone calls, and discreet visits from highly placed FBI officials and were receptive to charges that King was "following the communist line." Hoover's chief lobbyist on Capitol Hill, Deputy Director Cartha D. DeLoach, routinely briefed members of Congress on the material in the King monograph. After an office visit from DeLoach, Senator Thomas J. Dodd (D-Conn.), moderately liberal on the civil rights issue and a supporter of King, criticized King's Vietnam position and backed away from the civil rights movement. Presidential aide Harry McPherson began referring to King as "the crown prince of the Vietniks." Roger Wilkins, the highest-ranking black in Johnson's Justice Department, recalled that after King came out against the war, Johnson's "soul hardened against us then . . . and he liked very few of us."[13]

President Johnson wanted to know what was behind King's Riverside Church speech, and the FBI was quick to respond. A stream of FBI intelligence summaries designed to set off whistles and bells poured into the Oval Office. These summaries went directly to Mildred Stegall, the designated White House recipient of all sensitive FBI reports, usually captioned PERSONAL AND CONFIDENTIAL AND NOT FOR FILES. Known as "the sphinx," Stegall was the personification of discretion, and she enjoyed the director's implicit trust. Hoover was confident she would make sure that all FBI reports reach the Oval Office.[14]

The sum and substance of these April reports was that King's antiwar view "parallels the propaganda line" of the American Communist party. If King's speech sounded as if it was drafted by Hanoi party bureaucrats it was not surprising, according to the FBI, because King was being steered by "concealed Communist" Stanley D. Levison and fellow traveler Harry Wachtel, formerly associated with Communist front groups. Levison, the FBI noted (incorrectly), wrote "Beyond Vietnam" for King. The bureau summaries concluded that King "is an instrument in the hands of subversive forces seeking to undermine our Nation" and that he was aware that his handlers were "two of the most dedicated and dangerous communists in the country."[15]

Was Stanley Levison, with his purported Svengali-like influence over King, the advanced guard of the Red Army? Devastating—if true. How-

ever, the FBI's own released records on Levison reveal a relationship diametrically at odds with the FBI's "Manchurian Candidate" version.

The bureau case file on Levison reveals that he came under intense FBI
scrutiny in the 1950s because he was involved in covert financial dealings
with the American Communist party (CPUSA). The surveillance lasted
about four years (1952 to 1956); when Levison's association with the
CPUSA declined, the FBI dropped its investigation. Not only was Levison
no longer regarded as a security risk, but New York agents tried unsuc-
cessfully on at least two occasions to recruit him as an informer. By 1956
Levison had cut all ties with the CPUSA and had turned his talents and
energies to the burgeoning civil rights movement.[16]

In 1962 Levison's name resurfaced inside the FBI when his close friendship with King was discovered. This fresh interest was justified by security concerns; the bureau needed to make certain that Levison had not
gone underground in 1956 only to emerge as a "concealed Communist"
influencing a civil rights leader who spoke and acted in the name of 12
million black citizens. Beginning in 1962, the FBI conducted a marathon
surveillance of Levison, including wiretaps, bugs, physical surveillance,
and surreptitious entries into his New York business office. Between 1954
and 1964, Levison's Park Management and Realty Company office in
downtown Manhattan was entered illegally by FBI "black bag" operatives at least 29 times. A wiretap installed on Levison's home phone in
May 1965, staffed by an around-the-clock team of FBI wiremen, remained
active until the first Nixon administration.

Despite this massive and costly surveillance the FBI never came up
with a lead that produced one scrap of evidence that Levison was anything other than a faithful and supportive friend whose only interest was
that King remain an effective civil rights leader. Had this operation been
conducted in an unbiased and professional manner by reasonable men interested only in the true nature of the relationship, the investigation could
have been terminated by the end of 1963. The FBI came up dry; the Levi-
son-King association was not a real or potential threat to the nation's security. The campaign of vilification continued, however, because Hoover
and his internal security executives needed this version of Levison—the
Soviet courier and KGB high-flyer—to undermine King with the White
House, Congress, and the press. In addition, the "take" from the Levison
wiretap produced a tremendous amount of high-grade intelligence on the
civil rights movement.[17]

Activities centering around the peace movement dominated much of
King's 1967 summer calendar. In April King appeared in Cambridge,
Massachusetts, to help launch "Vietnam Summer," a project developed
by Clergy and Laity Concerned (CALC). Patterned on Mississippi Summer of 1964, its goal was to recruit thousands of student volunteers to dis-

tribute leaflets and knock on doors. King joined with Joseph Rauh of Americans for Democratic Action (ADA) in a new pressure group calling itself Negotiations Now! He even briefly entertained the idea of running as a third-party "peace" candidate in the 1968 presidential election.[18]

Buoyed by the growing ranks of the antiwar movement, King, Andrew ("Andy") Young, and other SCLC colleagues began to focus on the idea of a march on Washington along the same lines as the historic August 1963 event. Young, initially skeptical about associating with the antiwar movement, emerged as the driving force inside SCLC for holding a peaceful and dignified peace march on Washington by the end of the summer. Young worked with the staff from the National Committee for a Sane Nuclear Policy (SANE), ADA, and CALC in ironing out strategy and organizational details. Levison was upbeat about the plans for a march, seeing tactical merit in bringing together the disparate anti-Vietnam summer projects into a memorable collective protest that would give dramatic meaning to the summer's antiwar activities. At the end of May, King and Young attended a peace conference in Geneva, "Pacem in Terris, II." The conference was an international blue-ribbon gathering of Nobel laureates, diplomats, writers, and others whose names were associated with the advocacy of nonviolent conflict resolution.[19]

Plans for moving ahead with the march on Washington were shelved with the news of rioting on an unprecedented scale in Newark, New Jersey, and several days later by even greater violence in Detroit. The Newark and Detroit riots left King despondent. "There were dark days before," he confided to Levison and Wachtel, "but this is the darkest." Deeply distraught, King's thoughts turned to depressing historical comparisons. The "giant triplets" of war, racism, and poverty were in the driver's seat in this era of Pax Americana, and he feared that his country was "headed the way of the Roman Empire."

King discussed the situation with his advisers and agreed to speak out on the rioting. Although he was distraught over ghetto blacks resorting to violence, King wanted his statement to focus on the conditions that led to riots and not on the rioters. Levison suggested that he write President Johnson, advocating a program like the Works Progress Administration (WPA) of the 1930s. A program with the same imaginative and dramatic qualities that employed the jobless when the nation was experiencing the hard times of the Great Depression should, Levison opined, be even more effective "now that the country is almost sick with money." King liked the suggestion, and Levison volunteered to draft a telegram under King's name to the White House calling for a large-scale federal effort, along the lines of the New Deal's WPA, to address the economic causes of the urban revolts. In back-to-back press conferences in Atlanta and Chicago, King called for an immediate and massive federal jobs program as the remedy for urban violence and fixed a large part of the blame for the summer's racial crisis on the "insensitive and irresponsible Congress." Given the prevailing reactionary mood on Capitol Hill, King's was a voice raised in the political wilderness, but he felt compelled to call for a politics of remedy and hope and to distance himself from those black leaders who held out to the ghetto poor only the thin diet of forbearance.[20]

For King, Vietnam-era America was in the throes of a profound moral and political crisis. Its credibility abroad was crumbling, its cities were convulsed by rioting, and its values were corrupted by materialism. The national leadership, especially Congress, responded with trivial and half-hearted measures and searched for scapegoats while stolidly resisting real solutions. The 90th Congress had rejected a civil rights bill and eviscerated the War on Poverty with deep cuts in a broad spectrum of programs designed to assist the poor. The House even voted down a $40 million measure to assist communities in exterminating rats. Arguing that this appropriation would reward ghetto rioters, conservative lawmakers laughed the "civil rats" bill off the floor. The same House membership gave clear sailing (377 to 23) to a bill that made inciting or encouraging rioting illegal.

If Congress continued to indulge in the politics of backlash it would only open the door wider, King was convinced, to greater oppression. He worried that if the cycle was not broken, white America would sooner or later acquiesce in a "right-wing takeover in the cities." In what proved to be his last thoughts on the national dilemma, King warned that America could not stand another summer of rioting "without a development that could destroy the soul . . . and even the democratic possibilities of the nation."[21]

By summer's end the peace movement had little to celebrate as far as Johnson's Vietnam policy was concerned. The bleak prospect that the Southeast Asian conflict might continue for many more months, even years, seemed stronger than ever. King found welcome reprieve from his own despondency by focusing on a new Washington project. An August 1967 Lou Harris poll appearing in *Newsweek* magazine revealed that a majority of white Americans favored aggressive federal action to deal with the problems of black citizens in the urban ghettos. In discussing the Harris survey with Levison, King concluded that the time was right to launch a dramatization of the poverty problem. Both men agreed that the nation's capital was the most promising location to draw national attention to the plight of America's underclass. Several weeks after the Harris poll appeared, King and Andy Young had lunch with the editors of *Time* magazine. When the table talk turned to the current racial crisis, the editors, Young recalled, were unanimous in their deep concern about the decline of the inner cities and gravely troubled about what it portended for the future. None of them backed away from the prospect that unless remedies were forthcoming, two more summers like 1967 could give rise to repressive countermeasures by right-wing extremists.[22]

King was convinced that the behavior of an unresponsive Congress did not reflect the public mood. A dramatization of poverty would underscore in a graphic way the deplorable social costs of the war and could galvanize enough public pressure on the White House and Congress to force a reassessment of national priorities and erode support for the stalemated Vietnam conflict. The Washington project was at the top of the SCLC's agenda at the Arlie House retreat in Warrenton, Virginia. King summoned his senior staff and key board members to this mid-September meeting to brainstorm about the new protest tactics that did not rely on the good will and political support of the federal government. Marian Wright (now Marian Wright Edelman, founder and president of the Children's Defense Fund), a lawyer for the NAACP's Legal Defense Fund in Mississippi, originated the idea of bringing a group of poor people from Mississippi to Washington to stage sit-ins at the headquarters of the Health, Education, and Welfare Department (HEW) and the Labor Department. King ran with Wright's core idea, envisioning waves of disinherited, the nation's hitherto invisible hyphenates—poor-Americans—camping out on officialdom's doorstep until the federal power promised to take action to eradicate these deplorable conditions. After a week of intense discussions, the SCLC committed itself to going forward with the idea of a massive civil disobedience campaign, now christened the Poor People's Campaign (PPC), scheduled for the spring of 1968 in the nation's capital.[23]

Serious planning for the Poor People's Campaign began during a five-day retreat beginning on November 27, 1967, at Frogmore, South Carolina. King told his aides that the SCLC would have to raise nonviolence to a new level; a massive civil disobedience campaign would be necessary to arouse a moribund Congress and pressure it into passing an Economic Bill of Rights for the nation's poor. Jobs and income—the right to live—were the main goals of the Washington spring demonstration; the programmatic details would be worked out later. King impressed upon his staff that the tactics had to be "nonviolent, but militant, and as dramatic, as dislocative, as disruptive, as attention-getting as the riots without destroying property."

Was King planning to tie Washington in knots? When reporters later pressed him about the campaign's tactics, King sidestepped specific details and focused on the moral dimensions of the crisis. King wanted to avoid highlighting the civil disobedience aspects until the SCLC could undertake a "real job of interpretation" with its largely black and white middle-class supporters who were certain, as Levison phrased it, to have "great trouble" with the program. King consistently drew analogies to his movement's earlier Birmingham and Selma campaigns. "The Poor People's Campaign was a Birmingham-like movement," he averred, centered "substantially around economic issues."[24]

Although King was pointedly reserved about the campaign, Andy Young took some pleasure in speculating openly about SCLC's possible plans for the nation's capital. Massing a few hundred marchers on the heavily traveled bridges connecting the capital with Virginia and Maryland suburbs would create a rush-hour nightmare of the first magnitude. Although, Young quickly added, this would be a "last resort" kind of civil disobedience tactic.

Young was not shy about revealing other possible nonviolent tactics calculated to disrupt life in the nation's capital. "A thousand people in need of health and medical attention sitting around District hospitals," Young volunteered, "would dramatize the fact that there were thousands of people in our nation in need of medical services." A continually replenished army of the poor, he continued, willing to face arrest because "they had nothing to lose," could tie the nation's capital into knots. Other ideas tossed around at the Frogmore retreat included a "call-in" to tie up the White House switchboard and a mobilization of the District of Columbia's black community to hold local protests and to selectively boycott downtown businesses, all calculated to apply pressure to the Congress.

Stanley Levison hit upon the notion of erecting a shantytown in the heart of the capital, patterned after the 1932 Bonus Army's tent city that played such havoc with President Herbert Hoover's blood pressure. Levison thought the idea had great value as a public relations gambit that would be good press copy. However, he gladly deferred to Jack Greenberg, the director of the NAACP's Legal Defense and Educational Fund, who proposed transporting a sharecropper's shack still in use by a poor Mississippi black family to the Smithsonian and presenting it as a gift to the nation, a kind of living exhibit of how some American citizens still lived in the world's richest nation. Greenberg, with all too rare foresight as it turned out, was leery about plans to set up and administer a tent city along the Mall, fearing it might distract from SCLC's core purpose of demonstrating the plight of America's poor.[25]

Even though King emphasized continuity, the underlying reality was that the Poor People's Campaign was a radical departure from all previous SCLC projects. For one thing, the movement was not just a black affair. King and his staff envisioned bringing to Washington thousands of the nation's disadvantaged in an interracial alliance that embraced rural and ghetto blacks, Appalachian whites, Mexican Americans, Puerto Ricans, and Native Americans. Coordinating the campaign with leaders of nonblack contingents essentially meant that the SCLC was faced with building a movement from scratch under great financial and time pressures. In launching the poor people's army, King was proposing nothing less than a radical transformation of the civil rights movement into a populist crusade calling for a redistribution of economic and political power. America's only national civil rights leader was now focusing on class issues and was planning to descend on Washington with an army of poor to shake the foundations of the power structure and force the government to respond to the needs of the ignored underclass. The marching and praying that symbolized the movement for racial justice for a decade had given way to the tactics of militant nonviolence that threatened the daily business of the federal government.

King was not optimistic about the outcome of this planned campaign in confrontational politics. He knew this was a desperate gamble in domestic brinkmanship, but he was driven to the conclusion that there were no viable alternatives: It was either massive civil disobedience or riots. If nonviolent direct action failed as an instrument of social change, King believed that the nation might "be plunged into holocaust—a tragedy deepened by the awareness that it was avoidable."[26]

The planned Poor People's Campaign became the major front in the FBI's stepped-up campaign to contain the rising tide of black militancy and intensify the bureau's secret war against King.

On the first working day of 1968, Hoover alerted 22 FBI field offices about King's plans to conduct a massive civil disobedience action in the nation's capital. To counter the SCLC-sponsored spring mobilization, Hoover directed his agents to make certain that all channels of information-sharing with liaison sources, particularly local police, state police intelligence units, and regional military intelligence groups, were operational. Stressing the vital need for accurate intelligence, the Hoover directive advised each field office to mobilize its ghetto informers to report on activities of SCLC representatives recruiting for the Poor People's Campaign (PPC) and to prepare separate case files on each recruiter.

Operation POCAM[27] was the first major opportunity for the FBI to activate its Ghetto Informant Program (GIP). The GIP was the bureau's response to White House pleas to the Justice Department after the 1967 urban riots to set up an early-warning system to forecast escalating tensions and likelihood of future violence in America's ghettos. The program was conceived in October 1967, and before it was a year in operation, the FBI had recruited more than 3,000 contacts or "listening posts." These intelligence "assets" provided the FBI and the White House with a steady stream of information about sentiments and activities in America's black communities.[28] For agents in the field, the intent of Hoover's first directive regarding the PPC was unmistakable: POCAM had a top priority, and FBIHQ wanted a steady supply of hard information. Field offices that fell short of these expectations were chided by Washington headquarters to comply with the program.[29]

FBIHQ relied heavily on what the director characterized as "excellent" sources in New York, Chicago, and Atlanta. The New York field office was a rich source of intelligence on the SCLC's overall strategy and plans for the Washington mobilization. FBI wiretaps furnished almost daily information about the upcoming Washington campaign, particularly the taps on Levison, Bayard Rustin, and Clarence Jones—a trio who comprised a vital component of the SCLC's "brain trust.[30]

In Atlanta, the site of SCLC's home office, the FBI employed additional techniques to spy on King and his movement. James A. ("Jim") Harrison, the comptroller for the SCLC and a member of the organization's executive staff, had been a paid bureau informant since the fall of 1964. Harrison, designated by his bureau symbol number AT-1387-S, fed his control agent valuable information about SCLC's finances, meetings, travel and demonstration plans, along with generous dollops about internal politics, personal matters, and office gossip. Much of FBIHQ's information about the Frogmore conference, as well as a list of names of recruiters for the PPC, originated with AT-1387-S. Harrison developed into an extremely reliable source, and the bureau rewarded him handsomely with an annual stipend of almost $10,000.[31]

Hoover's January 4, 1968, directive ordered each field office to initiate a "discreet investigation" to develop background information on all SCLC activists recruiting for the PPC in order to determine potential candidates for the FBI's Rabble Rouser Index. Bureau officials loosely defined a rabble-rouser as any person demonstrating a penchant for fomenting racial discord or disorders that threatened "domestic security." These purposely vague and open-ended criteria provided a virtual carte blanche to any agent to open a file on almost any citizen engaged in political activities that FBI officials deemed a danger to domestic tranquility.[32]

Relying chiefly on information from Harrison, identifying regional POCAM recruiters and coordinators posed no special investigative challenge. Within a few weeks, FBIHQ had compiled files on SCLC recruiters in at least 17 major cities and the District of Columbia. The nature of the information in their files included past and current political activities as well as personal matters and trivia; virtually all of the intelligence was unrelated to criminal or violent activity.[33] That none of the recruiters qualified for the Rabble Rouser Index probably generated no surprise within the FBI, because most of them were either ministers, SCLC representatives with years of experience in the civil rights struggle in the South, or community leaders from northern cities affiliated with church-sponsored civil reform programs or Quaker social action groups. Nonetheless, a basic FBI interest was served in that these background workups provided the excuse for compiling political files on American citizens, a compulsion that all political police worldwide find impossible to resist.[34]

Despite the scope of operation POCAM, the director and his executive officers were not satisfied with the bureau's intelligence-gathering efforts. The widespread attention and publicity King was receiving with his threatened Washington "camp-in" generated a continuous flow of requests for information from official Washington, especially from the Johnson White House.

As a master bureaucrat and practiced hand at feeding selected information to presidents for almost half a century, Hoover knew that if he could stay ahead of the administration's call for intelligence, the FBI could shape the White House's perception of King's upcoming campaign.

Pressure from the top galvanized agents in the field to resort to more aggressive techniques of gathering information. One approach that met with at least some success was to recruit SCLC recruiters and coordinators to become FBI informers. Bureau efforts to co-opt a sensitively placed SCLC staffer or recruiter with reliable information about the dynamics of a black community was an essential precursor to employing disruptive operations.[35] In addition, wiretaps on some regional recruiting offices and information volunteered from secretaries and other SCLC office personnel helped keep the FBI current about the levels of interest and commitment to the PPC in the black communities.[36] The so-called "pretext" phone call or interview was a prized surreptitious technique in these operations. FBI agents posing as feature story writers, newsmen, citizens interested in more information about the SCLC's spring mobilization, or potential sympathetic benefactors, generally had success soliciting information from unsuspecting recruiters and office secretaries.[37]

During the first week in February, King spent several days in Washington canvassing for support for the poor people's movement. During his short stay he spoke to the SCLC executive board, a wide spectrum of local civil rights leaders and black ministers, members of the D.C. Chamber of Commerce, Student Nonviolent Coordinating Committee (SNCC) leaders H. Rap Brown and Stokley Carmichael, and members of the Washington press corps. He consciously played down tactics and concentrated on the goals of the Poor People's Campaign. He pledged that the SCLC's tactics would be "nonviolently conceived and nonviolently executed." Consensus, not conflict, was the message King gave his Washington audiences.[38]

By March the SCLC was starting to make some headway in its preparations for the PPC. The quota of 200 volunteers was being met in some cities. "Philadelphia already has 600," Andy Young enthused. "Every place is running over." Levison shared Young's delight in these figures and reported his own good news: Contributions from district mailing were running "well ahead of last year."[39] The outpouring of support in the nation's capital was a solid indicator that the PPC was grabbing the public's imagination. Before SCLC staffers fully settled into their Washington headquarters, more than 75 volunteers had formed a dozen committees to plan for alternative housing, transportation, freedom schools, medical and sanitation needs, and other contingencies.

The SCLC staff was off the mark quickly because Bernard Lafayette, one of King's lieutenants and a veteran of the Nashville sit-ins and Freedom Rides, had worked for the American Friends Service Committee (AFSC) organizing community projects in Boston and Chicago. His link with the Quakers was important because AFSC agreed to support the PPC with money and staff. Two key figures responsible for setting up and running the SCLC command post at Fourteenth and U Streets, N.W., Anthony Henry and William Moyer, were AFSC staff members from Chicago and were recruited by Lafayette for the Washington mobilization.[40]

By the end of March, the FBI's list of organizations endorsing the PPC was impressive. It included most of the liberal church and community action groups in Washington: Interreligious Committee on Racial Relations, Council of Churches of Greater Washington, Cooperative Lutheran Parish Council, Jewish Community Council of Greater Washington, Potomac Presbytery, Baptist Ministers Council, Greater Washington Unitarian Ministers Association, the local chapter of the NAACP, Black Student Union, Washington Teachers Union, National Association of Social Workers, and SANE.[41]

As prominent clergymen and religious groups endorsed the SCLC's spring mobilization, Stanley Levison commented that with the Washington Jewish Council in King's camp, "you know the sentiment is running in your favor. These are the real power boys. They are the leaders of the Jewish Community Council all over the country." The council represented 140 synagogues and Jewish organizations in the Washington area. The Interreligious Committee on Racial Relations (ICRR), a blue-ribbon panel of some 50 Protestant, Catholic, and Jewish religious leaders, endorsed the campaign and characterized SCLC's goals as "basic to any standard of human dignity." The group included such religious luminaries as Catholic Bishop John S. Spence; Rabbi Martin S. Halperin, president of the Washington Board of Rabbis; black Bishop Smallwood E. Williams of the Bible Way Church World Wide; and Methodist Bishop John Wesley Lord, the panel's chairman. Patrick Cardinal O'Boyle, the former ICRR chairman, joined the list of church men supporting the poor people's movement.[42]

Certain that King was going to lay siege to the seat of government, Hoover consulted with the FBI's top brass to devise ways to intensify the campaign to destroy the civil rights leader and disrupt the SCLC's Washington mobilization. In early March bureau chiefs and supervisors held a "racial conference" at FBIHQ to come up with strategies to sabotage the Poor People's Campaign. The conferees decided that circulating falsehoods and rumors would have negative effects on SCLC recruitment efforts. The campaign would spread stories "about the lack of funds and organization. Fears of economic reprisal and personal safety" were calculated to dissuade potential participants. The rumored threat that government welfare checks would be cancelled if recipients of federal assistance showed up in Washington was especially targeted at the South's black population. All FBI field offices involved in project POCAM were directed to shape their own distinctive campaigns according to what would play best in their respective locales.[43]

By March the Hoover Bureau's campaign against King was virtually on a total war footing. In a March 21 "urgent" teletype, Hoover urged all field offices involved in the POCAM project to exploit every tactic in the bureau's arsenal of covert political warfare to bring down King and the SCLC. At the end of the month he shot off another directive to the same SACs, notifying them to have on his desk by April 10 the list of informers each office recruited to come to Washington for the duration of the poor people's camp-in. The director was calling up the "reserves" for what was shaping up among FBI elites as an impending showdown.[44]

The FBI's March offensive turned into a no-holds-barred exercise in character assassination. Hoover ordered a quick update of the King monograph for distribution among top government officials to remind them of the "wholly disreputable character of King." This assignment went to Special Agent George C. Moore, the newly appointed head of the Racial Intelligence Section, who took up the task with élan, volunteering his section to undertake an "exhaustive file review" and prepare the update "in a hard-hitting manner."[45] The revised monograph, a 39-page report entitled "Martin Luther King, Jr.: A Critical Analysis," was a compendium of sections on Communist influence on King and the SCLC and on King's opposition to the Vietnam War. It concluded with two sections of lurid accounts of King's alleged sexual activities. The report took pains to link the war issue and the Poor People's Campaign, alleging that King's Communist "confidants," namely Levison, Wachtel, Bayard Rustin, and Clarence Jones, were conspiring to use the poor people's army to provoke violence in Washington in order to undermine the government's commitment to the war in Vietnam.[46] A week after dissemination of the report, Moore informed his division chief, William C. Sullivan, that it was "received very favorably by the intelligence community."[47]

Reports to Washington headquarters from FBI field offices indicated that the sanctioned campaign of intimidation, Red-baiting, disinformation, and disruption were having an impact on SCLC's recruitment for the Poor People's Campaign.

For example, the FBI field office in Birmingham, Alabama, had activated its network of racial informants, ghetto tipsters, and liaison sources to filter anonymous rumors throughout the black community that welfare recipients who participated in the PPC would be "cut off" from their benefits. The spurious threat of economic reprisal was an unalloyed success. Although metropolitan Birmingham had a black population of more than 300,000, by early March FBI Birmingham reported that the SCLC recruiter had only 40 names on the muster roll. The campaign of intimidation continued throughout April, and by late May the FBI's list of Birmingham participants for the Washington demonstration had increased by only three names.[48]

Similar COINTELPRO tactics were used in the neighboring state of Georgia. When SCLC's Hosea Williams led a march through his hometown of Savannah to drum up recruits for the PPC, the turnout from the black community was disappointingly small. The FBI frustrated Williams's recruitment drive by spreading stories through cooperating press, radio, and television sources that essentially depicted Williams as the SCLC's Pied Piper who would take gullible blacks to Washington and leave them stranded, broke, and sick. The Savannah SAC estimated that the planted stories discouraged at least 200 blacks from joining the ranks of the poor people's army.

Some COINTELPROs exploiting the fear factor required less planning and coordination. For example, Sullivan approved the planting of six FBI photographs of "militant and aggressive looking" black youths taken at a PPC rally in Cleveland, Ohio, with friendly media sources. The obvious intent was to promote the image of the SCLC's spring mobilization as synonymous with potential violence and risk-taking.[49]

Having advance information about King's every movement helped the FBI to ambush his recruiting and fund-raising forays, especially in the South, with Red-baiting operations. Alerted in March that King was preparing for one of his whirlwind tours to galvanize support for the PPC in Virginia, the FBI connived with elements of the local John Birch Society to thwart these efforts. The bureau and the Birchites set up a front organization called TACT (Truth About Civil Turmoil). Several days before the SCLC leader was scheduled to visit the capital of the Old Confederacy, TACT planned to sponsor a public lecture in Richmond by a Julia Brown, who would speak about the Communist penetration of the civil rights movement and especially King's links to the American Communist party. Brown was billed in the Birchite advance publicity as a derring-do black patriot and "secret operative" who had infiltrated the civil rights movement for the FBI and had witnessed the machinations of the Communist conspiracy to use the movement to undermine the American social order. Brown operated like a one-woman "truth squad," except that she was on the FBI payroll and was peddling disinformation throughout southern Virginia, lecturing to audiences in Petersburg and Danville just before King's scheduled appearances in these cities. The Richmond FBI was confident that Brown's preemptive strikes would damage King's cause, reporting to FBIHQ that "[unmasking] King's subversive connections will be effective as a counter-intelligence activity."[50]

Although it is impossible to gauge the full extent of the FBI's wrecking operations against the Poor People's Campaign, that they had an impact is unquestionable. SCLC insider and King confidant Harry Wachtel observed that the constant surveillance had a chilling effect on all movement leaders. "It affected the strategies and tactics," he lamented, "because the people you were having strategies and tactics about were privy to what you were about. They knew your doubts. . . ." Suspecting that FBI summaries of confidential SCLC political discussions and PPC plans would end up in the Oval Office was in itself a powerful inhibitor. Near the end of March 1968, King was troubled because recruiting volunteers for the poor people's army was slow. There were pockets of enthusiastic support in Washington, New York, and Philadelphia, but SCLC's broad appeals in Alabama, Georgia, and other parts of the South were going largely unheeded. Some of the SCLC's problems were self-inflicted; however, the FBI's unwarranted, extensive, and aggressive clandestine activities took a decided toll.[51]

Adding to the growing uncertainties about the campaign's viability was the issue of finances. "Where is the money to come from?" a troubled Levison rhetorically queried an equally bewildered William Rutherford, SCLC's newly appointed executive director. Rutherford admitted that the organization's finances were "a mess" and that current expenses contracted in mobilizing King's poor people already were running ahead of incoming funds. SCLC was experiencing a serious financial shortfall even before assuming the costs of erecting a "shantytown" equipped to house and feed thousands of marchers expected to take up residence for a summer-long protest, an undertaking unparalleled in the history of American protest movements. Understandably, King's staff was not elated when he decided to heed the cry of the powerless and oppressed Memphis sanitation workers and enlist his moral prestige and international reputation in their struggle.[52]

two

The Road to Washington
Goes Through Memphis

ON FEBRUARY 11, 1968, the eve of Abraham Lincoln's birthday, several hundred black sanitation workers proclaimed by a show of hands that self-liberation was still a hope that could stir action. The following day the city of Memphis, Tennessee, was hit with a garbage strike. What started as a "wild cat" job action soon escalated into a racial confrontation, then into a compelling civil rights struggle of national importance, culminating in an assassination triggering a storm of racial fury that stunned white America. For one dark moment this southern river city served as a microcosm of the domestic forces in racial conflict during this traumatic decade.

The 1968 Memphis sanitation strike attracted little national attention until local blacks persuaded Dr. King to enlist his moral support on the side of the striking garbage workers. At the time, neither King nor the supporters of black democracy in Memphis (or the nation at large, for that matter) were aware of the FBI's active involvement in this local labor dispute. Weeks before King agreed to come to Memphis, FBI Director Hoover had approved a domestic surveillance program against the strikers and their allies in the black community. For King, the cry of the powerless and oppressed brought him to Memphis. For Hoover, Memphis became another front in the FBI's stepped-up campaign to contain the rising tide of black militancy and another opportunity to carry forward the bureau's secret war against the black civil rights leader.

From the outset, the FBI characterized the dispute as a "racial matter" with potential internal security ramifications. Armed with the assertion that the nation's security was endangered, the FBI began a massive political intelligence operation that covered nearly every aspect of the Memphis black community's organizational life associated with the strike. Unhampered by respect for the rights of labor, the First Amendment, or a citizen's right to privacy, the FBI intruded into lawful political activities without any indication that specific crimes in violation of the federal law were imminent. The methods the bureau employed in its comprehensive and unwarranted urban surveillance were suggestive of a police state.[1]

For the first five decades of this century, Memphis and "Boss" Edward H. Crump were synonymous. During this period of heavy-handed machine rule, race leaders gained small concessions for the black community as a reward for keeping a lid on racial dissent. White Memphians came to expect that blacks would deal and not act in the tidy political universe presided over by powerful Boss Crump. During the early 1960s the long shadow of Crumpism still influenced white racial attitudes. Taking pride in the orderliness of relations between the races, Memphis had experienced no major racial troubles since Reconstruction days; most whites were convinced that the past would continue as a guide to the future.[2]

Along with accustomed racial stability, the city's economic life encouraged white Memphians to anticipate a future of bright promise. More than one third of the cotton produced in the United States during the early 1960s was bought and sold each year along historic Front Street in Memphis. The Bluff City was home to the world's largest hardwood market; it was the key rail center between St. Louis and New Orleans and one of the South's major distribution centers. City officials were quick to point out that the flip side of the coin of economic and industrial good times was social progress, noting that Memphis had more housing projects and improved low rent housing than any other city of comparable size in the South. Moreover, beginning with the Crump era, blacks exercised the vote without harassment. By the 1960s nearly 85,000 Memphis blacks were registered and increasingly politically animated in local politics and government. For most white residents the city's motto—City of Good Abode—was not an empty boosterism but a fitting description of postwar Memphis.[3]

By the mid-1960s, however, the shock waves of the civil rights movement rudely jostled white expectations in Boss Crump's river town. Prominent black leaders of Memphis gravitated toward nonviolent direct action to confront racial repression. This newfound militancy originated more out of a growing sense of frustration and disillusionment than in any supreme confidence that black Memphians would overcome. In 1965 Rev. Samuel B. ("Billy") Kyles, the black pastor of the Monumental Baptist Church, threatened one of the largest breweries in the city with a boycott unless the company ended its discriminatory hiring practices. The threatened economic action produced negotiations, and ultimately the brewery agreed to hire black workers. This one victory was quickly eclipsed by more numerous examples of white resistance to the rising tide of black expectations.

Police brutality was a major grievance among blacks and a pressing, tangible target for civil rights activists. A 1966 study by the U.S. Commission on Civil Rights reported on the abrasive relations between the Memphis police and the black community. Rev. Kyles, who moved to Memphis from Chicago in 1959, observed that the police department's approach to communicating with the black population was all too depressingly predictable: When "the niggers are getting out of hand . . . the only way to put them back in their place is to crack them across the skull."[4]

No one in Memphis was more outspoken and determined to hold the police accountable for their actions than Maxine Smith, the executive secretary of the Memphis branch of the NAACP. Articulate, assertive, demanding, and fiercely committed to the civil rights struggle, Maxine Smith was regarded by many of the older black citizenry as a stand-up lady and for over a decade something of a legend in the city's racial history. During the full-blown racial crisis of 1968 she battled with city officials on every front on behalf of blacks who reported being victimized by police mistreatment and abuse.[5]

Smith was a native Memphian born into a working-class family. She attended the city's public schools and then left Memphis to complete her formal education. She received her undergraduate degree from Spellman College in Atlanta, where she was a classmate of Dr. King's older sister. After her Spellman years, Smith earned a master's degree at Middlebury College in Vermont. She returned to Memphis in 1955, but not before doing some college teaching in Texas and Florida. Smith left the college classroom when she married an Air Force dentist, Dr. Vasco A. Smith, Jr., a fellow Memphian, and they decided to return to their hometown, where he could start a practice and they could raise a family.[6]

Sometime before the sanitation strike Maxine Smith; her husband, Vasco, the NAACP vice president; and Jesse H. Turner, a prominent local banker and president of the Memphis NAACP chapter, privately agreed among themselves to provide information about local racial matters to the Memphis FBI. There is nothing, however, in the released FBI files on its Memphis surveillance that hints at the possibility that the NAACP executive leadership was intriguing against the interests of their own race for money or self-promoting reasons. On the contrary, considering the racial tensions in Memphis at the time, it was a sound decision, albeit perhaps risky, for the NAACP leadership to cooperate with the federal agency. Providing information to the local FBI allowed the Smiths and Turner to try and sensitize the bureau to the legitimacy of the grievances of the black minority, not the least of which was systematic police harassment. The FBI's own files reveal that the information furnished to the bureau by the NAACP officers was to keep it apprised of the grave potential for violence if the Memphis police persisted in their provocative practices against the sanitation strikers and their supporters. The Smiths and Turner acted in a principled manner, hoping to moderate police harassment tactics by appealing to the federal authorities on the scene and thereby strengthen the odds favoring a peaceful settlement of the strike. The FBI's released documents clearly indicate that although the Smiths and Turner cooperated with the local field office, they were not "snitches" or "police spies."

Apparently this relationship remained superficially cordial for the duration of the sanitation strike. The Memphis FBI characterized the Smiths and Turner as "reliable sources" who were "most familiar with the inner workings of the Memphis branch of the NAACP."[7] Nevertheless, the Memphis FBI made no effort to persuade the Memphis Police Department (MPD) to moderate its approach to the black population. Actually, during the strike and the related violence, the bureau winked at incidents of excessive police force against the strikers and their allies. When the right opportunity arose the FBI resorted to a stratagem to destroy these dedicated and effective community leaders. When the FBI was required under the Freedom of Information Act to release to the public the more than 2,000 documents in its Memphis Sanitation Workers Strike file, it failed to mask out the names of the three top NAACP officers and their FBI designation "Extremist Informants." The names of scores of informants who reported to the FBI during the strike are all meticulously and properly withheld. The FBI has a deserved and virtually untarnished reputation for protecting the identity of its confidential sources. Much of the bureau's celebrated success as the nation's premier law enforcement agency is based on its not breaking trust with its sources. In the case of the Smiths and Turner, however, the bureau intentionally exposed them as FBI informants to compromise their reputation and standing in the community in which they lived and served as racial leaders and staunch advocates of equal treatment under the law.[8]

In order to try and remedy the situation, a group of black and white moderates calling themselves the Memphis Committee on Community Relations (MCCR) attempted to persuade the city's police commissioner to institute reforms, especially a civilian review board. The commissioner's office agreed to integrate the department's squad cars and ban the term *nigger* over the police radio but rejected out-of-hand the call for a civilian review board.[9]

MCCR's failure over the review board issue quickened the pulse of black militancy in Memphis. In the spring of 1967, Turner and Vasco Smith withdrew from the MCCR, expressing their loss of faith in the efficacy of racial accommodationism and moderate tactics. In a parting shot, Turner declared that injustices were "not corrected by meek requests but by firm and forceful demands accompanied by spectacular aggressive action."[10] Turner, the Smiths, Rev. Kyles, and other like-minded black community leaders refused to support the white liberals' choice for mayor in the 1967 municipal elections and instead ran their own candidate on a platform calling for a variety of municipal reforms, with a civilian review board heading the list. To further the interests of the estimated 250,000 black citizens, these protest leaders increasingly felt constrained to substitute the politics of race for the shopworn and ineffective politics of moderation. These developments pointed to the fact that on the evening of the sanitation workers' strike the racial climate in the Bluff City was becoming more polarized.[11]

Memphis had never been a strong union town. In a city dominated by whites, white workers never regarded themselves as part of the working class; that was a role delegated to blacks. As late as 1967, Memphis, the twenty-second largest city in the nation, had never signed a contract with any union. One black Memphian, Thomas Oliver Jones, a man obviously unimpressed with tradition, was determined to make unionism the key to black advancement. Jones focused his considerable energies on organizing the Memphis sanitation workers, the most oppressed workforce in the city.[12]

"Carrying the Man's garbage" was such a low-paying, insecure, and dangerous job that black Memphians left the work to displaced rural migrants who flocked to the city after World War II as farm mechanization pushed them off the land. The Memphis Sanitation Department actively recruited Fayette County blacks because they were industrious, tractable, and eager to work. By the 1960s, most of the 1,300 sanitation department employees were black and unclassified city workers. "Unclassified" was the city's euphemism for raw exploitation: It meant that the workers had little job security and were not covered by workmen's compensation.

T. O. Jones, a short and feisty man, had learned unionization in a West Coast shipyard before the recession of 1958 forced him to return to Memphis, where he took a job as a garbage collector. For the next 10 years, he doggedly tried to organize his fellow black workers. In 1963 Jones and more than 30 of his union converts were fired because of their organizational activities. A year later Jones surfaced again, this time as president and chief organizer for Local 1733 of the American Federation of State, County, and Municipal Employees (AFSCME), part of the American Federation of Labor—Congress of Industrial Organizations (AFL-CIO) and one of the fastest-growing unions in the country. The AFSCME was chartered by the state, but the city of Memphis refused to extend recognition to the local chapter. In 1966, Local 1733, reflecting the rising level of black militancy within the community, organized a strike in response to poor working conditions and low wages; the city responded with a court-ordered injunction forbidding any strike by municipal employees. The strike folded, forcing the indefatigable Jones to bide his time until the intolerable working conditions precipitated an incident that would force a showdown with the Memphis city officials.[13]

In January 1968 Jones found his incident when 21 black sewer and drain workers were sent home because heavy rains made work in the sewers impossible. The black workers received only two hours of "show up" pay, whereas their white coworkers and supervisors remained "on the clock" until the rains stopped, and they were put to work and paid for a full day. Since Memphis sanitation workers earned less than $70 for a full week of work, any reduction in take-home pay turned normally hard times into a domestic calamity for any worker with a large family. Responding to the black rank-and-file anger, the following day Jones ordered all sewer and drain crews to strike, and he notified the city that he was prepared to negotiate a more equitable policy of "show up" on rainy days.

While Jones and city officials entered into informal discussions, the desperate plight of garbage collectors was dramatized by the sickening news that two black workers had been crushed to death on the job. The two men, trapped by a torrential rainstorm, took shelter in the barrel of their truck because city police forbade black employees from seeking refuge on the porches of white patrons along the collection route. A freak accident triggered a defective automatic bailer, and they were ground up like garbage. The horror of the tragedy was compounded by the disclosure that their families were not entitled to any benefits because the men were unclassified workers. Local 1733 held a strike meeting on Sunday evening, February 11, where Jones reported to the more than 400 workers present that the city refused to make any meaningful concessions on wages and working conditions. The next day, fewer than 200 sanitation employees reported for work.[14]

The "wild cat" strike on February 12 caught Memphis officials by surprise, but once the initial shock dissipated, they assumed a rigid stance. Henry Loeb III, the city's newly elected mayor, declared the strike in violation of the 1966 injunction and ordered the striking employees back to work. Although Loeb adamantly refused to meet with the black officials of Local 1733, he consented to talk to AFSCME national officers who were in Memphis to assist the local organization.

The first session in the mayor's office was staged to provide good theater but not much mutual trust. Loeb engaged in polite conversation until the television cameras started filming; then he stood at his desk, a commanding presence—Loeb was six feet, five inches tall, with a build like an All-American linebacker—and made statements into the camera about the strike's illegality and its danger to public health. These circuslike tactics infuriated the union officials, and the session ended in a shouting match.[15]

The mayor's theatrics were exceeded only by his old-fashioned southern paternalism when dealing with the striking black city employees. Throughout the duration of the strike, the one union demand that unfailingly left Loeb shaking his head in sullen opposition was the checkoff. In a city like Memphis, known for its low wages, the checkoff was essential to build a stable base for a local union; otherwise, men would be reluctant to pay union dues out of their pockets on payday. Loeb stubbornly maintained that unions were evil and characterized the checkoff system as a swindle by scheming union officials to enrich themselves at the expense of the innocent rank-and-file workers. Echoing his own plantation boss theory of racial noblesse oblige, the mayor insisted that he had been elected to be the garbage men's "keeper" and that he would never abandon his "moral obligation" to protect them from the machinations of the union. Whatever his motives, most of the black community regarded Mayor Loeb as a segregationist determined to break the strike, defeat the union, and stem the tide of black democracy.[16]

Initially, the mid-winter "wild cat" strike of 1,000 blacks drew only scant national attention. From the outset of the strike, however, the FBI characterized Local 1733's "work stoppage" as a racial matter with potential national security implications. On February 16, 1968, in a teletype assigned an "urgent" priority, the bureau's Memphis field office alerted Hoover that because the local branch of the NAACP had sided with the striking workers, the job action no longer would be regarded as a local labor dispute.[17]

Hoover agreed with this assessment. From this point on, all administrative memoranda from Memphis to FBI headquarters in Washington were routed to William C. Sullivan, head of the Domestic Intelligence Division, and Cartha D. DeLoach, the FBI's senior liaison executive officer with the Johnson White House and Capitol Hill. Moreover, having classified the strike as a security-related matter fraught with possible racial unrest, the bureau saw the need to alert military intelligence and keep it posted on the events as they unfolded in Memphis.[18]

"NO INDICATION TO DATE OF ANY BLACK NATIONALIST INFILTRATION. THIS WILL BE CLOSELY FOLLOWED THROUGH RACIAL SOURCES AND POLICE DEPARTMENT LIAISON. U.S. ATTORNEY, U.S. SECRET SERVICE, ARMY INTELLIGENCE AND POLICE DEPARTMENT, ALL MEMPHIS, HAVE BEEN ALERTED." The abbreviated language of the bureau's plaintext teletype advised Hoover that a full-scale domestic political intelligence operation was under way. In the following weeks, FBI agents and their sources monitored all public demonstrations supporting the sanitation workers: church prayer meetings, fund-raising rallies, daily marches, picketing of downtown stores, and public grievance sessions involving workers and representatives from city hall.[19] During the course of the nine-week strike, closed strategy sessions conducted by Local 1733 and its supporters and executive sessions of the city council were penetrated by FBI informers.[20] From the beginning of the strike, these intelligence-gathering activities and intrusive techniques placed the FBI within the politics of a local labor dispute.

During the last week in February events took a dramatic turn when the strike was transformed into a civil rights struggle. To prove to the community that he was not heartless, Mayor Loeb authorized city funding of food stamps for the strikers' families, but he would not budge on any of the union's key demands: the checkoff, union recognition, and an immediate raise in wages. The city council, frustrated over Loeb's rigidness and increasingly troubled that the strike could escalate into a racial confrontation, tried to improvise a speedy solution to the dispute. Even some of the deepest-dyed conservatives on the council lost patience with the mayor. When Gwen Awsumb, the only woman on the 13-member council, chided Loeb for being the "most stubborn and hard-headed man" that she had ever met—the spunky Awsumb opposed union recognition but favored an immediate wage raise—His Honor took this as a compliment, retorting that mulishness was a mark of a good administrator.[21]

For two days, February 22 and 23, council members met intermittently with the mayor, the striking workers, AFSCME officials, and local black ministers in search of an arrangement that would end the strike and put the sanitation crisis behind them. The first session opened on Thursday morning, the 22nd, in the lavishly appointed wing of the new city hall, the site of the city council chambers. The council chambers had a seating capacity to accommodate about 400. Very few workers were in attendance, and most of the morning was taken up with union officials and local ministers reiterating their major demands: union recognition, a dues checkoff, and an immediate increase in wages. With the noon hour approaching, a spokesman for the council brought the union officials and ministers up short when he announced that the council would like to hear directly from the workers themselves. Jerry Wurf, the international president of AFSCME, saw this as a ploy to divide the workers and the union and accepted the challenge. Wurf made a call to Union Hall, where most of the striking employees were meeting, to extend the council's "invitation."[22]

What began as an unpromising start in the morning session threatened to completely unravel by the afternoon. More than 900 workers squeezed into the posh council chambers in a show of solidarity with their union representatives. All the seats and all four of the red-carpeted aisles were filled with workers. Alarmed council officials warned that they were creating a fire hazard and until the aisles were cleared or they moved to a larger meeting site, no business could be conducted. O. Z. Evers, an old political wheelhorse from the previous administration, urged the crowd to stay "until the council recognizes the union, and recognizes that they can overrule the mayor." Other speeches that followed seconded Evers's sentiments. Rev. Ezekiel Bell, one of the more flamboyant pastors, won a chorus of approval when he stated that city hall belonged as much to the city workers as to any one, and they would stay until their demands were met or hell froze over. Some of the workers began singing "We Shall Not Be Moved." At about 3:00 P.M. Reverend Bell phoned his church and ordered up about 300 to 400 sandwiches to be sent over to city hall. It finally dawned on the council membership that an army of rank-and-file Public Works employees were prepared to occupy the seat of government until their demands were addressed.[23]

Caught in a bind of their own making, the council devised a quick-fix strategy to temper the workers' resentments and persuade them to peacefully end their sit-in. Late Thursday afternoon a three-member "strike committee" of the city council informed union representatives that they supported the union's key demands. These concessions meant little unless they were accepted by a majority of the 13-member council. The likelihood that a council majority would favor a resolution supporting union recognition, dues checkoff, and a wage increase was virtually nonexistent. Under Memphis's newly installed mayor-council form of government, all real executive and administrative power resided squarely in the mayor's office. As long as Loeb remained unyielding, the council, for all practical purposes, was handcuffed. Only a handful of council members were ready to try and supersede the mayor and force him to accept concessions, even if it meant battling Loeb in the courts. Not understanding the workings of government, many strikers snatched at the "strike committee's" resolution as a victory for their struggle. Jerry Wurf and the other AFSCME officials knew that the committee's resolution would never pass the council, but for their own reasons they apparently never told the rank-and-file. At six o'clock that evening 900 satisfied sanitation workers cleaned up the residue of their picnic lunch and peacefully filed out of council chambers after agreeing to meet Friday to hear the city council's recommendations.[24]

Friday afternoon the full city council assembled at the Ellis Auditorium to deliver a prepared statement to the workers and their union representatives. All of the strike-related meetings and demonstrations were routinely monitored by the Memphis police as well as the FBI. The Friday meeting was no exception. Before the scheduled meeting some of the top brass of the MPD intelligence division secreted themselves in the projection booth at the top of the auditorium, outfitted with walkie-talkies, binoculars, and a tape recorder. Once the meeting started, inspectors, captains with the intelligence unit, and detectives were detailed to mingle with the crowd in the auditorium. That morning at Union Hall T. O. Jones appealed to about 600 workers to stay "cool" and "come to the meeting in a peaceful manner" to avoid any trouble with the police. He urged his audience to get the word out to friends and coworkers to make the meeting; Jones wanted to pack Ellis Auditorium with rank-and-filers and their allies.[25]

That afternoon about 1,000 workers and their supporters jammed into the auditorium, only to be told that the city council had limited powers and could only make recommendations to the mayor. The city council chairman then read off a list of the full council's recommendations, not one of which addressed the workers' major demands. The council recommended that the strikers return to their jobs and leave their union representatives to complete the negotiations with city officials. It was only then that the full shock of recognition set in among the rank-and-file: All of Thursday's hectic negotiations, the jawboning, the sit-in threat, and the promised concessions had not changed a thing. Thursday's "victory" was a victory in quicksand. As soon as the proposal was read, all but two of the council members filed out of the auditorium under police escort. All in all it was a dismal performance. Whether intended or not, the retreating council members left a meeting hall packed with angry workers who felt they had been betrayed and treated like backward children.[26]

Back in the Ellis Auditorium union leaders and black ministers knew they had to do something quickly to defuse the bitter anger and emotional outbursts of the workers. Some kind of protest had to be made. After a hasty conference it was decided that a march would be a ready-made catharsis, drawing away the anger and cooling tempers. The impromptu march would start at the auditorium and move south for about three miles through the center of downtown Memphis to the Mason Temple, where a mass rally would allow the workers to vent their protest over the "sell out" by the city council. The march route was cleared through the fire and police director's office and approved by the mayor with the proviso that the demonstrators walk in an orderly fashion in a line eight abreast and with a police escort.

The marchers were in a festive mood when they stepped off into the thin sunlight of a late winter afternoon. One of the ministers in the march remembered there was a lot of "laughing and talking more or less in a picnic fashion." Rev. Richard Moon, the white chaplain at Memphis State University, recalled that he and his marching companion, a black minister, were carrying on a pleasant conversation at the front of the column with one of the escorting foot patrolmen. They were trying to convince their escort that as a city worker his paycheck would benefit if the sanitation workers won their demands. Moon remembered that they had gone about six blocks and had just about convinced the white officer that they were marching for him too, when their attention was drawn sharply to a commotion to the rear of their position in the line of march.[27]

Ed Gillis, a black employee with the Public Works Department and a union supporter, happened to be at the spot where the trouble erupted. According to MPD radio tapes, about the time the front of the march reached Main and Gayoso, police squad cars began crossing the median strip and started herding the marchers, funneling them toward the curb in front of Goldsmiths Department Store "to keep them four abreast." Gillis, who was over 70 at the time, recalled how one of the police cars crossed the white line and bumped him twice. When Gillis glanced into the squad car, the driver "looked around at me and rolled his eyes." Just behind Gillis a second squad car brushed up against Gladys Carpenter, a black woman who had placed herself between the men and the police car, thinking that the police would not try the same thing with a woman. Ms. Carpenter was a plucky civil rights veteran, having participated in the Selma to Montgomery march and the Meredith March in Mississippi. When the back wheel of the police cruiser ran over her foot, she cried out in pain. If the police were looking to incite the marchers, they had their incident. Almost instantaneously about 15 to 20 men in the vicinity of Ms. Carpenter began to rock the squad car. As if on cue, all along the line of march blue-helmeted riot police poured out of the escort cars and began to mace and club the marchers.[28]

During the melee, nearly all of the black pastors and the international officers of AFSCME identified with the sanitation workers' cause were maced. Rev. James M. Lawson, Jr., pastor of the Centenary Methodist Church and long-time civil rights activist, rushed to the scene at the first indication of trouble, urging the marchers: "Let's keep marching. They're trying to provoke us. Let's not let them provoke us." Lawson sprinted the distance of about two car lengths and barely reached the crowd surrounding the squad car when he was hit on the side of the face with the stun gas. At that instant, as he turned from the chemical spray, Lawson took in a spectacle he recalled clearly more than two years later: "I [saw] then all the way up the line the police over their squad cars, out of their squad cars using cans of mace on everybody." Reverend Moon was maced right off but not before the same tableau was etched in his memory of that Friday police action: "Every policeman along the line for three blocks pulled out his mace can and started macing everyone."[29]

That same Friday Mayor Loeb dashed any residual hope that a negotiated settlement would end the dispute when he ordered the city attorney to prepare an injunction against the striking workers. Growing increasingly obdurate, Loeb opted to fight the union in the courts rather then negotiate. Moreover, before the end of the month, Loeb had garbage trucks back on the street. The skeleton force was manned by white supervisors, nonstrikers, and replacement workers and was convoyed through city neighborhoods by police escorts. The mayor was confident that his office would escape any unfavorable political repercussions from the garbage pile-up and would get the city through the remainder of the winter without a public health crisis. Content that he held all the high cards, the new mayor sat back and waited for the union to fold.[30]

The evening of the incident, Memphis Director of Public Safety Frank C. Holloman met with a group of angry citizens in the Peabody Hotel in response to a complaint against the MPD. In attendance were Jacques Wilmore, the southern regional director of the U.S. Civil Service Commission (who registered the complaint), and several members of his staff, along with others who were parties to the complaint, including the Reverends James Lawson and H. Ralph Jackson, Jesse Turner, and Braxton Bryant, executive director of the Tennessee Council on Human Relations. The mood of the meeting was heated and confrontational. Most of those in the room with Holloman were personally irate because they had been in the afternoon march and were gassed; some, like Lawson, were sprayed repeatedly in the face at very close range.[31] Holloman dismissed all accusations of excessive force leveled at the police and, despite all the first-hand experiences offered at the meeting to the contrary, insisted that the gassing had not been indiscriminate. Memphis's top cop countered the criticism of the macing, insisting that it was a humane law-enforcement tool and far less drastic than a police nightstick or a .38 caliber bullet.[32]

The Memphis police after-action report on the February 23 incident was upbeat. Lt. Ely H. Arkin, Jr., head of the MPD intelligence unit, noted that this was "the first time the Memphis Police Department was confronted and attacked by a large and unruly crowd. The police," the report continued, ". . . reacted coolly and efficiently [and] prevented a serious tragedy from occurring. . . ." Arkin credited the mace for the success of the operation.

FBI agents on the scene monitored the violence. A bureau memo sent to Washington headquarters and to the regional military network approved of the type of force used "to disperse the recalcitrant and obstructive crowd. . . ." and noted that "the mace worked most satisfactorily." Only once, and then inadvertently, did the issue of excessive force surface, when the memo noted that a 56-year-old black male phoned the police to complain he had been gassed and clubbed. "He was arrested," the memo continued with a sort of bureaucratic straight face, "and taken to John Gaston Hospital for treatment."[33]

Loeb's union-busting tactics, the rebuff by the city council, and the macing forged a unity and militancy in the black community that had been absent since the racial and political struggles of Reconstruction days. Maxine Smith was certain that the chemical gassing—an incident that was over in 15 minutes—was a turning point in the city's racial history. Its consciousness-raising impact on black Memphians, Smith observed, was equivalent to "turning the dogs loose in Mississippi or spraying the hoses in Birmingham."[34]

Rev. H. Ralph Jackson's "baptism by mace" was a telling example of what Smith meant by a "turning point." Never active in the civil rights movement, he was regarded by outsiders and Memphis's young angry blacks as a "Tom" minister. Among his ministerial brethren, however, Dr. Jackson was well regarded. As director of the minimum salary division for the African Methodist Episcopal Church in America, Jackson held down a prestigious and highly responsible position. Earlier in the year Mayor Loeb had cited him as one of the city's outstanding civic leaders. The only reason Jackson found himself in the front ranks of the march that Friday afternoon was because he had witnessed the actions of the city council at the Ellis Auditorium and wanted to protest their rebuff of the sanitation workers.

Reverend Jackson was one of many maced by the police when they attacked the line of marchers. He came away from the incident convinced it was provoked by racist police who would "not have maced ministers of the white community." What began as a mild curiosity about a labor dispute was transformed into a passionate attachment to a cresting civil rights struggle in his hometown. In anger Reverend Jackson took to action. He joined the more than 150 black leaders to help form an organization calling itself Community on the Move for Equality (COME). COME's members included elderly pastors and one-time racial accommodators, converts to nonviolent direct action, and angry black youths. During the strike crisis Jackson served as COME's treasurer and headed a strategy committee, the action arm of the new organization, a post he shared with other pastors, community leaders, and the NAACP's Jesse Turner. AFSCME officials, rendered helpless by the mayor's temporary injunction, were forced to step aside but gave their blessings to the new organization.[35]

COME took over the direction of the protest movement, mobilizing the black community behind the strike and the broader civil rights struggle. To pressure the white establishment into meeting the union's demands, COME's strategy was to boycott downtown stores and the city's two Scripps-Howard newspapers, which, blacks maintained, consistently gave the strike bad press. Downtown Memphis became the scene of almost daily marches dramatizing the boycott and calling for the city to meet the demands of the striking sanitation workers. Workers, college and high school students, and other members of the black community filled nightly prayer meetings and morale-building sessions in the churches and in less than a week raised $15,000 for the strikers' relief fund. Meanwhile, downtown merchants reported that sales were significantly down. While Mayor Loeb worried about a possible garbage buildup, COME was using the garbage strike to build up black unity.[36]

As the circle of support for the sanitation workers widened, drawing from all elements of black Memphis, the FBI stepped up its surveillance. As the Memphis field office caseload expanded, the bureau's intelligence capabilities floundered under the weight of the new assignment. The challenge was more than an operational one—monitoring the activities of the civil rights activists and racial militants now encompassed linking these activists with potential criminal or subversive conspiracies in violation of federal law, which would have justified the FBI's sweeping surveillance program in the first place. In the Memphis operation, the bureau resorted to outmoded techniques and political notions ("subversion," "overthrow," "sedition," and so on) to establish ties between the old "Communist Menace" and the new racial unrest of the 1960s. The effort proved fruitless; but as the racial confrontation progressed, the FBI—desperate to prove Hoover's pet thesis of Communist infiltration and control of the civil rights movement—indiscriminately targeted for surveillance all individuals and groups connected in any way with the protest movement.[37]

One leader the FBI concentrated upon was the young, able, and energetic chairman of COME's strategy committee, the Rev. James M. Lawson, Jr. His emergence as the most influential local leader in the sanitation workers' cause seemed natural considering Lawson's career or "calling" as an activist dedicated to combating war, racism, and poverty. During his undergraduate days at Baldwin-Wallace College in Berea, Ohio, Lawson joined the Fellowship of Reconciliation, the oldest pacifist organization in the country. Lawson's attachments to pacifism took on greater scope when he became a convert to A. J. Muste's revolutionary pacifism. In 1951 Lawson refused to cooperate with the Korean War draft. Although eligible for a ministerial deferment, he refused to exercise this option and was sentenced to three years in prison. After 13 months in federal prison and a three-year stint as a missionary in India, Lawson returned to the United States just as the civil rights movement was cresting in the South.

Before coming to Memphis in 1962, Lawson plunged into "Movement" politics, becoming an eloquent teacher of nonviolent direct action and a keen tactician of confrontation politics. As a divinity student at Vanderbilt University in 1960, he organized one of the first sit-in protests in the Nashville business district. While finishing his divinity degree at Boston University, Lawson helped organize a new direct action group, the Student Nonviolent Coordinating Committee (SNCC). In 1962 he accepted the chairmanship of the Memphis Area Project (MAP), a part of the federal government's War on Poverty. A strong exponent of nonviolent direct action, Lawson was convinced that only the shock of boycotts and demonstrations could overcome white resistance to social change in Memphis.[38]

Pastor Lawson's central role in black democracy's struggle in Memphis made him a prime candidate for FBI surveillance. The FBI investigative file on Lawson failed to determine whether he was a fellow traveler, but the file with its negative bias strained to find clues of subversive intent. Excluding any reference to his conspicuous pacifist antecedents, the file noted that he organized vigils in downtown Memphis protesting the American presence in Vietnam. These weekend antiwar demonstrations in 1967 were attended, according to a source within the MPD, by a handful of black and white students and community activists. Several participants were identified by the FBI as "card carrying" members of the W.E.B. DuBois Clubs of America, a youth organization characterized by the bureau as a Marxist-oriented front of the American Communist party whose "primary emphasis" was to develop "mass resistance to the draft."[39]

The inferential link between Lawson's strike-related activities and the bureau's perceived security threat centered on his successful efforts in mobilizing the black youth of Memphis behind COME's protest movement. Involvement of black youth in social action was only a preliminary stage, the bureau asserted, of a larger strategy: to prepare cadres for the massive demonstration against the Vietnam War scheduled for late April by the National Student Mobilization, which, the FBI carefully noted, "has many Communists and Communist sympathizers in its organizational staff." All the pieces seemed to come together, vindicating Hoover's suspicions, when a local source informed the FBI that Lawson planned a trip behind the Iron Curtain at the end of March to attend a peace conference in Prague, Czechoslovakia. With this revelation, Lawson's investigative file was upgraded from "Racial Matter" to "S-C" (Security Matter—Communism). The Lawson case was a good example of how FBI false alchemy made a mix of black and white come out Red.[40]

Other pastors, especially the more militant members of COME—variously referred to as "incipient interlopers" and "rabble rousers" in the FBI files—also came under bureau scrutiny. The FBI's interest in Reverends Ezekiel Bell, Malcolm Blackburn, and Harold Middlebrook, for example, was mainly to build a domestic intelligence file on these younger civil rights activists within the Memphis black community. Political intelligence-gathering in their cases took on heightened intensity when sources reported that the sanitation strike was only a forerunner of other planned job actions and racial activities in the months ahead. All rumors, allegations, and observations from informers and tipsters about a subject's personal habits, political views, and associations fell into the widespread surveillance net cast by Hoover's security police and were transmitted to the Memphis police and regional military intelligence.[41]

As the strike continued, the scope of the FBI's political intelligence operation against individuals and groups became so sweeping as to verge on the Orwellian. On March 7, for instance, Mayor Loeb held his usual "open house" to discuss the city's problems and the common concerns of its citizens. On this particular Thursday the session turned argumentative. Eighteen fashionably dressed women, described by the press as representing a "fairly broad cross-section of business and professions," crowded around the mayor and accused him of inflaming racial tensions by needlessly protracting the strike through his inflexible opposition to the checkoff system. These good Memphians, venting their civic concerns at the invitation of the mayor, attracted the attention of the Memphis field office. All of the 18 names appearing in the story carried by the *Memphis Commercial Appeal* were indexed by the bureau.[42] This practice meant that their names were fed into the field office files, checked against any previously compiled FBI file, and ultimately "warehoused" as part of the permanent record of this domestic intelligence operation.

The FBI file on the Memphis operation revealed that any name connected with the strike or related activities was routinely indexed in this fashion. Frequently a summary of the data related to indexed individuals or organizations was disseminated throughout the intelligence community. In one instance, a bureau memorandum recorded that Memphis police arrested five black youth for skipping school to participate in one of COME's downtown demonstrations. The names of the truants, ranging in age from 13 to 16, were indexed along with a summary of the circumstances surrounding their arrests and were distributed to the Memphis branch of the Secret Service and to Army, Navy, and Air Force intelligence services.[43]

Of all the activist elements in the Memphis black community coming under FBI scrutiny, youth was a special concern. Well before the sanitation strike, Hoover alerted the Memphis field office to keep FBI headquarters informed about an incipient Black Power group calling themselves the Invaders after a current popular television program. In late 1967 a number of college-age blacks, conditioned by the Vietnam War, the civil rights struggle, and the bleak economic prospects confronting black youth, created what they envisioned as a loose coalition called the Black Organizing Project (BOP). According to FBI estimates, the BOP never exceeded 100 members, most of whom were high school dropouts. Most of the BOP's executive officers were young men and women enrolled in the area's colleges and universities. Charles L. Cabbage, one of the recognized leaders of BOP and a recent graduate of Morehouse College in Atlanta, returned home to work for an antipoverty organization headed up by Reverend Lawson. Although the BOP was little more than a paper organization, its Black Power goals, extremist rhetoric, and active efforts to recruit high school and college students made it a high-priority target for bureau surveillance.[44]

Along with the FBI, the Memphis police were equally alarmed at what they characterized as the growing "Negro activist movement" within the city and had been compiling police files on black youth for several years. During the summer of 1967, senior Memphis police officials took extraordinary actions indicating just how serious they were about confronting the "subversive" menace to the social order.[45] During the summer of 1967 Memphis experienced a bout of "riot fever." Residents of the Bluff City were shocked to learn that city commissioner Claude A. Armour had declared a five-day "Alert" (July 27 through 31) and called for 1,000 members of the Tennessee National Guard to patrol the downtown area as a precautionary measure against racial violence. If Armour's actions mystified Memphians, it was understandable. The only protests with racial overtones the city had experienced since the beginning of the 1960s were the occasional NAACP-sponsored peaceful demonstrations against department stores to persuade them to liberalize their racial hiring practices and the weekend antiwar vigils of small interracial groups of students organized by pastor Lawson.

The only public explanation for the July alert from Commissioner Armour's office was the cryptic comment: "We are concerned that rumors of violence might lead to violence." However, the Memphis press was not as constrained. It carried stories of racial tensions and violence on the national scene, implying that city officials responsible for the public safety might not be overreacting.

On the first day of the alert the lead story in the morning paper was a grim account of the Detroit riot. Along with their morning coffee, Memphians were transfixed by pictures of sections of Detroit's inner city that looked like a war zone. A companion piece on the front page quoted the chairman of the House Un-American Activities Committee, Edwin E. Willis (D-La.), that "subversive elements had a hand in the riots that have rocked the nation." Willis announced that he was contemplating congressional hearings on the urban rebellions. The following day the *Commercial Appeal* carried the headline that President Johnson had named a special advisory committee to study the causes of the riots that had plagued the nation for the past four years. Another story featured a deeply agitated Whitney M. Young, head of the National Urban League and the most moderate of the nation's civil rights leaders. Stressed to the breaking point by the Detroit riot, Young told Congress that America must either "liberate or exterminate the Negro." Memphians who experienced a twinge of panic during the July alert, wondering if Memphis would be the next "Detroit," could be excused if reason gave way to fear.[46]

Calling out the National Guard, as one exasperated city official complained, was unwarranted and based on "totally unfounded rumors." Police lieutenant Frank Kallaher, recalling the 1967 threat of a "hot summer," attributed the alarm to stories of conspiratorial "underground meetings" by local black militants. "A lot of people," he quipped, "went off the deep end." The problem was that the domestic intelligence capability of the MPD was so amateurish that it could not distinguish between rumors and hard information. Probably most of the rumors about turning

Memphis into another "Detroit" originated with the Black Organizing Project. During the sanitation strike this kind of war of nerves directed against white Memphis was a favorite BOP tactic.[47]

For many years the NAACP had been the only sustained black activist movement in Memphis. Virtually without exception, young blacks were politically inert; when they did run afoul of the law it was for criminal acts; rarely, if ever, was it for crimes that were politically motivated. But by 1967 the Memphis police became alarmed at the sudden burgeoning of black youth organizations, especially on the college campuses: Owen College was home for the Afro-American Brotherhood; a Black Student Union took root at LeMoyne College; and at largely white Memphis State University a handful of black students drafted a constitution for a Black Student Association. All of these campus organizations were affiliated with the BOP. This rising tide of self-assertion and race pride among black youth was taking place in every community across the country with a large black population. Memphis differed only in that it was so late in developing. But the Memphis police viewed these largely disorganized black youth as menacing advocates of Black Power and their embryonic stirrings as a threat to the racial peace of the community.

Soon after the July alert the MPD began to upgrade its fitness in domestic intelligence and riot control. The first order of business was the reorganization of the Inspectional Bureau, the law enforcement unit responsible for both criminal and domestic intelligence work. The reorganization ended the mix of responsibilities by creating a Domestic Intelligence Unit (DIU). This four-man unit, or local "red squad," was tasked with collecting, evaluating, and acting on political intelligence.[48] Lt. Ely H. Arkin, Jr., the officer in charge of the DIU's daily activities, admitted that the unit was set up specifically to deal with BOP-Invader elements in the black community. In addition to the formation of a "red squad," a push was made to get more officers enrolled into the FBI Academy, the MPD opened its own riot training school at the Armour Center in Memphis, and a sniper squad was added to the force.[49]

During the course of Memphis's racial crisis, relations between the FBI and the MPD resembled a textbook version of cooperation between local and federal law enforcement agencies. There appeared to be none of the instances of paranoia revolving around issues of control, refusal to share file resources, or attempts by the bureau to shoulder aside the local police and grab the headlines that historically marred relations between Hoover's agency and local police functionaries. Frank Holloman, the Memphis director of public safety, characterized this relationship as "unique."

Holloman's own career was impressive testimony to this special relationship. Before joining the Loeb administration in January 1968, he had spent 25 years with the FBI, with bureau postings in Jackson, Mississippi;

Atlanta; and Cincinnati and a seven-month interim appointment as special-agent-in-charge of the Memphis field office. Holloman was professionally close to Hoover, having served seven years as inspector in charge of the director's Washington office. When Holloman became Memphis's top cop he brought with him the FBI's intelligence techniques and political standards to serve as a model for that city's police force. As soon as he assumed the directorship, his first priority, according to Holloman, was to push "for a good, efficient intelligence bureau" and to make sure there was always "a two-way street in terms of the flow of information" between the MPD and the FBI.[50]

By the beginning of 1968 the Memphis police force had a complement of 850 men, about 100 of whom were recently recruited black officers. Most of the black officers were detailed to exclusively black neighborhoods in north and south Memphis; others spent a lot of duty hours in the plainclothes detail, monitoring and reporting back to the DIU any information from public meetings, conversations, or street talk related to the strike and any black organizing activities. The DIU, generally referred to by the MPD as "Intelligence," had undercover police enrolled in Memphis State University and all the black colleges in the greater Memphis area. Using a student cover made it easier for police spies to collect intelligence on campus activities, associations, and reading material like campus newspapers, newsletters, and mimeographed handouts deemed political in nature or, more specifically, carrying a Black Power message. The MPD cultivated certain college administrators and heads of campus security to gain access to student records and help in identifying photos of students who attended rallies in support of the sanitation strikers, participated in Reverend Lawson's antiwar demonstrations, or were suspected of some affiliation with the BOP-Invaders. The red squad also made it its business to gain access to the bank records of individuals and organizations it targeted for political surveillance.[51]

During the late 1960s and early 1970s local police, especially in the larger urban centers, were adding to their forces political surveillance squads. A fundamental impetus for this burgeoning of red squads grew out of a public that was increasingly alarmed about the civil disturbances that were convulsing American cities and that demanded that the police be prepared to take effective countermeasures. Moreover, federal agencies, like the Law Enforcement Assistance Administration, at the insistence of members of congress who were feeling considerable pressure from their constituents, made funds available to local police to upgrade their domestic intelligence capabilities.[52]

The MPD's creation of a local red squad and the amassing of political files on suspected "subversives" was in lockstep with law enforcement developments that were nationwide in scope. As was the case with other

big city police forces, the accelerated growth of the MPD's political surveillance operations left the police hard pressed to supply agents to meet
the new intelligence demands. With professional advice and direction
from the local FBI, the DIU moved to close this gap by developing a stable
of ghetto sources, paid informers, and specially screened infiltrators.

The DIU's most adept undercover officer was Marrell McCullough,
code-named "Max," or Agent 500, who infiltrated the Invaders shortly after the start of the sanitation strike. McCullough was a Vietnam-era veteran with three years of military police experience. A native of Mississippi and a recent graduate of the MPD's training academy, Agent 500
took to his undercover assignment with considerable flair. Using the
cover of a "warehouse worker," he quickly established himself as a
trusted member of the Invaders, and in time he became a confidant of
some of the younger members of COME's strike strategy committee. Lt.
Frank Kallaher bragged about "Max," confiding that his performance as a
strident black militant was so convincing that "half . . . the department
would have given their eye teeth to have locked him up." The DIU
alerted the FBI about McCullough and routinely turned over to the bureau summaries of his intelligence reports.[53]

Hoover's directive on the BOP-Invaders reflected a larger concern,
namely, the FBI's nationwide COINTELPRO against designated Black
Nationalist-Hate groups. The director's justification for launching this
sweeping and costly domestic operation was to obtain preventive intelligence. Presumably, the FBI would use this information in thwarting potential or planned domestic unrest by violence-prone individuals and organizations. Approved in 1967, the program was directed against all
black activist organizations, including groups that eschewed violence but
fell under the FBI label of Black Hate because they militantly opposed in-
stitutional racism. One of the bureau's goals under the program was to
prevent any "long-range" growth of militant nationalist organizations,
especially among the young.[54]

The BOP came closest to approximating a Black Nationalist or Black
Power movement in Memphis. At best it was a fledgling movement with
worthy goals but exercising only a tenuous influence among the upcoming generation of Memphis blacks. Furthermore, it had no organizational
links with any of the Black Hate groups receiving special attention from
the Bureau's Domestic Intelligence Division. The BOP's professed purpose was to create a comprehensive community program to reach the
hard-core, bitter young adults isolated from the larger society and facing
daily choices between passive acceptance or self-destructive rebellion.
The range of programs envisioned by the coalition included an activities
center, neighborhood cooperatives, liberation schools for the teaching of
black history and black arts, and a work training program to improve the

employment opportunities for ghetto youth. In concept the program was no more subversive or un-American than Pride, Inc., a community action receiving federal funds and already in place in the nation's capital.[55]

Stymied by a lack of funds, community support, and active membership, the BOP leaders hoped to exploit the garbage strike to gain leverage within the Memphis community. Although the organization's goals addressed legitimate needs, the shrewd tactics its leaders employed only intensified racial mistrust, making a troubled situation even more explosive. Senior BOP officers consciously set out to shock Memphians, white and black, into supporting their program by raising the specter of racial violence.

Whenever possible they used public rallies supporting the strike as ready-made forums to harangue, insisting that capitalism and black liberation were incompatible and that Memphis "should be burned" or purged by a "good race riot." Cabbage and close associate John Burrell Smith gained a certain notoriety by poking fun at "Tom" ministers on the COME strategy committee and by urging blacks to "get guns" instead of marching and praying. In this calculated campaign to attract black youth with racial bravado and inflate their own credibility, Cabbage and Smith cultivated the impression that their coalition was actually a formal unit of SNCC. The main purpose behind this posturing was to work a subtle kind of blackmail: Either the BOP received recognition and financial support, or Memphis could expect a ghetto uprising. The implication that only the BOP could prevent racial violence alarmed the NAACP-COME leadership. In early March, mostly at the insistence of Reverend Lawson, the BOP leadership was invited to join COME, partially because of COME's limited influence with high school and college youth but largely to effect better control over Cabbage and his cohorts.[56]

On all counts, at least superficially—extremist rhetoric, intransigent racial militancy, and self-proclaimed formal links with SNCC, one of the bureau's designated Black Hate groups—the BOP met all the criteria to be included in an FBI political intelligence-gathering operation. Since the BOP executive officers became part of the COME coalition directing the strike and the civil rights struggle, the monitoring of their activities provided the FBI with new and prized intelligence conduits into the black community. Although the BOP was the group most intensely under surveillance in Memphis, the bureau ultimately was forced to conclude that Cabbage's organization was really a "local group led and operated by Memphians" with only a "possible fraternal relationship" with SNCC. The bureau made its intelligence "audit" of the BOP available through FBI liaison sources to federal agencies responsible for funding local community programs like that envisioned by the BOP.[57]

Since the BOP's broadest support originated among the area's college youth, the bureau had an operationally convenient justification to probe all the centers of higher education in Memphis. The Memphis field office had a file on every campus student organization supporting the sanitation strike in Memphis. This intelligence operation went to college in the guise of casual informers and tipsters, mostly bona fide students who reported occasionally to a bureau agent; college administrators and staff personnel; campus security police; and racial and security informants who had regular contact with an FBI case officer. During the course of this campus surveillance the bureau failed to uncover any groups influenced or controlled by violence-prone extremists. Actually, the campus probe had trouble detecting even the faintest pulse of any political life at all.[58]

The Memphis State University (MSU) student body was more energized by the garbage strike than students of all of the other neighboring institutions. Despite a student enrollment of about 15,000, all MSU campus activities centered around a handful of the white student membership of the Liberal Club and a few black students representing the Black Student Association (BSA). Eddie Jenkins, one of the campus organizers of the BSA, recalled that the Liberal Club did all of the planning of strike-supporting activities because the BSA charter had not yet been approved by university officials. Given the conservative nature of the MSU administration, activist blacks like Jenkins were reluctant to openly endorse any campus activity related to the strike until the university recognized the BSA campus charter. For the most part, the relatively few black students at MSU, like the overwhelming majority of white students, remained detached and apathetic during Memphis's racial crisis.

The Liberal Club staged a campus rally in support of the strike in early March, but fewer that 50 students participated. Subsequent Liberal Club efforts to galvanize the campus with sponsored marches all fizzled; even the *Tiger Rag*, the campus student newspaper, gave no coverage to the Liberal Club or strike-related news. Nonetheless, Liberal Club activities were monitored by the campus police, and the university's director of security provided the names of some of the students who participated in the March rally to the FBI which, in turn, informed the MPD.[59]

From the FBI political intelligence perspective, however, operationally habituated to the style of excess, the Liberal Club loomed as the center of campus radicalism and possible subversion. All information relating to the group was classified with the caption IS-C (Internal Security—Communism), which justified the full range of coordinated surveillance by campus security, the MPD's red squad, and the FBI. As with other targeted campuses, MSU, particularly the Liberal Club, provided the bureau with no evidence of any planned violence or civil disturbances. The last pieces of intelligence in the Liberal Club investigative file noted that the group planned to sponsor a "Students for Eugene McCarthy" rally and join in the COME-organized picketing of stores in downtown Memphis.[60]

As the strike dragged on, tempers shortened and the odds favoring serious racial violence shot up. Pent-up grievances gave vent to random incidents of vandalism, trashings, and fire-bombings. Beginning in March, on any given day the Memphis police blotter recorded a rash of trash fires, civil discord, ugly racial confrontations, and property violence against white businesses in black neighborhoods. Several of the Loeb family businesses near the ghetto areas were vandalized. The police reported that several homes of black sanitation workers who refused to honor the strike were targets of crudely fashioned fire bombs. In a single day, rumors that outside agitators from Chicago and Atlanta were headed for Memphis, a report of a bomb threat at the Booker T. Washington High School, and news that the police had confiscated weapons from student lockers at Porter Junior High School all crossed the desk of DIU's Lieutenant Arkin.[61]

Community leaders, trying to hold the line against the erosion of black patience and restraint, had their own litany of grievances. Blacks were angered by what they regarded as uniformly unfair coverage of the strike by the city's daily newspapers. The black community's resentment over the February 23 police action was further exacerbated by police actions it characterized as "harassment type" arrests and overt surveillance by plainclothes officers covering all public strike-related activities by the black community. The overall effect, black leaders complained, produced a chilling atmosphere of intimidation. Gerald Fanion, the director of the County Department of Human Relations, was arrested for jaywalking as he left a mass rally for the strikers. Fanion's arrest became an instant cause célèbre among blacks. The reaction was so sharp that police director Holloman made a public apology, dropped the charges, and had the arresting officers disciplined.[62]

COME leaders, convinced that time was no ally and that their cause needed national attention, invited prominent black figures to Memphis. On March 14 Roy Wilkins of the NAACP and Bayard Rustin of the A. Philip Randolph Institution spoke to a modest turnout of about 900 strikers and their allies at the Mason Temple. Four days later, at the entreaty of Reverend Lawson, King came to Memphis.[63]

The call from Memphis caught King and the SCLC in full-swing preparation for the Poor People's Campaign. Hesitant to add to the SCLC's agenda at a time when support for its own April campaign was flagging, King was reluctant at first but finally relented. The civil rights leader could not flinch in the face of human needs, and after all, the plight of the black sanitation workers was in microcosm the Poor People's Campaign itself.

On March 18 King spoke to an overflow crowd of 15,000 at the Mason Temple. The church was packed wall to wall with striking workers and their friends and supporters. COME "broke every fire ordinance" that night, Rev. Billy Kyles recalled; "every available space was taken." King drew strength from the huge turnout, the unity of the black community, and the fact that their struggle had kept faith with the principles of nonviolence. He told Jesse Epps, AFSCME field representative, that Memphis "was a rejuvenation of the movement." King paid tribute to the Memphis movement for "highlighting the economic issue" and "going beyond purely civil rights to questions of human rights." He delighted his audience when he exhorted them to "escalate pressure" and force Mayor Loeb to say yes when he would rather say no. He electrified the crowd when he urged all black Memphians to "unite beyond class lines" and close the city down with a massive work stoppage. Thunderous applause and cheers reverberated throughout the church, punctuated by cries of "Yeah!" "Yeah!" "Yeah!" Before the evening ended, King promised to return to Memphis and lead a protest march that would turn Loeb and his administration around. Thus, a local labor dispute–cum–civil rights struggle was spontaneously grafted onto the SCLC's planned Washington spring project.[64]

March 22 was the day King picked to return to Memphis to inaugurate the Poor People's Campaign. When a freak blizzard covered the city with more than a foot of snow, Lawson and King agreed to reschedule the march for the following Thursday (March 28). For those Memphians anxious to see the negotiations resume and the strike ended before King returned, the storm was a welcome reprieve. Many Memphians, black and white, saw the hand of providence at work. One Memphis housewife reflected this private hope when she told friends that "the Lord sent the snow to give us another chance . . . to settle it now."[65] Even before King's first visit on March 18, a concerted effort was under way to reopen the stalled talks between union and city officials. By March 26, union, COME, and city officials, meeting at the Claridge Hotel in downtown Memphis, had hammered out the form of a possible settlement through a memorandum of understanding. Had Mayor Loeb intervened favorably at this crucial point in the mediation process, he could have ended the strike and lifted the enervating siegelike atmosphere blanketing the city. But Loeb held back, refusing words of encouragement or timely concessions on the key interrelated issues of union recognition and the checkoff system. The mayor's obduracy ensured that the March 28 turnout would be cast as a protest demonstration instead of a victory parade celebrating the end of a racial dispute that threatened the social peace of Memphis.

three

Memphis: Days of Rage, Days of Sorrow

MARCH 28 WAS UNSEASONABLY HOT and seemed to grow hotter and more uncomfortable by the minute. The crowd of somewhere between 10,000 and 15,000 gathered at the Clayborn Temple AME Church, located in the heart of the Beale Street ghetto, was impatient to start the march demonstrating the solidarity of the black community.[1] Most of the marchers were middle-aged blacks who represented all sectors of the community: clergy, politicians, teachers, college professors and students, sanitation workers and their families, office and staff workers from the black insurance companies located in Memphis, and AFL-CIO union members from out-of-state locals. A large contingent of high school students joined the assembled crowd.

As the marchers waited for the command to step off, a sea of bobbing and twirling signs declared semaphore-like the diverse temper of the crowd. Intending to set the tone of the demonstration and capture the spirit of the movement, COME had hundreds of signs professionally printed with the message "I AM A MAN" distributed to the sanitation workers and their allies. Other signs, mostly handmade, ranged from the defiant to the ribald to the sassy and vulgar: "MACE WON'T STOP TRUTH," "GARBAGE STINKS. SO DOES LOEB," "LOEB EATS SHIT," and "FUCK YOU MAYOR LOEB."

The two-hour delay in starting the march, the growing heat, and the rowdy antics of black teenagers combined to take some of the edge off the early festive mood of crowd. Black youth wove in and out of the crowd chanting "Black Power" and "Loeb eats shit," completely indifferent to the efforts of the COME marshals to keep them in line. More unsettling was the stripping of the placards from the sticks, leaving defiant youth with three-foot-long weapons. Maxine Smith, located at the front of the demonstration waiting to welcome Dr. King when he arrived, admitted to no apprehensions about the march and expected no trouble until she saw "some strange people holding those sticks." Before King arrived at Clayborn Temple to lead the march, Reverend Lawson, the ministerial alliance, and the parade marshals had lost control of the situation.[2]

There were ominous signs that the March 28 demonstration might inspire violence even before the first marchers assembled at the Clayborn Temple. During the early morning hours (1:00 to 7:00 A.M.), the MPD reported 11 instances of what it characterized as "strike-oriented harassment and vandalism"—off the chart for a six-hour period even for tension-ridden Memphis. By 9:00 on the morning of the march, the police had responded to reports of trouble at five Memphis high schools. The most explosive situation occurred at Hamilton High School, a predominantly black school in South Memphis.[3]

Before first period classes began, hundreds of Hamilton students were milling around the school grounds talking up the march and trying to recruit classmates with friendly persuasion and threats to cut school and join the demonstration. Hamilton's principal, determined to fill his empty classrooms and get on with the school day, called the police to end the disruption. Police units arriving on the scene were met with a shower of rocks and bottles; the police responded by charging into the mass of students. For the better part of an hour students engaged in a running battle with the police in which "considerable force," according to one police official, was needed to "quell this disturbance." During the melee a 14-year-old girl was beaten over the head by the police and had to be rushed to the hospital. After an hour of battle royal, despite the use of clubs and mace, the police still could not gain the upper hand.

Reports from Hamilton prompted police director Holloman to phone COME headquarters, specifically requesting that Rev. Harold Middlebrook come to Hamilton High School. Middlebrook, a native Memphian and one of the more militant clergy in the ministerial alliance, was the youth director for COME and was known and trusted by many of Hamilton's black youth. Middlebrook's presence at the school was instrumental in ending the fracas before it spread into the surrounding black neighborhoods. It was touch and go for a time because some mothers, Middlebrook recalled, showed up on the school grounds with guns to stop "those kids from being brutally beaten by those police. . . ." Middlebrook barely had time to collect himself before a call came in from COME asking him to play peacemaker at Lester High School. After peace broke out at Hamilton High, hundreds of angry, boisterous teenagers, some still bloodied, joined other high school students fresh from their own earlier skirmishes with the police, at the Clayborn Temple. Many of them were now hot for revenge, ready to "zip it up" at the first opportunity.[4]

King's hectic schedule kept him from stepping off with the first line of marchers. He arrived at Clayborn Temple with staff aides after the march was already in progress, and after a hurried conversation with Reverend Lawson, the King party joined the demonstration after it had covered one city block. What happened next is still unclear. The familiar strains of "We Shall Overcome" welling up from the line of marchers was suddenly interrupted by sounds of shattering glass. Scores of black youth, including some with the logo "Invaders" scrawled across their jackets, armed with lengths of pipe, bricks, and long pine poles, were smashing windows and looting stores along the Beale Street march corridor. Pressing down hard on the heels of the rioters came a flying wedge of MPD riot police. At the first indication of violence, King's aides flagged down a passing motorist and whisked him away from the scene.[5]

Phase one of the Poor People's Campaign had turned into a riot. The situation grew uglier by the minute as police used mace and wooden batons on looters, peaceful demonstrators, and innocent bystanders alike as the blue-helmeted police wedge swept inexorably eastward along Beale Street. At the close of the violence-marred day the MPD reported one fatality—a 17-year-old black male shot by the police—and more than 50 hospitalized and approximately 125 arrested. The damage to the stores along Beale Street was later estimated at $400,000. The governor of Tennessee, at Loeb's request, sent 4,000 National Guardsmen into Memphis to enforce a dusk-to-dawn curfew.[6]

The action of the Memphis police at the high schools, especially at Hamilton High, and at the riot scene pushed to the forefront the long-standing, inflammatory issue of police brutality. Records of the emergency room at John Gaston Hospital, the medical facility receiving most of those injured during the riot, lend some credence to eyewitness allegations that the police reaction was excessive and indiscriminate. Most of those requiring emergency treatment were teenagers and young to middle-aged black males, but some of those treated for lacerations of the head, arms, and legs were 12 and younger, male and female. A handful of patients were senior citizens; the oldest was a woman of 75. Underscoring the depths of racial hostility in strife-torn Memphis were reports from some of Gaston's black nurses that their white counterparts cheered every time an injured black was wheeled into the emergency room.[7]

The March 28 violence left the local forces identified with the Memphis movement in a state of stunned bewilderment and bitter resentment against the police and at a loss about the future of the civil rights struggle. For King, the rioting, looting, and violence were a public relations disaster that threatened to erode away support for his planned Poor People's Campaign. For the parents of Larry Payne, the one fatality claimed by the day's violence, it was a family tragedy from which there was no recovery.

From the very moment that Payne was pronounced dead on arrival at Gaston Hospital from a shotgun blast point-blank to the chest, the MPD treated the killing as an open-and-shut case of self-defense. According to the police file, the 17-year-old Payne, who resided with his mother and younger brother at the Fowler Homes, a low-income housing project in south Memphis, had joined with other teenagers from the project in looting the Sears, Roebuck store on South Third Street after others had smashed the display windows during the rioting. According to the police, Payne was spotted carrying a portable television from the vicinity of the Sears store and disappeared down a stairwell into the basement of the apartment complex at Fowler Homes where he lived. The police did have probable cause that Payne had committed a felony. Officer Leslie Dean Jones, a white patrolman with six years on the force, chased Payne, cornered the youth in the basement, and "shouted eight or a dozen times," he later testified, "for him to come out with his hands over his head." It was the patrolman's testimony that when Payne emerged from behind the basement door he came at Jones with a large butcher knife. Fearing for his life, Jones discharged his sawed-off 12-gauge shotgun into Payne's chest. Jones was never placed on temporary leave or reassigned to desk duty while the MPD launched a formal investigation into the homicide. The Payne homicide, Director Holloman announced on March 29, was a clear case of self-defense and no administrative action was contemplated.[8]

In actuality, the key evidence in the death of Larry Payne pointed in the opposition direction, contrary to the official police version of self-defense. During a 1971 civil suit for damages brought by Payne's parents against the Memphis Police Department, the then chief of police, Henry Lux, admitted that Homicide Division was unable to lift any fingerprints off the butcher knife. Equally startling was the revelation that the knife, the retrieved shotgun pellets from Payne's body, and the victim's clothes were all deep-sixed in the Mississippi River five months after the shooting, since, according to Lux, there was no criminal indictment pending. In the crucial area of chain-of-evidence, Jones testified that soon after the shooting he gave the butcher knife to a "tall, big lieutenant in a white helmet" whom he could not later identify and that the MPD officer left the scene with the knife before the police photographers showed up to take pictures of the scene of the shooting.[9]

Almost a dozen Fowler Homes residents claimed to be eyewitnesses to the shooting. All of them testified in 1971 that when Larry Payne exited the basement he had both hands above his head as he approached patrolman Jones. In fairness, these statements have to be treated as coming from ex parte witnesses. As one FBI source noted, Payne was very popular with the residents in the project. Moreover, since this was a matter of white on black violence involving the police, there was little likelihood that any eyewitness would freely come forward to support patrolman Jones's version of the shooting. Harder to dismiss was a newspaper picture appearing in the black-owned *Memphis Tri-State Defender* showing the dead youth slumped against the wall of the basement stairwell, his mouth and eyes still open and both hands raised above his head.[10]

What the MPD represented as an open-and-shut case in actuality reeked of police improprieties, bordering on an official coverup. It was clear that law enforcement officials had misrepresented key facts in the Payne file and destroyed material evidence, thereby obstructing any independent attempts to uncover what really happened in that stairwell on March 28 at the Fowler Homes public housing project. The FBI had a keen interest in the Payne case, as it did with all the events surrounding the March 28 riot. However, the bureau's interest in the Payne homicide was strictly political, focusing on whether COME would try and exploit his death "to build up support for their over-all movement."

Despite all the compelling evidence to the contrary, bureau officials never entertained the presumption that there might be grounds for a federal investigation into whether Payne was unlawfully deprived of his civil rights. The bureau simply shrugged off its law enforcement responsibilities and never questioned the MPD's official version of the Payne homicide.[11]

One of the FBI's high priority claims for conducting its intelligence operations was to deter violence. Despite the agency's massive intelligence-gathering operation covering virtually every strike-related aspect of black community life, neither the bureau nor the MPD took any preventative measures to try and head off the March 28 violence. In less than a week, however, the FBI and the Memphis police came up with an explanation for the eruption of the violence. Both law enforcement agencies agreed that the riot was unorganized and limited to the petty criminal class and juveniles who were out "to get Whitey" and quickly followed the lead of these "Beale Street professionals." According to one highly placed source, the Invaders played no part in the riot.[12]

The source exonerating the Invaders was the police spy Marrell McCullough. "Max" was at the Clayborn Temple on the morning of the march, and he reported back to his superiors that the Invaders were lying low and did not engage in the rioting and looting.[13] However, McCullough was only one of an unspecified number of police spies and FBI informers at Clayborn Temple that morning. In addition to McCullough and probably other police sources, the FBI had at least five informers, one of whom had infiltrated the Invaders, who provided coverage on the Invaders.

Three of these informants were at the demonstration. All three reported seeing kids with Invader jackets distributing two-by-fours to impressionable and unruly teenagers. Several of these informers noted "common criminal types" circulating among the crowd gathered around the church. The FBI's own records clearly indicate that the bureau had information an hour or two before the start of the ill-fated march that violence was a real possibility. Moreover, the FBI's information was corroborated by the intelligence reports generated by MPD police sources.[14]

Despite early warning signals that the demonstration might erupt in violence, neither the FBI nor the MPD made any effort to warn COME or King and his party. A source at American Airlines in Memphis had informed the local FBI office of the exact time King was expected to arrive at the city's Municipal Airport from Atlanta. The bureau had plenty of lead time to reach King when he and his party deplaned and warn him that the march might incite violence. In 1978, the House Select Committee on the Assassinations concluded that the FBI was innocent of any "plan to disrupt the march" but censured the bureau for "unwarranted neglect" in its failure to alert the march organizers of the potential for serious trouble.[15]

COME undertook its own investigation to sort out what triggered the riot. Using press photos of the looters and reliable sources to work the streets, Lawson and the march organizers came up with the same conclusions the FBI settled upon. Lawson was clear in his own mind that the Invaders had nothing to do with the events of March 28. The trouble was sparked, he was convinced, by the petty criminal class who staked out their territory around Beale Street—the pool hall crowd, pickpockets, pimps, the guys wearing tank tops and wraps around their heads—the "professionals" who lived hand to mouth, hustle to hustle, on the edges of crime. With the downtown economic boycott in effect for weeks, the supply of trusting souls and pushovers they targeted for their scams had dried up and so had their livelihood. The March 28 demonstration was a golden opportunity to score big, and they had planned to turn it to their advantage.[16]

Singling out the Beale Street criminal element for igniting the riot cannot excuse COME's own incautious and miscalculated actions that helped set the stage for the March 28 troubles. Lawson and the older clergy in the ministerial alliance failed to establish any rapport with the Invaders, let alone the hard-core disaffected street people who populated the ghetto encircling the Clayborn Temple. The relationship between the senior clergy of the ministerial alliance, especially Lawson, who was the driving force behind COME, and the leaders of the Invaders was one of mutually reciprocated distrust. Trying to work with Cabbage, John Smith, and others was, Lawson complained, exhausting and futile. For a year he tried to convert them to the philosophy of nonviolence as the only sure way to effect substantive racial reform, but they refused to be weaned. In return, the Invaders regarded Lawson as their chief rival among the established leaders in the black community. Although Lawson at once impressed and intimidated them with his shrewdness and intelligence, the

Invader lieutenants were put off by what they saw as an overbearing personality that refused to entertain any views other than his own. Convinced that the Invaders had no sympathy for the sanitation workers and were using the strike to strengthen their own power base in the black community, COME kept the Invaders at a very long arm's length.[17]

Locking the Invaders out from any meaningful role in organizing the March 28 demonstration was a grave tactical error on COME's part. For all their faults, the Invaders did have influence with Memphis's black youth. Instead of attempting to marginalize the militants, Lawson and the ministerial alliance should have made every effort to win their conditional support for a peaceful march by inviting them to sit in on COME's strategy sessions.

On the day of the march the Invaders were conspicuously absent. Those Invader officers who are on record claim they avoided the Beale Street–Clayborn Temple area altogether or did not participate in the march because they anticipated serious trouble.[18] Calvin Taylor, one of the original Invaders and a senior at Memphis State University majoring in journalism in 1968, contended that the racial tension was so volatile in the city that "if 20,000 people marched . . . all the police would have to do is look the wrong way and the place would have blown up." Ron Ivy, a member of the BOP and one of the founders of the BSA at Memphis State University, was convinced that the March 28 demonstration would not be peaceful because COME had no influence with many of the high school kids, especially those who sported Invaders' jackets and fancied themselves as "revolutionaries." Ivy was also leery about a trouble-free demonstration because COME had neglected to open up any lines of communication with "the cats that hang out on the corners of Beale Street all day with rags on their heads." Some of the Invaders' post facto analysis was certainly self-serving, but events demonstrated that after isolating the militants COME went ahead without qualms, comfortably certain that the march had the support of all those elements of the black community that mattered. Admitting that none of the march organizers "thought in terms of violence," Rev. Billy Kyles, an active member of COME, when reflecting on the riot noted that all the Invaders "wanted was recognition really. I think it was a fault on our part," he continued, "that we didn't take the time to try and come together."[19]

The onus for the March 28 violence rested on many shoulders: the FBI, MPD, COME, "the cats from downtown," and the Invaders for their rabble-rousing of impressionable black kids from the public housing projects. All contributed in different ways, wittingly or not, to virtually ensure that the planned peaceful march would erupt into a storm of lawlessness and rioting. It was a day of torment that the City of Good Abode had not witnessed since the turbulent days of the Reconstruction era.[20]

Although King was the headline attraction and honored guest-leader of the march, he shared none of the culpability for the outcome. King was not the culprit—he was the prime victim of the day's events. He offered to lead the March 28 demonstration because he was uplifted by the enthusiastic outpouring and solidarity of Memphis's black community. After his March 18 address before an overflow crowd at Mason Temple, he told Kyles that the struggle taking place in Memphis had "that old movement spirit." King was gratified and moved by the fact that after five hard weeks of organized protest and marching there had been no violence, except at the hands of the Memphis police. Racism and economic injustice, the issues of the Memphis movement, were exactly the ones, King confided to Lawson, he wanted to bring before a national audience with the Poor People's Campaign.[21]

These were the considerations that inspired King to graft the Memphis movement onto the SCLC's planned spring project for the nation's capital. King and the SCLC took no part in the planning of the March 28 protest demonstration. It was not SCLC's practice to move in and take over planning and organizational responsibilities from local civil rights groups. Past experience proved that this was always bad politics and usually ended in pointless trials of mutual recriminations. Because King's calendar was so tight, his staff had the burdensome job of juggling his commitments to get him to Memphis for the rescheduled March 28 demonstration. When King and his party arrived at the Clayborn Temple, they assumed that Lawson and the COME organizers could deliver on their promise that everything was under control and that all of the elements of the black community were solidly behind the demonstration. SCLC had no information or suspicions that would have caused it to question these assurances.

The FBI seized upon the March 28 violence as a way to undercut King's reputation as a man of peace and nonviolence. There is good reason to conjecture that the FBI's inaction on March 28 in the face of threatened mayhem was a deliberate decision on the part of bureau agents. The riot was custom-made for Hoover's top priority campaign to embarrass King and to discredit the upcoming march on Washington. To that end, bureau officials in Washington and Memphis orchestrated a campaign aimed at saddling King with responsibility for the Memphis riot. The Racial Intelligence Section of the DID, responsible for running COINTELPROs against designated Black Hate groups, generated several blind memos for distribution to "cooperative media sources." The purpose of these FBI-authored editorials was to depict King as a hypocritical, demagogic, faint-hearted scoundrel who fled the scene of a riot he provoked by his own heedless actions.

One of these inflammatory concoctions, entitled "Do As I Say, Not As I Do," likened King to a "judas goat leading lambs to slaughter . . . and when the violence broke out, he disappeared." This bureau exercise in character assassination went on to underscore King's alleged hypocrisy: "The fine Hotel Lorraine is owned and patronized by Negroes but King didn't go there from his hasty exit. Instead King decided the plush Holiday Inn Motel, white-owned, operated and almost exclusively white patronized was the place to 'cool it.' There will be no boycott of white merchants for King only his followers." The other blind memo disseminated for planting with a "friendly" news source emphasized that King could not control his own followers and that "vandalism, looting, and riot" stuck to King like lint on velvet. "Memphis," the memo ominously concluded, "may only be the prelude to civil strife in our Nation's Capitol [sic]," if the Poor People's Campaign were not abandoned.[22]

This attempt to discredit King through FBI-generated press releases was a standard FBI technique rooted in the notion that if enough mud was thrown, some was bound to stick. The fact that none of these allegations were true is evidenced in the FBI's own records on King and the March 28 violence. On the dozen or more occasions since 1958 when King visited Memphis, he almost always stayed at the black-owned Lorraine Motel unless he was a guest at some private home. Since the bureau had King under blanket surveillance, this was not news to the FBI. More importantly, the day after the riot, the FBI had in its possession a complete account of the circumstances that brought King and his party to the Holiday Inn Rivermont. The records reveal that Lt. M. E. Nichols of the MPD decided to take King to the Rivermont.

At the first signs of trouble, King's aides, uncertain of what was happening but concerned about King's personal safety, tried to commandeer a white panel truck, but the driver refused to help and sped away. For a moment, Abernathy recalled, it looked like they would be caught up with part of the crowd "like fish in a closing net" as a cordon of police moved toward them. Just then Bernard Lee flagged down a passing white Pontiac occupied by two black women. The women recognized King and agreed to assist him and his party by driving them away from the danger. Lee took over the wheel and the Pontiac proceeded to the intersection of McCall and Front Streets, which was blocked by a crowd of 50 or more marchers and reporters. Fortunately at this point, Lieutenant Nichols, working crowd control on a motorcycle, happened on the scene. He cleared the crowd away from the Pontiac, and after he determined that King was in the back seat, offered to escort King and his aides to a safe place. Nichols quickly and professionally sized up the situation and decided on the Rivermont because it was far removed from the riot scene. Nichols escorted the Pontiac with sirens wailing to the Holiday Inn Rivermont on Riverside Drive far from the downtown chaos. He stayed with the King party until they were assigned rooms.[23]

Both of these bureau editorials received Hoover's OK and were "handled" on March 28 and 29 respectively, which meant that the bureau found outlets with friendly newspaper editors. According to one bureau official, the FBI did "enjoy favorable relations" with the *Memphis Commercial Appeal*. During the next several days both Memphis dailies carried editorials about the riot and King's "awesome credibility gap" and reflected on whether the March 28 violence was merely a dress rehearsal for larger forms of "non-violence" if the PPC descended on Washington, D.C. The *Commercial Appeal* published a cartoon editorial of a timorous King fleeing the riot scene under the caption "Chicken A La King."[24]

Were these Memphis editorials FBI inspired? There is no unassailable connection, just a circumstantial link. However, the House Select Committee, in its investigation of FBI efforts to smear King by press manipulation, concluded that a bureau-influenced editorial did appear in the *St. Louis Globe-Democrat*, a newspaper with a "close relationship" with the FBI in the past. Entitled "The Real Martin Luther King" (March 30–31, 1968), the editorial's salient thrust was viciously anti-King:

> Rev. King is more dangerous than Stokley Carmichael because of his non-violent masquerade. He continues to talk non-violence even as it erupts all about him. He purports to be genuinely distressed when it breaks out after his incendiary speeches or during marches he leads.
>
> Memphis could be only the prelude to a massive bloodbath in the nation's capital in several weeks.
>
> Rev. King has lost all claim to being a responsible leader of his people. Unless he is checked, he could wipe out most of the impressive civil rights gains made by Negroes in the recent years and further divide Americans at a time when unity and moderation are desperately needed.

The House Select Committee branded this *Globe-Democrat* editorial inflammatory and concluded that "it might have placed Dr. King's life in danger."[25]

The committee ignored the Memphis editorials and focused on St. Louis newspapers because the House investigation was intent on pursuing its pet theory that St. Louis was the center of an assassination conspiracy that took King's life.[26] Regardless of the merits or shortcomings of the House Select Committee's conjectures, clearly the committee's arguments put forward to satisfy its conclusions that the St. Louis editorial was FBI inspired can be used to make the same case for the Memphis editorials. The circumstances in both cases are virtually identical. In both St. Louis and Memphis, the unavoidable conclusion is that these FBI smear tactics exacerbated anti-King feelings and encouraged violent action to check this "rabble-rouser" because he was a clear threat to law and order and even the very security of the nation.[27]

Manipulation of the press was just one of the COINTELPRO strategies employed to discredit King and diminish his cause. By artfully managing all intelligence reports channeled to the White House, top-level government officials, and congressional leaders, the bureau was in a position to influence opinions about King and the Memphis violence at the highest reaches of the government. William C. Sullivan, head of the DID, selected the "pertinent parts" of the intelligence picture that were forwarded to the White House, Department of Justice, Congress, and appropriate government agencies. Sullivan's direction of this operation was straightforward and neatly summarized in his instructions to the Memphis field office to "get everything possible on King" and "stay with him until he leaves Memphis." Sullivan was especially interested in the names of the two women in the white Pontiac and "whether there is any indication of improper action on the part of King since he has been at the Rivermont Hotel."[28]

The FBI's campaign to saddle King with the responsibility for the Memphis riot found ready converts on Capitol Hill. Anti-King legislators, briefed on bureau reports of the riot, delivered emotional speeches to their colleagues linking the Memphis violence with the upcoming SCLC's scheduled march on Washington. Powerful West Virginia Democratic Senator Robert C. Byrd led the attack, characterizing King as a "self-seeking rabble-rouser" whose actions "undoubtedly encouraged" the outbreak of rioting and looting. Byrd ended his diatribe by calling on the Department of Justice to block any march led by King. Arch-segregationist Senator John C. Stennis (D-Miss.) suggested that the invitational violence inherent in the proposed Poor People's Campaign be left at the "city limits" and that only King and a small delegation of the poor "symbolically" present their case to the nation's lawmakers. Other legislators agreed with Byrd and Stennis that King should be enjoined against carrying out his plans for the Washington spring mobilization. On the evening of the abortive march, President Johnson appeared on national television and warned that "mindless violence . . . will never be tolerated in America."[29]

A leader of more ordinary stature would have abandoned the Memphis campaign and tried to ride out the wave of unfavorable national publicity. King, however, began immediately to lay plans for a new demonstration. Despite the great risks, King had little choice but to return to Memphis and live down the label of cowardice fostered by the FBI-inspired editorials. Although shaken and despondent over the March 28 violence, King felt compelled to reestablish his reputation for nonviolence by leading a peaceful march in that troubled riverfront city. The politics of the moment compressed all other considerations into one stark undeniable relationship: No Memphis, no Poor People's Campaign.

However, for the next 24 hours while King and his party took refuge at the Rivermont, there was much agonizing over whether the principles of nonviolence and the SCLC's vision of the Poor People's March had any future at all. The afternoon of the riot, a delegation of COME ministers came to apologize to King and found him in bed with the covers pulled up around him. Billy Kyles recalled that King "wasn't angry . . . but he was upset." But the two SCLC staffers staying with King, Rev. Ralph D. Abernathy and Bernard Lee, made no effort to hide their sense of betrayal by the Memphis ministers for placing the SCLC in a situation that could turn violent without alerting them to the possibility. With Lawson taking the lead, the COME ministers blamed the violence on the Invaders. This was the first that King had heard of this small group of young militants.[30]

That evening, after the COME party had left, King's earlier surface composure gave way to undercurrents of bitterness and depression. The television images of the day's looting and violence preyed on his mind. King worried that the national press would be hot on his heels, blaming him for leading a mass march that turned violent. Then there were national black leaders like Roy Wilkins and Bayard Rustin and "that stripe," he gloomed to a trusted adviser, who would use the Memphis incident to undermine his reputation as a man of nonviolence and his influence with the nation's black population. Abernathy tried to lift King's spirits, but all efforts at reassurance and consolation were in vain.

Exhausted but unable to sleep, King spent the evening on the phone talking to friends and family, trying to exorcise the nightmare of the day's events and seeking advice on how to recover from the public relations setback of Memphis. In a conversation with Stanley Levison, a dejected King confided that he was thinking of calling off the Washington campaign. Levison tried to reassure him that his pessimism was the result of his physical exhaustion and that Lawson and the local clergy were responsible for the trouble. Levison refused to accept King's notion that the Poor People's Campaign was doomed, arguing that the facts exonerating King would soon surface and the crisis would blow over. Nothing seemed to shore up King's spirits, and at one point late in the evening he told Abernathy, "Maybe we'll have to let violence run its course. Maybe people will listen to the voice of violence. They certainly won't listen to us."[31]

One of King's late-night calls on March 28 was to Hosea Williams at SCLC's Atlanta headquarters. Concerned about King's depressed state of mind and his second thoughts about the Washington march, Williams discussed the call with his colleagues, including secret FBI informer Jim Harrison. Harrison reported the conversation to his bureau case officer in Atlanta, who in turn passed this valuable intelligence tidbit to senior bureau officials in Washington. A check of the logs of the FBI's phone tap on Stanley Levison provided firsthand confirmation of the Memphis news. These sources provided Assistant Director Sullivan and the DID with a working outline for a sure-fire plan to play on King's anxieties and discredit the upcoming Poor People's Campaign.[32]

Friday morning, the day after the abortive march, King had his first meeting with the Invaders at his Rivermont suite. King had sent word out that he wanted to meet with the militants to learn about their grievances. Charles Cabbage, Calvin Taylor, and Charles ("Izzy") Harrington showed up at King's suite because they wanted to assure King that they had nothing to do with the rioting. Abernathy met them at the door and carefully checked them over. He recalled they "were well dressed, well groomed; and I didn't see any signs of weapons, so I ushered them in." Abernathy, of course, had no way of knowing that one of the trio was probably an FBI informer. When King entered the room he was surprised to see Cabbage. King had met Cabbage before when Hosea Williams recommended adding him to SCLC's staff as a field organizer in Baltimore, but there was some mixup about finances and Cabbage had returned to Memphis.[33]

This helped to ease the initial tension, but the real icebreaker came when King recalled that Cabbage was a fellow Morehouse graduate. King was all attention as Cabbage did most of the talking for the Invaders, explaining that they had been wrongfully accused of precipitating the violence. Cabbage blamed Lawson and the COME ministers for exiling the Invaders to the fringes of the Memphis movement. In defending the Invaders, Cabbage's unspoken message that the march would have been peaceful had the ministers brought the Invaders into the planning was not lost on King and Abernathy. Later Calvin Taylor was more forthcoming. He remarked: "It was not our intention that the march erupt into anything. However . . . we must take part of the blame simply because we represented the element that did break it. But these people were not controlled by us. . . . I felt a little bit ashamed," he confessed, "because I know for a fact that we were partly responsible for the riot, and there weren't any two of three ways about it."[34]

King did not accept Cabbage's claims that the Invaders were totally innocent of Thursday's riot, and he let the Invader leader know without raising his voice.[35] In any case it was too late for recriminations. What King was desperate to understand was why a riot had broken out in the ranks of a demonstration he was leading. He wanted to know why Cabbage had not approached him, as one Morehouse man to another, when he was in Memphis earlier in the month and warned him of the danger of violence. Lawson, King went on, never told him about the tensions between the ministers and Black Power elements in the community. To the contrary, Lawson led King and the SCLC to believe there were no militants in the city. As Taylor recalled, Cabbage shot back: "Well, then it was just a trap . . . because we have been here trying to talk to Lawson . . . he won't hear us." Taylor, whose attention was riveted on King throughout the meeting, noticed the dispiriting effect Cabbage's remarks had on their host. King told the threesome that had he known of these hostile dynamics, he would have called off the march. King related that when he arrived late at the march he sensed some hazard. "The people were trampling over my feet . . . crowding around me. The atmosphere was just wrong."[36]

Before the meeting broke up King promised he would speak to the COME ministers and see that the Invaders were brought into all future planning affecting the black community. He impressed upon his visitors that it was essential that SCLC return to Memphis and carry off a peaceful demonstration. Picking up from Cabbage's earlier latent inference—that an orderly march depended upon Invader support—King raised the key question: Could he count on their cooperation? Cabbage saw this as an opening to appeal to King for financial help to get the Invaders' community action programs up and running. King agreed that programs like those Cabbage described were needed and said he would try and find funding and administrative assistance for the Invaders. Cabbage pledged all-out support for the second Memphis march, tentatively scheduled for April 5, and volunteered the Invaders to help King recruit people for the Washington spring project. When the trio left King's suite they were elated. Cabbage, contemptuous of all authority (Taylor branded him "sincere" but a hell-raiser), felt compelled to point out to the others that they had just left the company of an "extraordinary man." "We will get our program going," Cabbage enthused, "because that man is good for his word."[37]

When King left Memphis late Friday afternoon, he was determined to return to lead a peaceful march. The following day he met with his SCLC staff to prepare the groundwork for the return to Memphis. Events of the past few days made it incandescently clear to King that the Poor People's Campaign would either live or die in Memphis. As he learned early in the Saturday planning session, this view did not receive the enthusiastic support of the group; some of his top aides even spoke out openly, saying that it would be a mistake to get bogged down in Memphis. For King, this sounded like cut-and-run talk. He was disheartened that some of his closest friends and advisers would not stand with him when he needed them the most. As the morning session dragged on without a consensus, King excused himself but not before venting his anger and frustration at his irresolute colleagues.

This rare display of anger and his sudden disappearance had a salutary effect on King's aides. Somewhat ashamed of their foot-dragging and dissidence, they agreed to resolve their differences and prepare to launch the Poor People's Campaign with a nonviolent demonstration in Memphis. By the end of the afternoon session it was agreed that an advance team of staffers would leave that night for Memphis to set up meetings with the Invaders, prepare to hold workshops with black youth on the principles of nonviolence, and repair the damage of the March 28 violence.[38]

King, Abernathy, Andy Young, and party arrived in Memphis on April 3 at about 10:30 A.M. on Eastern Airlines Flight 381. Normally this short flight from Atlanta to Memphis was always on schedule. Flight 381, however, was held up on the runway for more than an hour while the luggage was rechecked because of a bomb threat aimed at King. After the plane was cleared for takeoff, King turned to Abernathy "and gave a dry laugh: 'Well, it looks like they won't kill me on this flight.' "[39]Abernathy tried to assure King that he was in no danger, but he had witnessed these bouts of foreboding and preoccupation with death before, and he knew his friend would have to work through this cold and dark mood himself.

When the King party deplaned at Gate 17 they were met by an orderly crowd of about 20 well-wishers and some news media people. COME assigned Mrs. Thomas Matthews to pick up the King party and take them to the Lorraine Motel.[40]

Elements of the MPD were also in the vicinity of Gate 17 when King arrived in Memphis. Inspector G. P. Tines assigned two black plainclothesmen, detective Edward E. Redditt and patrolman Willie B. Richmond, to "keep a continuing surveillance" on King and report back on all his contacts while he was in Memphis. A security detail of four senior white MPD officers, headed up by Inspector Don H. Smith, met King at the airport. Inspector Smith's regular duties at this time were with the MPD's "Intelligence" or red squad. Smith later reported that when he approached Reverend Lawson at the airport terminal and identified himself as part of the security detail for Dr. King, Lawson mildly but firmly rebuffed him, inferring that COME was not interested in cooperating with the Memphis police on security matters. Earlier that morning while awaiting King's arrival, Mrs. Matthews was questioned by a lieutenant in Smith's detail about security arrangements and was told point-blank, according to the MPD, that COME had not asked for police protection for King. No one in Smith's detail ever approached King directly at Metropolitan Airport about the need for police protection.[41]

Tines's report, written after King's assassination, contains much that is self-serving and one glaring omission that strongly argues that surveillance or intelligence and not King's security was the MPD's priority concern. That COME and the SCLC rejected police offers of protection for King was probably true and reasonable given the prevailing hostility between the black community and the Memphis Police Department, even allowing for shading in Tines's account.

Several days after the February 23 macing incident, an emotional Billy Kyles, addressing a mass meeting at St. Paul Baptist Church, stated what was on the minds of many blacks in the audience: "This was a labor issue in the beginning, but it is a race issue now, and we are at war."[42] The overreaction of the police on March 28 and the Payne homicide only reinforced Kyles's reading of the racial situation in the minds of black Memphians. COME and the sanitation workers were also angered by the

MPD's persistent overt surveillance—the police routinely used black officers in mufti who were known in the black community—of every strike-
related public meeting and outdoor demonstration since the beginning of
the walkout. COME and their sympathizers regarded this as a calculated
war of nerves on the part of the police to intimidate and break the spirit of
their movement. COME complained strenuously about this to the city
council and Director Holloman but to no avail.

"You are a dirty black son of a bitch who has sold his race out" was the
invective screamed over and over again at Louis McKay. McKay was an
MPD undercover officer assigned to the DIU to spy on the sanitation
workers. The unfortunate McKay was spotted monitoring a mass meeting at Union Hall, manhandled by some of the strikers, dragged to the
stage, and publicly vilified before he was released. McKay might have received rougher treatment if Cornelia Crenshaw, who was at the meeting
and had earned the strikers' gratitude by distributing food to their families, had not interceded on his behalf.[43]

Detective Redditt and patrolman Richmond, who carried out the lion's
share of surveillance for Lieutenant Arkin's red squad, were both threatened by irate movement blacks that if they continued showing up at
COME meetings they would end up in the hospital or worse. Redditt reported that while he waited at the air terminal for King's arrival he was
confronted by Mrs. Matthews, who threatened him, pointing a finger at
the detective and promising to "get him" and "I am going to shoot him."[44]

This complete breakdown of trust in the MPD by COME and its movement allies convinced the local leaders not to cooperate with the police on
any security arrangements for King. Had they known of an April 1 assassination threat against King's life, COME and the SCLC might have reacted differently.

On April 1, four days after the riot, Helen Perkins, a reservationist with
American Airlines in Memphis, received a phone call from a man who
"spoke in a clear, precise and emphatic voice." The caller, believed to be a
local white male, left the following message: "Your airline brought Martin
Luther King to Memphis and when he comes again a bomb will go off
and he will be assassinated."[45] The threat was immediately reported to
the Memphis bureau. Crank calls and written threats against King were
not uncommon occurrences.[46] This threat commands attention because it
was one of two bomb threats against King in as many days, because it
was believed to be a threat from someone in Memphis, and because of the
indefensible manner with which the FBI treated this incident. The file
records that the Memphis bureau advised FBI Washington headquarters,
the Secret Service, MPD, the Shelby County Sheriff, the 111th Military Intelligence Unit, and the Federal Aviation Administration but never notified King and his family. Memphis FBI agent Burl Johnson notified the

Memphis police of the threat. The decision for keeping King in the dark about this threat on his life could only have originated at the highest reaches of the FBI—the office of Director Hoover.

The FBI set up a separate headquarters file on this incident captioned "Threat to American Airlines & Dr. King, Jr., Memphis, Tenn., 1/4/'68" (149-121) instead of filing it under the bureau's main Murder of King or MURKIN file. In my opinion, the sole purpose behind this creative record keeping was to conceal file 149-121 from any future independent investigation into the King assassination. Then on May 28, 1968, the FBI closed file 149-121 on the grounds that "all information furnished by unknown person making the . . . call was untrue." All these manipulations point incontrovertibly to an FBI admission of guilt. It was official bureau policy, stated unequivocally in the FBI manual and reaffirmed by Hoover in October 1964, that any "victim of threatened bodily harm" unaware of the threat was to be notified immediately by a bureau agent.[47] In addition to "unwarranted neglect," the record in the King case lays the bureau open to charges of reckless endangerment of King's life. The top law enforcement officials of the MPD were also aware of the April 1 threat on the day it was made but failed to alert COME or King when he arrived in Memphis on the morning of April 3.[48]

As America's foremost paladin of the poor and oppressed and an unwelcome critic of Johnson's Asian war, King attracted a host of enemies. King learned to coexist with the danger, accepting the reality that his might not be a long life, but he never allowed threats of assassination to cripple his spirit or interfere with his work. In the privacy of his parents' home, he spoke openly about possible attempts on his life, trying to prepare his mother and father for any eventuality.[49]

King was prepared to persist with the Poor People's Campaign regardless of the risks. He was not, however, the kind of man who played or flirted with death; nor was he a fatalist. When King was the keynote speaker at the SCLC-sponsored "Ministers Leadership Training Program" in Miami, Florida, in February 1968, he received a bomb threat. An anonymous call was made to the FBI's Miami office and one to the switchboard operator at the Sheraton Ambassador Hotel where King was staying. The caller in both instances wanted to know King's room number so he could kill him without injuring others in the hotel. In this instance, the Miami field office followed the FBI manual and notified King and the local authorities of the threat. According to Billy Kyles, who was with King at the time, the Miami police let King know that they were taking the threat seriously and strongly urged him to stay in his hotel suite until he left Miami. Convinced of the legitimacy of the threat and persuaded that the police were concerned about his safety, King readily accepted their protection and remained in his rooms for two nights.[50]

It is impossible to state with confidence that King would have lived to lead a second Memphis march even if the FBI and MPD had reacted like their Miami counterparts in the Ambassador Hotel incident. However, if they had taken warranted action, it is likely that the SCLC, once alerted, would have come up with some precautionary measures or even agreed to cooperate with MPD personnel who could advise them on security matters. King might have agreed to some restrictions on his movements and a legitimate security detail that was not too obtrusive. King was not in the habit of refusing police protection, even when his work took him to Memphis. This might have been enough to deter any attempt on his life while he was in Memphis.

Furthermore, it should have been obvious to Director Holloman and the Memphis Police Department, even if they were not sympathetic to King and his cause, that it was in the self-interest of the city authorities to do their utmost to see that nothing happened to this international figure while he was in Memphis. Already shaken by a riot that attracted national attention, the City of Good Abode was in no shape to carry the weight of national guilt for a crime as heinous as the assassination of Dr. King. In failing to alert King of the threat on his life, both law enforcement agencies raised the odds considerably favoring a successful attempt.[51]

The Washington bureau elites were determined to keep a tight surveillance rein on all King's movements, contacts, and plans as he prepared to return and after he arrived in Memphis. On April 2, citing the Memphis violence and linking it with the upcoming march on Washington, Hoover requested that the attorney general approve a wiretap on SCLC's Atlanta offices and its recently opened local headquarters in northwest Washington. Attorney General Ramsey Clark had already rejected an earlier Hoover request for a phone tap on the Atlanta offices, maintaining that there was no "adequate demonstration of a direct threat to the national security."[52] Hoping that the March 28 riot might have caused the attorney general to rethink his position, Hoover went on record again with the April 2 request and asked for a "prompt reply" so the "Bureau may fulfill its responsibilities in the field of internal security." Clark squelched this latest overture with icy silence. He did not bother to respond to the importuning director until January 1969 and then only to deny the April 2 request.[53]

The denial of the wiretaps did not handicap the Memphis bureau's intelligence-gathering operation targeted against King and the SCLC. The Memphis FBI and the MPD engaged in a highly successful joint venture in information sharing. There was little that went on at the Lorraine Motel involving King and SCLC's planning for the rescheduled April 8 march that did not cross the desk of either FBI agent William H. Lawrence or the DIU's Lieutenant Arkin. At the time of the sanitation strike, Lawrence was a veteran case officer, having spent more than 20 years working out of the Memphis field office. His specialty was developing and running racial informers. Lawrence was instrumental in helping the MPD to bring on line its intelligence unit, or red squad, where he and Lieutenant Arkin developed close professional ties that matured over time into an active social relationship involving their families.

Lawrence was the case officer for the five FBI informers assigned to cover the Invaders, at least one of whom had infiltrated the group. Arkin's prized intelligence asset was "Max," designated minister of transportation by the Invaders because he was the only one in the group with a car. This overlapping coverage, augmented by other sources, provided the FBI and the MPD with detailed information on who was conferring with King and what was discussed. For example, a 17-page memorandum reported what took place at a strategy session at the Lorraine Motel on April 2 involving SCLC, COME, and members of the Invaders. The sources for this lengthy intelligence report were police spy McCullough and Lawrence's man inside the Invaders, probably one of the threesome who met with King on the morning of March 29. On the evening of April 3, King and his SCLC staff met with Cabbage and a few other Invaders to ensure their support for the April 8 demonstration and outline what steps SCLC would take to advance their grassroots program in Memphis. McCullough contributed to a 12-page intelligence summary of this evening session, but the major source was SCLC staffer Jim Harrison. Harrison had arrived in Memphis with the King party on Wednesday morning and attended the strategy session before his scheduled flight back to Atlanta that evening.[54]

While preparing for the second Memphis march, King was struck down by an assassin's bullet. A few minutes before 6:00 P.M. on the evening of April 4, King left his room at the Lorraine Motel after a long, taxing day of staff meetings. He walked out onto the balcony to relax before dinner at Reverend Kyles's house, joking with members in his party waiting below in the motel's courtyard. At 6:01 P.M. an assassin's bullet hit King in the face, exploding on impact and slamming him away from the balcony railing and over onto his back.[55]

Marrell McCullough was the first person to reach the fallen civil rights leader. He had recently returned to the Lorraine after spending most of the afternoon chauffeuring SCLC staffers, the Reverends Jim Bevel and Jim Orange, around Memphis in his 1967 blue Volkswagen while they shopped for overalls. "Max" was using his cover as an Invader and blue-collar worker sympathetic to the strike to maintain continuous surveillance on King and his party. While he was waiting around in the parking lot making a mental note of all those present, he heard an explosion.

McCullough recognized that it was a rifle shot, and he sprinted up the stairs toward the stricken King. Almost simultaneously an unidentified man reached King and handed McCullough a towel that he used to apply pressure to a gaping wound starting at the right cheek and running down into King's neck. McCullough applied pressure for one or two minutes to try and stop the profuse bleeding, but he realized that for all practical purposes King was beyond help.

By this time a number of people had gathered around the stricken King. Abernathy moved in and relieved McCullough and cradled his dying friend in his arms. McCullough was suddenly conscious of two young college-aged women among the horror-stricken onlookers on the balcony. Clara Ester and Mary Hunt were COME volunteers who had come to the Lorraine that evening to introduce themselves to Dr. King. As they stared down at his motionless body and immobile eyes, they were on the verge of hysteria; McCullough intervened and walked them back down the balcony's outside stairs to the parking lot below. At 7:05 P.M. doctors at St. Joseph's Hospital officially pronounced King dead.[56]

The news of King's murder incited a wave of arson, looting, and sporadic sniping in Memphis and in more than 100 other American cities and produced a groundswell of pressure that Mayor Loeb could no longer resist. The day after the assassination, President Johnson dispatched Undersecretary of Labor James J. Reynolds to Memphis with instructions to impress upon the local white leadership that a quick settlement of the strike was in the national interest. As Reynolds flew over the capital, buildings near the White House were still burning from the rioting in black neighborhoods sparked by the news of King's assassination. Tennessee's Governor Buford Ellington urged that the city and union spokesmen reopen talks and arrange for a quick settlement of the strike. Prominent elements of the white business community who had consistently opposed all compromise with the union now insisted that Loeb work for an expeditious end to the strike. The recognition that the black community was prepared to continue the boycotting and demonstrations well into the summer partially explains the volte-face of the mayor's former supporters. Many businessmen were also fearful that Memphis would invite derisive treatment at the hands of the national press as a "southern backwater" and "decaying river city" unless this dark chapter in the city's history was ended amicably and without further delay.[57]

All these converging pressures set in motion the negotiating process that ultimately produced an agreement ending the sanitation workers' strike. On April 6, Loeb, Reynolds, and Jerry Wurf, the international president of AFSCME, met in Reynolds's room at the Peabody Hotel in downtown Memphis. This was the first face-to-face meeting between Loeb and the union president since the abortive television session on February 21 in the mayor's office. The negotiations proceeded in a businesslike atmosphere with Reynolds as umpire and a constant reminder that Memphis's future share of federal funds hinged upon a quick and successful denouement. Ten days later Loeb and the union representatives agreed on the final terms of a settlement that met virtually all the union demands. Ironically, the final agreement employed almost the same language as that contained in the earlier Claridge Hotel "memorandum of understanding" submitted to Loeb on March 26. That evening the jubilant workers and their supporters gathered at the Clayborn Temple, where the union membership voted unanimously to accept the agreement, ending the 65-day strike.[58]

From the very outset, the problems inherent in the government's version of the King assassination were glaringly accented in the official solution to the crime. It seemed impossible that an unaided gunman could kill King and make a clean escape from an area that was literally swarming with police. According to Inspector Tines, at the time of the shooting there were "two tact units and five cars in close proximity." By Tines's calculation this added up to at least 44 of Memphis's finest in the vicinity of the Lorraine Motel. Moreover, at the time King was shot there were at least a dozen officers from Tact Unit 10 taking a rest break at the Butler Street fire station adjacent to the motel, less than 200 feet from the crime scene. Given these circumstances, gullibility was not a prime prerequisite for dissenters from the official story to suspect that King was set up. By the mid-1970s, when the Justice Department and several congressional committees in separate investigations publicly laid bare some of the "Hoover horrors" entailed in the FBI's five years of COINTELPRO operations targeted against King, it seemed impossible to think about the murder of King except in terms of doubt and conspiracy involving both the MPD and the FBI.[59]

Several months before the scheduled trial of the alleged assassin, James Earl Ray, Rev. James Bevel, representing the SCLC, told a news conference in Philadelphia that he had evidence that Ray was not the gunman. Abernathy supported Bevel's claims that King was the victim of a conspiracy.[60]

Although Bevel and Abernathy's 1969 allegations created only a temporary stir, two 1976 stories appearing in *Newsday*, a Long Island, New York, newspaper, had a more far reaching impact. The writer of these two hard-hitting news stories was Les Payne, a tough-minded, black investigative reporter for Newsday, Inc.[61] In his February 1 lead story Payne, citing unidentified sources, charged that FBI informers and an undercover police spy in the Invaders were instrumental in instigating the March 28 riot that forced King to return to Memphis where he was assassinated. In his second *Newsday* piece, Payne added a few more links to what he characterized as "a chain of curious circumstances" surrounding King's murder.

This story centered on the sudden removal of Edward Estes Redditt, a black detective with the MPD who, according to Payne, was assigned to King's security detail when he returned to Memphis to prepare for the second march. Redditt, who had to be Payne's chief source for this story, "had prepared a contingency plan," the article continued, "to enable the police department to apprehend an assassin had an attempt been made on King's life." Retired FBI agent and Redditt's superior, Director Holloman, ordered the detective to leave his post at the Butler Street firehouse on the afternoon of April 4 because there were two reported threats on Redditt's life. His removal, as Payne was careful to point out, came only hours before King's assassination. Detective Redditt protested his removal, but the MPD brass insisted that he accept a police guard and go home for his own safety. Redditt remained at home with his family under police protection for three days before returning to duty. The Redditt affair raised the serious allegation that King's security was stripped from him just hours before he was assassinated. The two Payne articles made a prima facie case for FBI and MPD involvement in the King assassination.

Payne's *Newsday* pieces set off alarm bells at FBI headquarters in Washington. His disclosures came at a most untimely juncture in the agency's history. The Hoover era of almost half a century had just recently come to a close with the death of "the Boss" who had shaped the agency in his own image, and the Justice Department was reviewing FBI files to determine whether the former director's vendetta against King was related to his murder. The new director, Clarence M. Kelley, ordered an in-house search of the records so the bureau could prepare a rebuttal to Payne's charges and forward it to the office of the U.S. attorney general.[62] Director Kelley wrote to Payne that a "thorough search" of FBI headquarters and Memphis field office files "resulted in no substantiation being found for the allegations" in his February 1, 1976, *Newsday* article. However, Kelley did notify Payne that his earlier request to examine the physical evidence in the King case had been granted.[63]

While reporter Payne received attention with his *Newsday* pieces, Mark Lane, who was a noted author, an early critic of the Warren Commission, lecturer, and law professor, had the credentials, connections, and ready funds to expand upon Payne's initial discoveries in the King case. Lane teamed up with television producer Abby Mann, who had counted King among his good friends, to make a television documentary of the life of the martyred civil rights leader. Mann had impressive credentials. He had written the film classic *Judgement at Nuremberg* and was the creator of *Kojak*, the long-running TV series about a crime-fighting, skin-headed, lollipop-sucking, tough New York police lieutenant.

Lane had learned about Detective Redditt from Les Payne, and he later introduced Redditt to Mann during their joint fact-gathering trip to Memphis. The chief purpose behind the Memphis trip was to interview Redditt, check his story against Payne's information, and talk to other local witnesses for independent corroboration. After three days of interviews and taping of witnesses, Lane was satisfied that "all Payne had written was established again. . . ." Through discussions, probably with COME ministers Kyles and Lawson, the two investigators learned about the mysterious removal of the only two black firefighters, Floyd E. Newsum and Norvell E. Wallace, from the Butler Street firehouse less than 24 hours before the assassination. These revelations, coupled with questions about the physical evidence in the case, were instrumental in persuading the membership of the Congressional Black Caucus, with Mrs. King's endorsement, to press the House leadership to support a resolution calling for the creation of a Select Committee on Assassinations to examine the facts behind the murder of King.[64]

On September 17, 1976, the House voted overwhelmingly to create a 12-member committee to investigate the assassinations of Pres. John F. Kennedy and Dr. Martin Luther King, Jr. A similar measure proposed by Congressmen Thomas Downing (D-Va.) and Henry B. Gonzalez (D-Tex.) had been languishing in the House for more than a year. According to a *Washington Post* story, it was the sudden push from the Black Caucus inspired by "new information" unearthed by Abby Mann and Mark Lane that moved the House to take positive action. The *Post* account noted that this "new information" featured the Redditt affair and the removal of two black firemen from a firehouse across the street from the Lorraine Motel.[65]

Lane's stock as a citizen investigator in the King case would rise or fall depending upon Redditt's veracity. Unfortunately for Lane, Detective Redditt turned out to be an accomplished self-promoter who completely misrepresented virtually everything Lane attributed to him. It is puzzling that Lane did not suspect that there was something shady about Redditt's story during the three days he was sounding out witnesses, some of whom were movement activists and very knowledgeable about the racial crisis in Memphis that reached fever heat during the sanitation strike. All of them knew that Redditt was an MPD intelligence officer who spied on Dr. King, the sanitation workers, and their allies and that he was distrusted and even hated by many in the black community.

Ed Redditt probably first entered into police intelligence work when he was assigned to MPD's Community Relations Division, an effective cover for penetrating the Memphis ghetto. As soon as the sanitation strike began he was transferred to Lieutenant Arkin's red squad, where he and his partner, Willie B. Richmond, surveilled activities related to the strike. This was a risky assignment requiring some professional cool, evidenced by the fact that both undercover officers received several threats against their lives. Soon after King's advance party of SCLC staffers arrived in Memphis on Sunday, March 31, Redditt and Richmond set up a surveillance command post at the Butler Street firehouse. They were assigned to report back to Lieutenant Arkin the names of all known Memphians, especially Invaders, who were meeting with the SCLC staff.[66]

The Redditt-Richmond detail was still in place after King arrived in the city. On the evening of April 3 both officers were ordered to cover a mass meeting at the Mason Temple. Before they had a chance to enter the church, they were called aside by Rev. Malcolm Blackburn, who warned them to leave because the tension was very high and Lawson was prepared to point them out after his remarks about the "cold blooded murder" of Larry Payne. Redditt must have unraveled when Blackburn ended the conversation with the news that the word was out that the two undercover officers were spying on the Lorraine Motel with binoculars from the Butler Street firehouse. It must have hit Redditt then and there that someone in the fire station had blown their operation.[67]

Lane's reporting that two black firefighters were suddenly removed from the Butler Street firehouse, more commonly identified as Fire Station No. 2, was accurate. In an interview with Justice Department investigators, Floyd Newsum, one of the black firefighters in question, reported that after he returned from the Mason Temple rally on the evening of April 3, where he was deeply moved by King's "Mountain Top" speech, he received a phone call at 11:30 P.M. from his immediate superior officer and was told not to report to Fire Station No. 2 the next day. The black fireman was temporarily reassigned to a fire company in a white neighborhood. Newsum was outspoken about his support of the striking garbage workers. He was aware and troubled that Redditt and Richmond were observing the Lorraine Motel and King through a peephole in a newspaper-covered window on a door at the rear of the firehouse. When he confronted Redditt about his activities, the detective said he was posted there for King's protection.

After King's assassination, Newsum's initial uneasiness about his sudden transfer became a consuming suspicion, and he forced himself upon his superiors for explanations but received only evasive replies. Later, however, a deputy chief in the fire department told him that the request for his removal came from the police department. As for the other black firefighter at Station No. 2, Norvell Wallace, his treatment was a replay of Newsum's story. Late in the evening of April 3, Lieutenant Wallace was suddenly transferred in the middle of his 24-hour shift to a firehouse near the Memphis airport. Assuming he was reassigned to bring an understaffed unit up to full strength, Wallace was surprised when he was detailed to a pump truck that was already fully staffed. He rode the pump truck as an extra fifth man for three months before returning to the Butler Street firehouse. It should be noted that Wallace was aware of the lookout post at the rear of Fire Station No. 2 and that he supported the strike largely through financial contributions; unlike Newsum, he discreetly avoided discussing the politics of strike in the workplace.[68]

Redditt's star witness status, highlighted by his public interviews, the multiple citations of his name in Lane's book on the King assassination, and his appearance on Abby Mann's television documentary on King, inevitably brought him before the House committee investigating the circumstances surrounding the King assassination. While under oath, all of Redditt's representations about the King case collapsed like a bad alibi. He admitted several times that he was assigned only to surveil King and not to provide protection. At least three times the MPD detective confessed that the "perimeter plan," the scheme he touted to seal off the area around the Lorraine Motel in the event of an attempt on King's life, was a hoax. He also disclosed under questioning that the removal of Newsum and Wallace from Fire Station No. 2 was the result of a memo he and Richmond wrote to Inspector Tines requesting Tines to try and secure their transfer. Newsum, it seems, was giving them "a hard way to go" about their spying on King and his party at the Lorraine, and they were afraid that either one of the black firefighters would broadcast their activities to the black community. The only defense Redditt offered up throughout his ordeal was that his words and intentions were misrepresented by someone "much smarter" than him, who can "write books overnight." The impression Redditt hoped to leave with the committee was that during his association with Lane, it was Lane who was doing the steering and not the other way around.[69]

The suspicious circumstances surrounding the removal of Detective Redditt on the day of the assassination were resolved to the committee's satisfaction and, for the fair-minded at least, the historic record.[70]

On April 4, while Redditt was manning his surveillance post at the fire station, he received a local phone call from a woman who accused him of betraying his own people and warned that he would pay for his treachery. Later that same day Philip R. Manuel, a staff member of Sen. John McClellan's Investigating Committee, was in Memphis discussing the upcoming April 8 march with MPD brass, when he was summoned to call his Washington office. Manuel was advised that a reliable source within the Mississippi Freedom Democratic Party had learned that there was a contract out on a black lieutenant in Memphis. (It turned out that Manuel, after returning to Washington that evening, phoned Memphis the next day advising that the threat was aimed at a black lieutenant in Knoxville.) In the face of these April 4 developments, Director Holloman ordered Redditt pulled off his post and sent home with police protection. Richmond took over for Redditt at the peephole in the rear of the firehouse. Given the fact that Redditt had already had his life threatened on two separate occasions by local black women, his superior officers acted promptly and correctly; there was simply no other responsible course of action open to them. Under these circumstances and given the fact that Redditt was never detailed to protect King, it was an outlandish mangling of the facts to assert that his removal was part of MPD policy to "strip" King of his security.[71]

On November 9, 1978, Director Holloman was a witness before the House Select Committee on Assassinations. Compared to most of his testimony during this session, his defense of the removal of Redditt was his finest moment.[72] However, in those critical areas related to King's assassination, Memphis's top cop gave the impression that he was little more than a figurehead director, outside the loop, always once removed from decisions affecting King's security. For example, he could not say who called off King's security detail on April 3 at 5:05 P.M. around the Lorraine Motel. Surprisingly, 10 years after King's assassination, Holloman blandly admitted that he had no personal recollection that the detail had been canceled until it was pointed out to him by committee staff during an executive session.[73] He pleaded ignorance when questioned why an all points bulletin (APB) was not dispatched to neighboring jurisdictions after the assassination. The shift commander of communications that day, Lt. Frank Kallaher, affirmed that because of the immediate deluge of radio traffic and "massive confusion" at MPD headquarters after the assassination he failed under the stress to send out an APB. Anticipating an outbreak of rioting in the city, Holloman's immediate response to the news of the assassination was to call the governor's office requesting National Guard units. A second call, one that Holloman never made, should have been to Kallaher, confirming that an APB had been sent out to Arkansas, Mississippi, Alabama, and Georgia.[74] Holloman's failure to pick up the telephone and order the dispatcher to send out an APB was an inexcusable dereliction of his most basic responsibilities, especially since the fleeing suspect had just killed the nation's leading and most controversial civil rights figure.

Throughout the November 9 afternoon session Holloman's testimony was a telling exercise in contrasts: His recollections about the surveillance on King tended to be assured and detailed while his memory about King's security arrangements was muddled and evasive. Holloman's performance before the House committee left an indelible impression that if there was a police conspiracy in the King assassination, it was a conspiracy of incompetence.

The matter of King's security or lack thereof—an issue that still looms like a dark cloud over the Memphis assassination—is made more complicated by the refusal of King and his party to accept police protection. It is unfair to the Memphis police to give the impression, as some researchers have, that on April 4 all police presence in the vicinity of the Lorraine Motel had collapsed or was intentionally stripped away.[75] The removal of the security detail from visual proximity to the Lorraine Motel at 5:05 P.M. on April 3 was at the request of a member of King's party. The next day Police Chief James C. MacDonald and Holloman decided to honor this request but assigned three or four tactical units, each unit routinely composed of three vehicles with three or four officers in each car, to patrol along a five- to six-block perimeter around the Lorraine Motel. Created as a quick reaction force to suppress urban rioting, the Tact units were not an adequate substitute for a security force detailed to work closely with the subject of a threat. In detailing the Tact units, a dual deterrent purpose was served, probably each not having equal weight with the MPD commanders—to secure Memphis against King and a replay of the March 28 violence and to be a deterrent against a possible attempt on King's life.[76]

Holloman could have taken options other than leaving Tact units in the field but out of visual range of the Lorraine Motel. He could have exercised his authority of office and professional judgment and refused to allow King and the SCLC to influence police security procedures. After all, the police were aware of three threats against King's life if he returned to Memphis, especially the April 1 threat the FBI reported to the MPD, and these were reasons enough for Holloman to override SCLC's requests that all police presence be removed from around the motel. Deploying Tact units in a perimeter mode may have provided some security, but a more effective deterrent would have been foot patrolmen. Officers on foot in the immediate vicinity of the Lorraine Motel were more likely to provoke second thoughts even among the boldest gunmen. However, the MPD's security arrangements did not include the cop on the beat. Even the FBI, which claimed it did not investigate the MPD in the King assassination, did do some checking and was surprised to learn that "no officers [were] assigned to a 'walking beat' in Memphis on the day Dr. King was killed."[77]

COME's refusal of police protection was the result of the racial crisis in Memphis and the total breakdown of trust between the city government, especially Holloman's police department, and the Memphis movement. The official police security detail that met the King party at the airport offering protection could not have inspired much confidence. These were all senior officers, including inspectors, one of whom was attached to MPD "Intelligence," and not the young and athletic types required to handle security functions. In addition, Redditt and Richmond were recognized hanging around Gate 17 when King deplaned. Their presence would have been enough to persuade members of the COME welcoming party that surveillance of King and not his protection was the principal reason for the police reception at the airport.

The purported police concern about King's security begs the question: Why did not Inspector Don Smith, who headed up one of the airport security details, approach King directly and alert him to the April 1 threat on his life? Why did the MPD join the FBI in what can only be characterized as a conspiracy of silence that endangered King's life? If both law enforcement agencies had alerted King that they were taking the threat seriously, King and his SCLC aides might have changed their attitudes about requesting police protection.

It was not King's practice to deliberately reject police protection, even when his civil rights campaigns brought him to Memphis. Many times before the sanitation strike when King came to Memphis, Reverend Kyles would call Commissioner Claude Armour and ask for two or more "soul brothers" to protect King, and Armour would respond, "They're yours." Kyles recounted how the black officers would beat him to the airport to pick up King. "They loved him too . . . and they would be right with him. . . ."

The kind of comparatively relaxed racial atmosphere Kyles recalled no longer existed in Mayor Loeb's Memphis. It was replaced by a mayor with an outworn, plantation-boss approach to race relations, a craven city council, and Loeb's hand-picked director of police who shared "His Honor's" racial views and political standards. By the time of the sanitation strike, Memphis authorities had adopted the instruments of the new urban political police of the mid-1960s: red squads, political files, target groups, police infiltrators, campus informers, mace, and Tact units. These new instruments of political surveillance, control, and intimidation were deemed necessary to keep a newly aroused black democracy in check.[78] It was Reverend Kyles who described race relations in Loeb's Memphis as a state of war existing between the white protectors of privilege and wielders of power in the Bluff City and the black community.

Facing extraordinary demands on his time to keep the Washington spring project on schedule, the probability was that King would not have returned to Memphis had the March 28 demonstration not been marred by violence. That the violence was unplanned and spontaneous, as most of the interested parties—FBI, MPD, and COME—contended at the time, should be accepted unless contrary evidence surfaces in the future. The simple truth is that we will probably never know with certainty what inspired the rioting that others exploited to either embarrass King and destroy his reputation or, with more terminal prejudice in mind, to kill him.

What is certain is that the Hoover FBI launched a raw, no-holds-barred covert campaign to blame King for the March 28 violence, hoping to ruin his reputation as a man of nonviolence and force him to scuttle his plans for the poor people's march on Washington. The demeaning and vicious anti-King editorials generated by the FBI's "dirty tricks" division superheated all the latent and active hatred centering on King for his civil rights crusading and his imminent spring march on the nation's capital. However, there is no reason to believe that the bureau's COINTELPRO campaign to exploit the Memphis riot was intended to force King to return to the city to lead a peaceful march. Intended or not, however, King's return to Memphis was in large part a consequence of FBI actions.

For those parties interested in getting a fix on King's movements and location to set up an assassination, Memphis was almost a made-to-order killing field. The press announced on April 1 when he was expected to arrive in Memphis and how long he was scheduled to stay. In laying out plans to assassinate King, the conspirators had to know that their target usually stayed at the Lorraine Motel when he was in Memphis. The location would have been confirmed as early as March 31 when the SCLC advance team checked in at Walter ("Bill") Bailey's establishment.

What the plotters did not know beforehand was the conspiracy of silence by the FBI and the MPD surrounding the April 1 threat on King's life. This culpable omission, still unexplained and unexplored, increased the odds in favor of a successful attempt on King's life. The odds were further inflated by the MPD's security arrangements for the civil rights leader. Surveillance of King was the main course at the head table that Holloman and the MPD commanders fell upon with great relish. Security for King sat at the second table and ate short rations. The MPD was more committed to employing its law enforcement tools to protect Memphis against King—and what it perceived as an inherent threat from a second mass march—than to providing King with little more than token security.

One does not have to be a committed conspiracy hobbyist to harbor a rational skepticism about the official solution to the King assassination. Delving into the crevices of the FBI's campaign to destroy King as a crusader for the poor and powerless raises deep-seated doubts about the good faith efforts of the government's investigation into his murder. Ex-FBI agent Arthur L. Murtagh best spoke to this concern when he appeared before the House Select Committee on the Assassinations and was asked his opinion about the investigation. Without equivocation, Murtagh thought it was incomplete and seriously flawed because "I just think it defies and assaults reason to think that the people who have been engaged in a 10-year-long vendetta against Dr. King are the ones who should be investigating his death. . . . "[79]

Nonetheless, having said all this, there is nothing in the released documents to support, and persuasive evidence to reject, assertions that the FBI and the MPD conspired to assassinate King.[80] Had Hoover and FBI elites actually planned to neutralize King by assassination, it is reasonable to assume they would have called off their COINTELPRO campaign against him and destroyed these records once the decision was finalized. Any truly independent federal investigation into the King assassination uncovering this kind of incriminating evidence would place the FBI at the top of its list of prime suspects. It is equally untenable and baseless to imagine that the Hoover FBI, a virtually independent security state within a state that had succeeded so spectacularly over almost 50 years under the operational premise that control was the name of the game, would conspire with parties outside the bureau to kill King. At the same time, neither agency was blameless. Their unwarranted actions and inactions significantly increased the odds favoring a successful assassination attempt on King in Memphis. In the matter of the King assassination, the FBI and the MPD must share the responsibility and condemnation for being accessories before the fact.

four

"The Poor People Are Coming!" "The Poor People Are Coming!"

THE NEWS THAT AN ARMY OF THE POOR was about to descend on the capital sent a chill down the collective spine of Washingtonians. The prospect of the dispossessed—no longer conveniently invisible—virtually camped out on the doorstep of Congress and executive agencies alarmed a Washington community recently shaken by an ordeal of rioting and arson following the King assassination. At best, the ruling mood on Capitol Hill was to look upon the Poor People's Campaign as a temporary affliction to be endured stoically. There were those, however—lawmakers and government officials—who were ready to exploit the capital city's anxiety for their own political advantage in the name of law-and-order racism.

Despite the dual blows of King's assassination and the firestorm of rioting in more than 100 American cities triggered by black rage, the SCLC decided to go ahead with the Poor People's Campaign. On April 29 Rev. Ralph D. Abernathy, the new president of the SCLC, arrived in Washington with the advance guard of the poor people's army, about 100 delegates, to present Cabinet officers and government leaders with the PPC's demands.[1]

Abernathy characterized this initial phase as a "test run," going through the motions of calling on the federal bureaucracy, and he gave the government 10 days to prepare a legislative reply before the SCLC returned with 3,000 to 5,000 demonstrators. For three days Abernathy led his rainbow coalition of America's poor—southern blacks, Appalachian whites, Native Americans, Puerto Ricans, and Mexican Americans—in well-publicized encounters with officials of the Johnson administration. The SCLC lobbying campaign dominated the Washington press, and the coverage was uniformly positive, treating the campaign cautiously but respectfully. "We will be back—not with 100 as today, but with 3,000 to 5,000 strong," Abernathy trumpeted at the close of the mini-campaign, "and we will demand answers."[2]

Abernathy was thrilled with the results, reporting to Stanley Levison that the delegates spoke movingly of their aspirations to Congress, Cabinet officers, and agency heads and that the powerful listened. Understandably, since this "trial run" was his first national exposure as King's successor, Abernathy drew additional pleasure from the success.[3]

On May 2 Abernathy led a rally in Memphis, officially inaugurating the Poor People's Campaign. The campaign began with a brief ceremony at the Lorraine Motel where SCLC's new president cemented a gold cross into the balcony floor where King was standing when he was shot. After the dedication several thousand well-wishers gathered at the Mason Temple to watch the first contingent of poor people step off on "march one" from Memphis to Marks, Mississippi, the first leg of this extraordinary march on Washington. Fittingly, Memphis was the kickoff point for the King-envisioned crusade to redeem the soul of America.[4]

King's assassination stirred a great groundswell of national support for the campaign. Blacks muted their criticism and rallied around SCLC's protest movement for human rights. Contributions reached an unprecedented volume by mid-May; the Field Foundation augmented this sum with a $275,000 grant to the SCLC; a single advertisement signed by entertainer Harry Belafonte running in the *New York Times* brought in $320,000. For the first time since the civil rights campaigns in Birmingham and Selma, Levison could report that the SCLC had no money problems. With access to a $1 million operating budget, the prospects for the PPC brightened considerably. Volunteers for the army of the poor were signing on in such numbers that the SCLC had no trouble exceeding the target of 3,000 demonstrators. "The poor are responding," Levison enthused. "The poor, almost for the first time this century, are really assembling to go to Washington." The first buses of campaigners were expected in the capital by May 11, and the following day King's widow, Coretta Scott King, was scheduled to lead the first protest march. Washington was about to witness one of "the greatest nonviolent demonstrations since Gandhi's salt march," Andy Young predicted. The PPC was gambling that it could ride the forces of history and bend them to humanitarian ends just as the civil rights movement overcame in 1963 with the historic March on Washington.[5]

Hoover anticipated that King's murder would energize the flagging poor people's movement. The day after the assassination, he expanded responsibility for project POCAM to every FBI field office in the United States. Despite King's death, the director and FBI elites were even more determined to destabilize the SCLC by expanding their surveillance and covert disruption campaign. Declaring that SCLC's "assault on Washington" was imminent, Hoover reminded his agents that project POCAM was "one of the bigger tasks facing the bureau at the present time." He directed the WFO to spare no expense in creating a preventive intelligence capability by the "full exploitation of valuable and expensive informant coverage." The director notified the WFO that the bureau expected a highly reliable intelligence product from the scores of seasoned informers assigned to Washington for project POCAM from field offices across the country.[6]

Broad-based black unity, presidential favor, and peace—conditions favoring the historic 1963 Washington march—had all but vanished by 1968 under the erosive events of the past five years. The mood on Capitol Hill was a mixture of apprehension, extreme caution, and fear. "Paranoia, literally," was Attorney General Ramsey Clark's strongest recollection of the prevailing atmosphere on the eve of the PPC's campaign. Members of the Southern bloc in Congress were the most vociferous in their opposition to the PPC, stirring up fears by harping on the potential for violence if the poor were allowed to come to the nation's capital. Leading this full-throated chorus of segregationists was Senate Majority Whip Russell Long (D-La.), who threatened to evoke censure or expulsion of any Senate member who advocated "bending the knee to lawbreakers." Long's fulminations were echoed by fellow West Virginia Democrat Robert C. Byrd, who lauded Chicago's Mayor Richard Daley for ordering his police to shoot and kill arsonists and to cripple and maim looters. Byrd associated himself with Mississippi senior solon John Stennis in urging the Justice Department to file a court order banning the PPC from the capital. Representative William C. Cramer (R-Fla.) drafted legislation prohibiting the army of the poor from using the federal park lands for their planned camp-in. Nine other lawmakers in the House either supported Cramer's resolution or proposed similar measures.[7]

From the campaign trail in Oregon, Richard M. Nixon, candidate for his party's presidential nomination and peddling his own program of "black capitalism" as a remedy for the ghetto poor, urged Congress not to negotiate under PPC pressure. Congressional liberals urged their colleagues on the political right to reject the politics of fear-mongering and respect the right of citizens to petition their government. But all the trilling by liberals about constitutional rights was drowned out by the stronger and more numerous voices of congressional conservatives. Liberal members of Congress, even if they were inclined, were initially stymied from mounting any concerted support for the campaign because PPC organizers never attempted to recruit their support.[8]

The siege mentality settling over Washington played into the hands of opportunists who were quick to exploit it for their own political ends. In the summer of 1967 Senate Democrat John L. McClellan of Arkansas, an ardent segregationist and chair of the Permanent Subcommittee on Investigations, had his subcommittee begin a marathon probe (lasting three years) into the causes of urban rioting. Even before receiving congressional approval, the chairman announced his emphasis would be "law enforcement rather than social causes underlining the disorders."

McClellan's attempt to ideologize the urban unrest of the 1960s was symptomatic of the polarization of attitudes about ghetto rioting. On one side of this fundamental conflict were those who argued that economic and social factors, namely poverty and discrimination, were the principal causes of urban unrest. If the government could ameliorate these environmental factors, they argued, the spreading epidemic of urban violence would subside. The Kerner Commission, appointed by President Johnson in 1967 to investigate the origins of the riots, argued forcefully in its *Report of the National Advisory Commission on Civil Disorders* that social factors were the determining cause of the nation's deepening racial crisis.

On the other side were the Arkansas senator and his numerous allies on Capitol Hill—political conservatives, segregationists, and authoritarians of every stripe—who dismissed these views as sociological twaddle and liberal propaganda. When a moderate voice on the subcommittee, Senator John Sherman Cooper (R-Ky.), tried to persuade his colleagues to also consider "social and economic factors involved," the opposition retorted that concern with social factors was tantamount to "condoning lawlessness." Convinced that ghetto rioting was the work of subversive agitators, McClellan's solution was to roll back the Great Society programs that allegedly coddled criminals and terrorists and to instill a renewed respect for law and order. McClellan's subcommittee began to work on an omnibus crime bill calling for stronger antirioting legislation, gun control, increased police training, and virtually open-ended discretionary authority for the Oval Office to use electronic surveillance against political dissidents.[9]

No one in Washington was a more ardent supporter of McClellan's law and order stand than the prestigious director of the Federal Bureau of Investigation. Hoover and the senator enjoyed a symbiotic relationship. McClellan's frequent requests for information from bureau files were always handled promptly. On occasion the FBI even spied on McClellan's rival, the Kerner Commission. Subcommittee staff members worked so closely with Hoover and Deputy Director Cartha DeLoach, the bureau's liaison with Capitol Hill, on the language and provisions of the omnibus crime bill that they could have claimed joint authorship with McClellan. The payoff for the bureau when the Omnibus Crime Control and Safe Streets bill became law in 1968 was its carefully crafted provisions. The FBI was rewarded with a substantial 10 percent increase in its budget to accommodate the expansion of the number of police officers permitted to attend the FBI's National Academy annual training program in riot control. With access to new law-and-order tax dollars, Hoover was able to expand his bureaucratic empire, inculcate more law enforcement officers with his views of subversion and racial matters, and pursue unchecked his own agenda in domestic surveillance and covert operations.[10]

On May 3 DeLoach took a call from the Arkansas senator. He assumed it was another routine request from the subcommittee chair; however, McClellan's call was anything but routine. McClellan related to the assistant director certain revelations from a secret subcommittee informant about a black militant group's plans to foment violence during the PPC and take over the campaign from the SCLC leadership. This conspiracy, according to McClellan, was hatched somewhere in Tennessee, and his source claimed intimate knowledge about the "master plan" because he sat in on the plotting. McClellan apparently placed a great deal of stock in the story because, according to DeLoach, he appeared deeply troubled. Although the senator refused to reveal his source's identity, McClellan asked that the FBI do a confirmatory investigation.

That same afternoon Hoover alerted FBI field offices in Tennessee and Alabama. Alabama was included in the investigation because nine days earlier before his subcommittee McClellan had taunted Ramsey Clark when the nation's chief law enforcement officer pleaded innocent to any knowledge about a conspiracy centered in Alabama. During this lengthy April 25 exchange, with the chairman doing his best to make the attorney general appear inept, McClellan identified Alabama, not Tennessee, as the alleged conspirators' home base.[11] Either the aging senator was muddled about his geography, or he was being less than frank with DeLoach. Three days after the May 3 phone call, DeLoach met with McClellan, and the senator handed over an affidavit from his mystery informer, named "John Silver," and informed DeLoach that Silver was living in Atlanta, Georgia. McClellan also gave the assistant director a copy of a speech he planned to make the next day on the Senate floor about the looming threat the PPC posed for the entire Washington community.[12]

McClellan's May 7 Senate speech was pure law-and-order theater. He accused Abernathy and the SCLC of defying authority and deliberately planning to violate public law for "the purpose of provoking an incident." He then shifted his sights and blasted the "permissive" liberals occupying the federal bench who struck down the District of Columbia's one-year residency requirement in determining eligibility for welfare. "Recruits for the march," McClellan bellowed, "are being told to go to Washington one night and get on welfare the next day," threatening to turn the city into a "Mecca for migrants." He ended his performance with a febrile recital of what lay in store for Washington as the first contingents of the poor people approached the city. According to the "evidence" unearthed by his subcommittee, the Arkansas lawmaker went on in Mc-Carthy-like fashion, organized groups of criminal-minded black militants were planning to infiltrate the ranks of the poor people's protest movement and unleash a reign of rioting, looting, and armed insurrection, using the "shantytown" camp as their base of operations. He described the seven main objectives of their "master plan." This was no drill, McClellan somberly warned his colleagues. "The subcommittee has received sworn information that this is actually being planned, and this information comes from within the militant movement itself." The pending omnibus crime bill was not mentioned in the speech but was conspicuously lurking in the wings. As floor manager of the bill, McClellan had no compunction against using the PPC to parade his scapegoating thesis about the cause of urban unrest and to whip up a false hysteria for his own legislative purposes.[13]

While the Arkansas senator went gunning for headlines, the FBI was searching for the conspirators. By May 7 SACs from Knoxville, Memphis, Mobile, and Birmingham all reported to Washington headquarters that their investigations had come up empty-handed; FBI informants and ghetto tipsters even had failed to come up with isolated rumors about militant blacks preparing to come to Washington with the Poor People's Campaign. Mobile reported that it contacted every source, confidential informant, and person in a position to know in 36 counties in southern Alabama and came up with nothing to confirm McClellan's allegations. Weary of the chairman's little game of deception, Hoover contacted an FBI source on the subcommittee's staff to find out "John Silver's" real name and learned that he was residing in Mobile and not Atlanta.[14] Hoover ordered Mobile to interview McClellan's source and to pin him down on the specifics in his affidavit to the subcommittee. Mobile sent back to Washington a reconstruction of the interview in a six-page teletype. The subject avoided specifics, according to the agents' report; was evasive, cagey, and hostile; and demanded money from his interrogators to continue the interview. The report noted that FBI sources in Montgomery and Mobile characterized "Silver" as "completely unreliable," "untrustworthy and . . . a police pimp."[15]

Hoover immediately called off the investigation, satisfied that McClellan's source was bogus and the senator's allegations groundless. McClellan, however, was busy keeping his revelations before the public eye. On May 10 he released a statement to the press that his office had turned over to the FBI the names of two of the gun-toting militants who were planning to turn the PPC into a riot. Later that same day the Arkansas senator went to Canossa. During an afternoon meeting in DeLoach's office, the senator was all contriteness and, according to the assistant director, he "hoped we would not expose him." After being reassured that the bureau had no such intentions, McClellan, searching for some face-saving consolation, asserted that his predictions on the Senate floor would still come true because "obviously militants would try and stir up trouble."[16]

Aside from a wrist-slapping lecture from DeLoach about first checking with the bureau before issuing press releases involving the FBI, McClellan suffered no other embarrassment because he never made any retraction or public apology. His intrigue in public deception was safe with Hoover; both public servants needed each other to nurture the law-and-order campaign, beginning with the enactment of the omnibus crime bill. Although not directly sponsoring McClellan's politics of fear campaign, the bureau jumped at the chance to exploit any hysteria it fostered. Chief of the Racial Intelligence Section of the DID George Moore, who was responsible for devising COINTELPROs against targeted black groups, proposed planting a story with cooperative media drawing attention to the large numbers of black youths traveling with some of the PPC caravans coming to Washington. The propaganda thrust of the FBI draft of the story equated young black with potential violence.[17]

Washington's first encounter with the PPC came on May 12, Mother's Day. Coretta Scott King led a contingent of 5,000 demonstrators through some neighborhoods devastated by four days of rioting sparked by her husband's assassination. The marchers were protesting Congress's 1967 amendments to the Social Security Act, intended to slow down the expansion of the nation's welfare rolls. The national lawmakers' answer to this "welfare crisis" was to cut funds for the Head Start program and fabricate new rules and regulations to drive women and children off the rolls. Joining Mrs. King in the Mother's Day march was Dr. George A. Wiley, the talented executive director of the National Welfare Rights Organization (NWRO). During the Great Society's heyday, the NWRO was the driving force behind the relief movement, championing the cause of America's most desperate citizens, a virtual pariah class—impoverished single women with dependent children, or mothers on Aid to Families with Dependent Children (AFDC).

Wiley and some of NWRO's top leadership had testified before Congress in the fall of 1967 against the proposed amendments and even staged a sit-in, a historic first, in the chambers of the congressional committee searching for a solution to the "welfare crisis." Driven to the end of his tether by this perceived outrage, Senator Russell Long, in a classic exhibition of blaming the victim, publicly denounced the AFDC mothers as "brood mares." Equipped with their own proposals for reform of the welfare system, Wiley and his "brood mares" were back in Washington demanding the repeal of the anti-welfare amendments. Although the NWRO's specific demands would require additional funds, none of the proposals were unreasonable. A full maintenance program, a key demand, had already received strong support from a great number of professionals studying the welfare system. Even President Johnson's own National Advisory on Civil Disorders urged adoption of a National System of Income Supplementation to reduce the accelerating racial trend that was moving America "toward two societies, one black, one white—separate and unequal."[18]

May 12, a Sunday, was just another work day for some FBI agents. The FBI's WFO assigned a detail of agents to monitor the Mother's Day protest from start to finish. Agents shadowed the march route, recorded the comments made by the scheduled speakers, and took names of prominent participants for later indexing: Mrs. King, Mrs. Harry Belafonte, Wiley, and most of NWRO's executive officers. The surveillance and indexing of citizens lawfully engaged in political activity was routine with Hoover's FBI, but the Mother's Day march provided a side commentary on the prevailing mood in the nation's capital.

A week before the scheduled march, Wiley wrote to Mrs. Wilbur Mills, chair of the hospitality committee of the Congressional Club, a fashionable social club located in northwest Washington that catered to congressmen and their wives. Wiley requested that a delegation of congressional wives meet with a small contingent of welfare mothers accompanied by Mrs. King at the club in a show of solidarity with the NWRO's protest aims. Senator Winston L. Prouty (R-Vt.) furnished a copy of Wiley's letter to the FBI and said that under no circumstances were the lawmakers' wives interested in meeting with Mrs. King and AFDC mothers. Wiley subsequently was informed by letter that the club was closed on Sundays and therefore a reception was impossible. The Vermont Republican, apparently speaking for the membership, brought in the FBI because of fear that the rejection might provoke a retaliatory attack on the Congressional Club. Prouty pointed out that Pride, Inc., the black community action group, was headquartered across the street. After a conference with Prouty, the FBI notified the Washington police, the Capitol police, and the 116th Military Intelligence Group about the threat of potential violence.

May 12 ended as it had begun, peacefully. The marchers gathered at Cardozo High School Stadium to hear Mrs. King speak about her husband's devotion to the ideal of nonviolence, while Mrs. Robert F. Kennedy and the wives of Senators Joseph S. Clark and Philip Hart looked on from the speaker's platform. There were no incidents or vengeful stampedes by the "brood mares," and most of the NWRO contingent returned to New York at the close of the rally.[19]

Jolted by King's assassination and the subsequent rioting, the White House scrambled to come up with some emergency measures to meet the national crisis. Harry McPherson, special counsel to the president, recounted in his memoirs that immediately after King's assassination, most

White House advisers supported the idea of a special presidential address to Congress outlining the causes of the domestic crisis and calling upon Capitol Hill to commit new funds to improve education, housing, and employment opportunities for the nation's poor. Presidential assistant Joseph Califano recommended a sweeping reassessment of budgetary priorities and promoted a list for new social expenditures totaling $5 billion, which the president could take to the Congress.20

A presidential appeal to Congress for programs to restore racial peace and tranquility never took place. Angry and fearful over the outbreak of ghetto rebellions and importuned by their outraged law-and-order constituents, Congress was in no mood to spend more tax dollars for social programs. The nation's lawmakers were hardly amenable to even listening to the voices of the poor and unrepresented or acknowledging their right to come to Washington to petition for a redress of their grievances. Given the sour atmosphere in Congress, to send new programs forward would have been futile, in President Johnson's judgment. Moreover, there was considerable uneasiness in the White House that even the existing Great Society programs could be in trouble.21

The paralysis gripping the administration was rooted in Johnson's decision in 1965 to commit American combat troops to the Vietnam conflict. While pushing his Great Society programs forward the president kept the public, Congress, and even the executive branch in the dark about the long-range consequences of this commitment. For two years Johnson lulled the nation with vain hopes that it could have its great society at home and fight a foreign war to contain Asian communism. In 1967 these vain hopes turned into grim realities when the president, fearing escalating deficits might trigger runaway inflation, went to Congress and asked for a temporary 10 percent tax surcharge. Only additional revenues from tax dollars would enable him to continue reform on the home front while he and his generals groped for a winning strategy on the war front.

Congress was unsympathetic with the Oval Office's dilemma and refused to come up with higher taxes to sustain his "butter and guns" policies. Representative Wilbur Mills (D-Ark.), the powerful chairman of the House Ways and Means Committee and a southern conservative with low regard for liberal reforms, jumped at this opportunity to inform the president that his account was overdrawn. Mills promised Johnson that he could have his tax increase but only if he cut domestic spending by $6 billion. Budget Director Charles L. Schultze reminded the embattled president, who really needed no coaching, that if he satisfied Mills, his domestic program would be a "shambles." For nine months the Oval Office resorted to delay tactics to salvage something of the existing Great Society programs, only to capitulate in the end on expenditures. In June 1968 Johnson, now a lame-duck president, signed the Revenue and Expenditure Control Act, which enacted the 10 percent surcharge but required the executive branch to slash expenditures by a crippling $6 billion.[22]

Under the prevailing political circumstances, White House advisers and their staffs had few options when formulating responses to the demands of the Poor People's Campaign. They were like men trying to swim in the sky. The leader they served was shortly to trade away the Great Society for an Asian war, a war that a growing number of his fellow citizens thought was mad. Nevertheless, the White House had to deal with Abernathy and show concern for the needs of the nation's poor, if only to strengthen the hand of movement moderates to try to ensure that the campaign continued in an orderly and peaceful manner.

Joseph Califano, smart, indefatigable, and not timid about assuming responsibility, served as the point man in this largely public relations operation, coordinating the efforts of the White House staff with department and agency heads. The tactics Califano and assistants Jim Gaither and Matthew Nimetz settled upon were planned responses that officials were to use in their discussions with PPC delegations. Administration spokesmen were directed to emphasize the accomplishments of the existing Great Society programs, pending legislation aimed at the plight of the poor, and future administration actions that might be taken if consistent with budget levels ("without commitments"). As the first PPC marchers arrived in Washington, the president's domestic affairs management team had its game plan ready: an invitation to dialogue, compassionate rhetoric, and, in the words of one staffer, "some small victories, if possible."[23]

The administration, unwilling to do more about social needs, was preparing to handle the anticipated consequences of its own incapability by mobilizing an awesome military-intelligence capability to respond to future urban unrest. The government had prepared a list of 124 designated "hot cities," and with the PPC coming to town, Washington leapfrogged to the top of the list. From March through May an administration task force met periodically to discuss preventive measures and iron out contingency plans in the event of new waves of rioting in the District of Columbia. The sessions were attended by members of the White House staff, Califano serving informally as the chair, with representatives from the Justice Department, Pentagon, Secret Service, and District of Columbia Mayor Walter Washington's office.

These strategy sessions had a grim, tight-jawed quality about them. This was especially evident when the task force contemplated any future ghetto revolts; it noted that "we must be prepared for guerrilla-type warfare, incidents in the suburbs, use of children, Castro-trained commandos, and various other possibilities. . . ." The discussions centered around such concerns as "response capability," "high-grade intelligence," "prepositioning of troops," "helicopter surveillance," "trouble spots," and "infiltrat[ion] of militant groups." The jargon was the lingua franca of the Vietnam War era, the language of men who were preparing for a civil war, a made-in-America Tet Offensive.[24] A March story in the *New York Times* estimated that officials in Washington would have 10,000 police and troops on standby for the Poor People's Campaign. By May Pentagon planners were ready to deploy 20,000 regular army troops in "a steady stream" into the capital over a 72-hour period, the first 5,400 within six hours after notification.[25]

Caught up in the siege mentality and the government's preoccupation with developing an early warning system to predict urban revolts, the Justice Department created the Interdivisional Intelligence Unit (IDIU). The origins of the IDIU were rooted in the 1967 Newark and Detroit riots, which were, in Califano's words, a "shattering experience" for Justice and the White House. The administration's response was to establish a national center to collect and analyze high-grade intelligence to predict when the next ghetto would blow. The Oval Office, increasingly hypersensitive about the politics of urban rioting, was obsessed with proving that these disorders were the work of a relatively small handful of subversive conspirators in the black community.

Fixated on the conspiracy thesis, the president and his advisers wanted to throw the book at racial extremists, especially Stokley Carmichael. The attorney general had the Justice Department work overtime to put together a case against this Black Power advocate to get him off the streets and behind bars. To the White House's chagrin, the department could not find evidence to indict Carmichael. To Clark's credit, he refused to manufacture a political case, arguing that likely acquittal would only elevate Carmichael's image even higher among ghetto youth.[26]

Actually, at this time Carmichael was not a clear and present danger. Since locating in Washington, D.C., in December 1967, he was under around-the-clock surveillance by relay teams of FBI agents. A few days after King's assassination, according to a former agent assigned to the WFO, Hoover set up a special 50-person squad to build a case against Carmichael on inciting to riot. Even his private bodyguard was a paid FBI informant. When Carmichael fled the country, he was probably under tighter surveillance than any other black American or any other citizen, for that matter.[27]

Although privately dismissive of the Oval Office's conspiracy thesis, Clark did move with alacrity to transform the Justice Department into a national command post for surveillance of the nation's black community. He proposed using FBI reports to compile an IDIU "master index" organized around a city-by-city scheme on "individuals and organizations." The information was computerized, providing the unit with the potential for a linkup with other government agencies to create a central data bank.

Responding to the administration's lament about limited intelligence sources, Clark proposed a "broad spectrum approach" to intelligence-gathering, one that would monitor all possible suspected riot conspirators in the urban ghettos. The attorney general authorized the FBI to "use maximum available sources, investigative and intelligence, to collect and report all facts" regarding any "scheme or conspiracy by any group."[28]

Assistant Attorney General John Doar, a legend within the Civil Rights Division during the Kennedy years, underscored the new intelligence-focus line of thinking in Clark's Justice Department. Doar recommended that ghetto-based staff with the Great Society bureaucracies—"the poverty program, the Labor Department programs, and the Neighborhood Legal Services"—be canvassed to "funnel information into this unit." Doar conceded that using advocates for the poor as Justice Department "agents" was getting into a sensitive area, but he thought the department could maintain "its credibility with the people in the ghetto" by keeping the identity of the IDIU secret. The IDIU also received daily intelligence summaries and reports from the U.S. Army, with the military making up the third component of this intelligence triad. The IDIU, characterized later by a U.S. Senate report as a "massive domestic intelligence apparatus," was in place and functioning by the time the PPC had set up its tent city within the shadow of the Lincoln Memorial.[29]

By early May the first PPC bus caravans began to converge on Washington. On May 7 the Southern Caravan, with symbolic gusto, began its journey with a march across Selma's Edmund Pettus Bridge to mark the spot where 600 black demonstrators were attacked by Alabama state troopers and mounted sheriff's deputies in March 1965. Over the next two days, crowds of well-wishers turned out in Chicago (Midwestern Caravan) and Boston (Northeastern Caravan) to celebrate the departure of hundreds of PPC demonstrators destined for the nation's capital. Press coverage of the departing columns of the poor people's army, although not uniformly friendly, was heavy.

Much media fanfare was directed at Marks, Mississippi, where 50 marchers set out with 15 wagons and 33 mules and horses to rendezvous with their motorized fellow campaigners in Washington. Dubbed the Mule Train Caravan, the wagon train was scheduled to wind its way across Mississippi to a point in Alabama where the mules, horses, and wagons would be transported by train to their final destination. Other caravans originating in Los Angeles, San Francisco, San Antonio, and Seattle were not expected in Washington until the end of the month. These caravans were variously designated as the Western, Southwestern and Indian Trails caravans, the latter because it was composed mostly of Native Americans representing the Flathead, Sioux, Yakima, Seneca, Tuscarora, and Hopi tribes.

While en route to Washington the caravans were under massive surveillance by the FBI, army intelligence units, Department of Justice agents, and state and local police forces. Hoover directed each field office along the routes to submit daily intelligence summaries to the bureau and to forward copies to the next field office as the caravans moved from one FBI "territory" to the next. Agents kept a running check on the number of demonstrators in each caravan, the destination of the next leg of the journey, the name of the carrier, and the license plate numbers of the buses.[30]

FBI agents solicited information about bus schedules, the person who ordered the buses, and the number of tickets purchased from cooperating officials of the bus companies patronized by local SCLC recruiters. In at least one instance, agents of the San Francisco office were allowed access to the PPC's bank account by the auditor of the Wells Fargo Bank in that city.[31]

Initially, the bureau was interested only in the names of recruiters, regional coordinators, and SCLC staffers, but as the caravans headed toward Washington, the FBI began collecting names of rank-and-file participants. The names of everyone connected with the PPC—whether those names appeared in the newspapers, on lists compiled by PPC recruiters and turned over to FBI agents by cooperating SCLC office staff, on copies of motel guest registration cards, or from informants and sources traveling with the caravans—went into the FBI's intelligence hopper for indexing. An employee of American Airlines upon request turned over to FBI agents the passenger list with the names of a 25-member delegation of campaigners who flew from Gary, Indiana, to Washington for the demonstration. One sharp-eyed agent out of the Cincinnati office picked the name of a white female physician who joined the caravan in that city off the identification tag on her luggage. An administrator of a small college in Indianapolis, Indiana, thought the FBI should be aware that 42 students accompanied by the college's president, dean, and a faculty adviser would be in Washington to observe the demonstration because they were "interested in civil rights legislation and not necessarily in sympathy with the Poor People's Campaign." After receiving the list of volunteered names, the FBI field office indexed 28 of the 42 names.[32]

The physical surveillance of the caravans, or "fisur" in FBI parlance, allowed the bureau to dredge up all kinds of raw intelligence to use later for its own tendentious purposes. Statistics vital to the bureau, for instance, were the race, sex, and age of the campaigners, with special attention to the number of known members of ghetto youth gangs. The director prompted agents to look out for black nationalists, alleged militants already on the FBI's computerized Rabble Rouser Index who might be traveling with the caravans. FBI agents and undercover military operatives, usually with U.S. Army military intelligence groups, routinely subjected the PPC participants to surreptitious photosurveillance at every stopover along the route. These photos were checked against the bureau's Black Nationalist Photograph Album; each field office had a copy of this "mug book" with its 8 x 10 glossies to identify any militants who might have "infiltrated" the ranks of the poor people's army.[33]

The two bureaucracies, FBI and U.S. Army, worked together smoothly in carrying out their surveillance mission. Hoover gave every appearance of being an IDIU team player and exhibited no undue concern about the army's intrusion into his domain of internal security matters. In part, Hoover's acquiescence was based on the military's ability to use large numbers of black intelligence officers to carry out "fisur" operations without attracting undue attention from those targeted for surveillance. Because of the bureau's hiring policies, the FBI had only 40 black agents out of a total force of 6,000 at the height of the Poor People's Campaign.[34] The FBI could also take credit for the army's work because the military could not go public with its surveillance on civilians campaigning for domestic reforms. Although not foolproof, "fisur" provided valuable intelligence. Using photos taken mostly by military intelligence operatives, the FBI was able to identify a handful of indexed blacks from the Rabble Rouser list who were making their way across America's interstates along with more than 3,000 other campaigners headed for Washington. Whether or not the figures were of any solace to Hoover, the combined intelligence efforts of the FBI and army apparently established that violence-prone black extremists had not "infiltrated" the PPC's caravans.[35]

These intrusive surveillance techniques were unworthy of a democracy and reminiscent of abuses by unchecked secret police of authoritarian regimes. Perhaps the most flagrant example of these excesses was the FBI's surveillance of the mule train. The Mule Train Caravan, one of the eight PPC caravans, originated in the dusty, down-at-the-heels town of Marks, in Quitman County, Mississippi. Marks was chosen by the SCLC leaders because in early 1968 King, who was no stranger to the misery of poor rural blacks in the South, visited Marks and was prostrated by the abysmal conditions of the black population, especially the children. The mule-driven wagon train was meant to symbolize an earlier time when black peasantry tried to coax a marginal existence off hardscrabble farms and to serve as a contemporary reminder that conditions had improved little, if at all, for their children and grandchildren in places like Quitman County.

The mule train was an instant success. The local black population turned out in droves to see a little bit of history and to learn something about the PPC and its business in Washington, and occasionally curious onlookers accepted invitations to join the march. The mules also generated, in Hosea Williams's words, "communications notoriety." The national press, including some large southern dailies, the three major television networks, and Britain's BBC, recognized good copy when they saw it, giving the mule train broad and sustained coverage. The SCLC "mule skinners" in charge of the wagon train were natural and shrewd showmen. They ensured that the protest march had a festive air with plenty of singing, joshing, and political high spirits. For example, marchers wore white armbands with the inscription "Mississippi Goddamn." The caravan's lead wagon, reserved for Abernathy and Williams, was drawn by two mules dubbed "Stennis" and "Eastland," after Mississippi's incumbent segregationist senators. Whenever circumstances permitted, Abernathy and Williams bantered with the crowds of onlookers and never failed to make some reference to the senators' "namesakes," igniting peals of laughter from an appreciative audience.[36]

Since the Mule Train Caravan enjoyed such a high media profile, the FBI could have kept track of its progress through the agency's news-clipping service and by liaison with the state and local police monitoring the mules and the small contingent of marchers (rarely more than 50) over every leg of the journey. The Mississippi state police, for instance, assigned 26 uniformed officers and three plainclothes investigators to cover the caravan until it crossed into Alabama. The bureau passed up this opportunity to "farm out" this operation and use its manpower for other law enforcement purposes. While the mule train took two weeks to trek over the back roads and highways of Mississippi, the FBI's field office in Jackson assigned 14 agents, one supervisor, and its network of informants and sources to an around-the-clock surveillance of the wagon train.[37] Intelligence summaries from the Jackson office kept Washington posted about the condition of the mules, how they were shod, the repair and maintenance of the wagons, and the cost of rented tents for an overnight encampment.[38]

On two consecutive nights the wagon train received permission to camp on private land owned by black farmers. The FBI indexed both farmers and noted that one farmer was a bus driver for the Quitman County school district.[39] The Jackson office routinely disseminated its intelligence on the caravans to the U.S. Army, Secret Service, and the local military intelligence group and OSI (Office of Special Investigations, U.S. Air Force) at Jackson and Oxford, respectively. Washington headquarters was notified by teletypes, designated "urgent," of every move the mule train made along its point-to-point march through Mississippi. The bureau's interest in the caravan's progress remained just as keen after it left Mississippi. In June the Atlanta field office reported that the mules and wagons were scheduled to be shipped by train from Atlanta to Alexandria, Virginia. The teletype identified the carrier and the numbers of freight cars carrying the mules and wagons to their destination just outside Washington.[40]

As the larger caravans—southern, midwestern, and northeastern—approached the final leg of their journey, FBI elites peppered the federal bureaucracy with daily summaries. Copies of these reports on the PPC went to the Oval Office, the Office of the Vice President, secretary of state, departments of the army and air force, all agencies responsible for intelligence, and the IDIU, with sanitized versions going to friendly newspaper reporters, "responsible Negroes," and congressional leaders. The summaries, based on carefully selected information, originated with Assistant Director Sullivan's Domestic Intelligence Division, the enclave in the FBI responsible for dirty tricks operations. Contrary to official FBI claims that its reporting is devoid of conclusions and recommendations, these summaries on the PPC caravans were so tendentious that they verged on pure invention—the contrived products of a disinformation campaign to manipulate the government's perceptions. The Hooverized version of the daily activities surrounding the caravans was tailored to emphatically prove that the director's warnings about the potential for violence were correct—the barbarians were at the gates!

This abuse of power and Hoover's manipulation of the political system to serve his own ends were nothing new. The old ringmaster had had presidents, congressmen, and government officials jumping through hoops to the score of his own personal agenda for years. What was different in this steady stream of FBI reports on the PPC was a new emphasis in the bureau's threat assessment. The Communist menace was conspicuously downplayed and emphasis shifted toward the dissidents in the black movement, the new clear and present danger confronting Hoover's America. The Black Menace had replaced the Red Menace as America's number one internal security threat.[41]

The caravans were an intractable source of frustration for SOG (Seat of Government), Hoover's euphemism for FBI headquarters in Washington, D.C. The dilemma facing the bureau was readily apparent in the daily situation reports from the field offices monitoring the eight caravans. For SOG, it was a classic scenario of "good news, bad news." The "good news" was, given that there were thousands of PPC campaigners—many of them teenagers away from home for the first time—ample opportunity existed for some rougher sorts to ignite violent incidents. The "bad news" was that, other than the violence provoked or directed at the campaigners by the police, the caravan phase of the PPC was remarkably free of any major incidents.[42]

The bureau's predicament, too much "bad news," was evident in the pseudointelligence summaries it circulated through the higher channels of official Washington. These reports were a dubious admixture of overripe allegations, rumors, distortions, exaggerations, and half-truths. SCLC's Jim Bevel, one report noted, was taking unkind shots at President

Johnson, calling him a "pimp from Texas." Matching vulgarity with vulgarity, an FBI summary rehashed a story about a rape charge in 1952 involving Abernathy. Readers of these summaries learned from unidentified FBI sources that "many people coming to Washington are determined to gain recognition . . . or they will take violent action." Another source reported that some campaigners were "talking about killing policemen" when they arrived in Washington.[43]

Heating up its war of nerves, the bureau played up the large numbers of teenage black males with the caravans, highlighting the fact that some were in groups with names like Milwaukee Commandos, Blackstone Rangers, and Invaders. In one incident a white counterdemonstrator at a large PPC rally in Boston was stabbed by a black man; the FBI asserted that "he was stabbed by an unknown Negro member of the campaign." Playing upon some racial discord that was troubling the PPC leadership, an FBI report drew attention to the dissension between black and white Quaker staffers at SCLC's Washington headquarters. Implying that the PPC organizers were losing control over the campaign, the report did not include an admission that the racial tension poisoning relations at the SCLC command post was exacerbated by an FBI COINTELPRO operation.[44]

Hoover was clearly unhappy with the composite intelligence picture on the PPC assembled from the daily situation reports from the field. On May 24, 1968, he fired off a directive to all continental offices, making known his dissatisfaction with their intelligence product. "To give a true picture of the situation," he admonished, "complete facts regarding the role subversive organizations and individuals are playing in the Poor People's Campaign must be dug out by penetrative investigations." The view from FBIHQ, the only one that counted, was that conspiratorial forces were using the PPC for their own nefarious purposes. It was up to the FBI's front line of defense, the agents in the field, to unmask these "subversive organizations" by resorting to "decisive, imaginative, and aggressive investigative efforts."[45]

Organizing, financing, and coordinating the transportation of thousands of poor citizens from every section of the country was no small accomplishment. Aside from road weariness, some hygiene problems, and delays, the caravans, almost without exception, made it to Washington free of major mishaps or ugly incidents. A good deal of credit for this tour de force in logistics and people management rested with the Justice Department, or specifically the Community Relations Service Division (CRS).

Established under Title X of the 1964 Civil Rights Act, the CRS was transferred from Commerce to the Justice Department in 1966. A key function of the division was to generate voluntary and peaceful resolution of civil rights disputes before the contesting parties opted for legal action.[46] The move from Commerce to Justice did not altogether solve the identity crisis that plagued the new division. CRS lawyers, whose main mission was reconciliation, did not feel at home in the Justice Department, the prosecutorial arm of the federal government. CRS was woefully understaffed and had to operate with a bare-bones budget, which added to morale problems.

CRS was in a state of limbo until 1968, when Roger Wilkins was appointed director, making him the highest-ranking black man in the Justice Department. Wilkins quickly turned things around. He was young, accomplished, and not afraid to take on responsibility, and he developed an instant rapport with the CRS staff. Moreover, he was a favorite of President Johnson and had the unstinting support and total confidence of the attorney general. Clark and Wilkins first met in 1965 when they were both part of a federal task force sent to the black ghetto in Los Angeles to investigate the causes of the Watts riot. For more than a week, they worked closely together in a highly stressful situation for 18 hours a day, every day. Their mutual professional respect and similar views about civil rights matters helped break ground for the maturation of a strong friendship that broadened to include their wives and families. The attorney general was instrumental in getting Wilkins appointed to head up the troubled CRS Division.[47]

The CRS assigned agents to travel with each caravan and to work directly and openly with the caravan leaders. This assignment had something of a "play-it-by-ear" quality in that agents were never certain what each day on the road held in store. CRS representatives had to be versatile, for they were usually called upon to play many troubleshooting roles: street lawyers, ombudsmen, facilitators, and morale officers. However, their overriding mission was clear enough: to see that the caravans proceeded along their course as smoothly as possible. A standard practice followed in every caravan was to have a CRS agent travel ahead of their contingent to the next stopover and check in with the local SCLC coordinator to make certain that accommodations were ready for the campaigners when their buses arrived. In almost all cases, the SCLC representative along with throngs of well-wishers from the black community had prepared hot meals and lodgings at local black colleges and churches and at private homes if there was an overflow.

Slipups occurred occasionally. When the Pittsburgh SCLC failed to prepare for the Midwestern Caravan, the CRS agents with this group contracted with the downtown YMCA to register and feed about 800 weary marchers. A CRS agent with one of the western contingents, anticipating a long and tiring trek from Salt Lake City to Denver, called ahead to the SCLC Denver office to arrange hot showers for the campaigners. A CRS official with another western caravan confronted the Greyhound Bus manager in St. Louis and insisted that the company provide clean buses for the next leg of the trip. The report filed with the CRS noted that dirty buses caused a serious morale problem. In Seattle, police denied permission to caravan buses to park on a downtown street to take on campaigners and their luggage. A CRS agent appealed to the U.S. marshal, who happened to be a friend of the chief of police, and arrangements were made to cover the parking meters in an entire city block until the buses were loaded.[48]

When the Northeastern Caravan reached Philadelphia on May 13, the poverty pilgrims were scheduled to take part in a rally in the city's northern ghetto. This initial rally was followed by a march to Independence Hall and a monster rally where Abernathy and other SCLC leaders spoke about the poor people's movement.

Race relations in the City of Brotherly Love were notoriously tense. A large part of the problem was the city's police commissioner, Frank L. Rizzo. Rizzo's approach to race relations was that of a law-and-order cop who wore his racism on his sleeve. During Rizzo's tenure as police commissioner Philadelphia became a police city. According to one author, Rizzo's style with demonstrators was "the night-stick style, a 'let-me-at-'em' passion that hungers for a victim. . . ."[49] The police commissioner and the city's black community shared a mutual and escalating hostility toward each other. Particularly offensive to blacks was Rizzo's practice of using cruising buses full of helmeted tactical police to patrol black neighborhoods.

Before the May 13 march and rally, CRS agents, caravan leaders, and the local SCLC president met with Rizzo to work out a modus vivendi to cool any developing trouble. Rizzo assured the caravan delegation that his riot police would keep a low profile during the demonstrations. If trouble did erupt, the commissioner promised that the first police response would involve only his community relations units, teams made up of black officers. The march and rally, which attracted a sizable crowd of more than 10,000, went off without a hitch. The caravan left Philadelphia free of incidents, and Rizzo even provided a police escort across the Ben Franklin Bridge to Camden, New Jersey.

Pending the approval of caravan leaders, CRS representatives arranged a meeting with elected officials and law enforcement officers in every city where a march and rally were scheduled. The run of things in Philadelphia, unique only in that it was a city on the IDIU's "hot cities" list, was a pattern repeated with the same success in a host of cities, including Camden; Columbus, Akron, and Toledo, Ohio; Atlanta; Louisville; Charleston, South Carolina; Greensboro, North Carolina; and Wilmington, Delaware.[50]

Most city officials and police chiefs probably suffered a case of nerves when asked to stand down their police forces or use only black cops at PPC rallies and were relieved when the caravans departed their jurisdictions. In some cities, especially in the South, CRS reports noted that law enforcement officials were "helpful and courteous" and "their presence has been welcomed by the marchers."[51]

CRS agents who rode the buses and helped keep tempers even, morale up, and trouble at bay were only part of the caravan story. The single most important guiding force, the one from which campaigners took their cues, was the caravan leader. Even though CRS representatives were indispensable in caravan life, their status was only advisory. The day-to-day decisions influencing the overall mood of the caravan—handling internal security, maintaining schedules, and enforcing discipline—were made by the caravan leaders.

The most effective leaders were usually veterans of the civil rights struggles and converts to King's philosophy of nonviolence. Albert Turner, the principal leader of the Southern Caravan, was a longtime civil rights activist from Marion County, Alabama, a charter member of the SCLC, and a veteran of the 1965 Edmund Pettus Bridge "massacre." CRS reports described him as an "excellent" leader and a positive force in the affairs of the largest of the southern caravans.[52] Turner insisted that time be set aside every day for workshops on nonviolence training. The workshops, a crash course in self-discipline, were to prepare campaigners for massive civil disobedience actions when they arrived in Washington and for the likely consequences—confrontation with the authorities, arrest, and jail. For most of the PPC demonstrators, the Washington camp-in would be their first experience in organized protest. Orientation and structure were doubly important because of the large numbers of teenage black males in some of the caravans, notably, the Northeastern, Southern, and Midwestern.[53]

A few of the caravan leaders either ignored the need for nonviolence training or made a perfunctory gesture in that direction. The Midwestern Caravan, whose nominal leader was Rev. A. D. King, Dr. King's younger brother, was negligent about planning workshops and left caravan discipline to a group of youths calling themselves the Milwaukee Commandos. Former street gang members, the Commandos were taken under the wing of Father James Groppi, a Catholic priest and militant community activist in Milwaukee. Groppi was adviser to the Milwaukee Youth Council, and the Commandos worked with him in his community reform programs. Since A. D. King was largely an absentee leader, the Commandos took on the heavy daily burdens of managing caravan affairs. The experience they gained with Groppi in Milwaukee paid off as CRS reports described the Commandos as effective caravan leaders.

To maintain control, all the caravans practiced rigorous self-policing. Numerous CRS and FBI reports documented that caravan leaders were not lax in dealing with suspected or potential troublemakers. Those campaigners considered too militant, substance abusers, and those with criminal records or who were generally unruly were summarily weeded out and sent home. For instance, when the CRS agents alerted Turner that among his youthful marchers were drug addicts, drug pushers, and even a fire alarm addict, they were all given bus tickets and ordered to return home. In Savannah, Georgia, one of the caravan leaders was sent packing for undisclosed reasons. In disciplining their own, the PPC leaders sent a clear message that there was serious business in Washington and those not up to the responsibility were not welcome.[54]

Detroit was the scene of the only major violence involving PPC campaigners. The "Detroit Incident," as it was captioned in the Justice Department reports, occurred on May 13 when the Midwestern Caravan made a scheduled stop to rest and drum up support with a march and rally. The FBI agents monitoring the caravan reported that the march and rally were orderly and without incidents. The trouble began when marchers returned from the rally to regroup at the Civic Center, better known as Cobo Hall, located in a predominantly black neighborhood. The marchers found police surrounding the caravan's communications car and a tow truck ready to haul the stalled vehicle away. Several Milwaukee Commandos blocked this action, explaining that the car had a dead battery but a new battery was en route, and they would move the stalled vehicle when it arrived.

As the standoff grew more tense, heated words were exchanged between the Commandos and the police, who demanded that the car be moved immediately, and crowds of neighborhood blacks began moving in on the circle of angry police and march marshals. Suddenly—virtually from out of nowhere—a column of mounted police appeared. When the crowd refused to disperse after exchanging words with the commander of the horse patrol, the commander reassembled his troop into ranks of four abreast and, according to an FBI source, charged into the crowd at "fairly high rates of speed." For the next 15 minutes pandemonium reigned outside of Cobo Hall as some of the marchers were clubbed to the ground and stomped by the mounted patrol, bent on savaging the demonstrators. Compounding the nightmare, while the horse troop was sweeping the street the foot patrolmen were forcing marchers who had taken refuge in Cobo Hall back out into the street and into the path of the mounted police.[55]

News of the Detroit violence drew immediate reaction from the Justice Department, FBI, and SCLC leadership. The attorney general's office ordered the bureau to interview the CRS representatives traveling with the Midwestern Caravan. The day after the incident, the FBI in Detroit interviewed Phil Mason, a black CRS agent with the caravan. Mason's account of the events outside Cobo Hall was sharply and exclusively critical of

Detroit's finest; he characterized the affair "as a gross case of police over-reaction." When Mason arrived at the scene of the incident, some march marshals had draped their bodies over the communications car and were singing "freedom songs." The CRS report, based on Mason's account, noted that when he approached the officer in charge of the mounted troop, identified himself as a federal agent, and requested that the commander withdraw his force to ease tensions, the officer ignored Mason's credentials and "caused the horse to step on his foot." "Other police on the scene," Mason's report continued, "physically manhandled, pushed, beat and otherwise assaulted innocent persons in the crowd." At least 15 persons were injured; six were hospitalized, treated, and released, with one exception. A young black woman with the caravan was knocked to the ground by a mounted officer and, suffering from hysteria, was kept in the hospital for further observation. Mason testified that he tried without success to get reports on her condition before having to leave for Cleveland with the departing caravan. Mason attributed the hospital's refusal to collusion between the police and the hospital staff.[56]

Mason's assertion that the Cobo Hall incident was a police riot did not sit well with Hoover and Sullivan's DID staff, who were responsible for shaping official Washington's view of the campaigners as the likely source of violence and not its victims. The Detroit Incident was just one example of the Justice Department and the FBI working at cross-purposes in the matter of the PPC caravans. The primary mission of the CRS officials was to troubleshoot for the caravans to ensure they reached Washington without incident. Conversely, FBI agents were looking for any derogatory information that could be used to undermine the PPC's credibility. Since their missions were in conflict, the unwritten policy of Hoover's agents vis-à-vis CRS representatives in the field was one of no assistance and no contact.[57]

To offset Mason's testimony, the bureau came up with its own witness to the Detroit Incident. Howard Royer, a white man affiliated with the National Council of Churches and the driver of the caravan's communications car, was interviewed by Cleveland FBI agents the day after Mason gave his account. The bureau singled out Royer although the march and rally were surveilled by at least one FBI agent, the Special Intelligence Bureau (red squad) of the Detroit Police, and elements of the Michigan State Police.

The reason for picking Royer was probably twofold: First, as a member of the caravan he was less likely to have his credibility questioned; second, and more important, Royer was an FBI source who had, according to the bureau, provided "reliable information in the past." Royer's testimony was certain to be more acceptable to the FBI than Mason's, and Royer would not question how his statement would be used. Royer reportedly only saw one person injured during the melee outside Cobo

Hall. He characterized the interaction between the crowd and the mounted police as merely "jostling" and nothing more. When it came to assigning blame, Royer pointed the finger at the patrolmen for insisting that the car be moved immediately and at the PPC marshals, who favored "militant nonviolence" and were anxious for a confrontation. Royer's account gave the bureau something to rework for its regular intelligence summaries circulated around official Washington. A May 15 report on the Cobo Hall incident blamed the violence on "young Negro militants who are arrogant and disruptive" and who, favoring "militant nonviolence," had "seized upon the incident to provoke a confrontation with the police." In the FBI version, mounted police or injured demonstrators were not mentioned. The Detroit Incident,[58] initially reported as a police riot, was transformed by FBI revisionism into a scuffle provoked by racial agitators. The FBI's treatment of the Cobo Hall affair was consistent with the bureau's reporting of the Poor People's Campaign.[59]

The Cobo Hall violence left emotions running high among the marchers and local blacks. Quick reaction to the situation by caravan marshals and local SCLC leaders, especially Rev. C. L. Franklin, a respected force in the black community, cooled racial tensions for the moment. Early the next morning national SCLC leaders Andy Young, Hosea Williams, and Rev. John P. Adams of the National Council of Churches arrived in the Motor City. They joined the PPC participants in a strategy session at Reverend Franklin's church that took up most of the morning. Mason was invited to give an account of the events of the previous day. The upshot of the meeting was a unified decision to keep the caravan in Detroit until Mayor Jerome Cavanagh met with them and gave assurances that the police officers responsible for the incident were disciplined. That afternoon Mayor Cavanagh, with some prompting from CRS Director Wilkins, apologized to the SCLC leadership and announced that two officers were suspended pending further investigation.[60]

With tensions eased, the Midwestern Caravan campaigners, weary and impatient to reach Washington, left Detroit for Cleveland that afternoon. In contrast to Detroit, the PPC's reception in Cleveland had all the trappings of a homecoming. Offers to house the campaigners from private homeowners, churches, and neighborhood centers were so abundant that PPC organizers had to decline additional outpourings of assistance. Faculty and students from Case and Western Reserve University coordinated a joint fund-raising drive to collect money to help with transportation expenses. Cleveland was more representative of the kind of receptions the PPC caravans experienced as they traveled America's interstates to their common destination. In Los Angeles, some Hollywood luminaries adopted the Poor People's Campaign as their own special cause and set up a support committee to raise funds. Actor Marlon Brando showed up at a rally in Albuquerque, New Mexico, to help galvanize support for the poor people's army. In St. Louis, some hospitals agreed to provide overnight accommodations for some caravan members. Students and faculty from numerous universities and colleges, including Montana, Wisconsin, Michigan State, Pittsburgh, Maryland's Morgan State, St. Louis's Washington University, Morehouse, Antioch, Haverford, and little St. Vincent's College in Pennsylvania, made the campaigners welcome and helped with the protest demonstration.[61]

By the end of May the SCLC had successfully massed its army of the poor in the nation's capital at a base camp christened "Resurrection City." The PPC did not arrive in Washington as a mendicant without resources. The SCLC had money and more influential support than any other twentieth-century American grassroots protest movement and had focused the attention of a traumatized public, if only fleetingly, on the plight of the nation's poor. It remained to be seen whether the SCLC leadership could mobilize these assets to wring some concrete concessions from a reactionary Congress and a distracted, increasingly isolated, and indifferent chief executive.

five

Resurrection City— Shantytown Among the Cherry Trees

RESURRECTION CITY, SOMETIMES REFERRED TO AS the City of Hope by SCLC planners, became a crushing weight that King's successors carried for six onerous weeks. The Washington campaign was turned into almost a perfect failure: It was poorly timed, poorly organized, and poorly led. After Resurrection City was leveled, Hosea Williams, who was never sanguine about the campaign, expressed relief that the government got them out of "that mudhole," a sentiment shared by the top SCLC leadership. The central failure of the Poor People's Campaign was that SCLC's real strength and mystique emanated from improvisational movement politics and not organizational acumen. By allowing itself to become bogged down in running a city, the SCLC surrendered all its best protest weapons: imagination, spontaneity, and élan.

King's assassination and the violence it ignited in America's black ghettos left a shaken SCLC leadership with one of the toughest decisions in that organization's short history: whether to abandon or go ahead with the Poor People's Campaign. Even under King's leadership, the campaign was a desperate gamble, and with his death the odds against a successful outcome considerably increased. Rev. Ralph D. Abernathy, King's successor, called for a staff retreat at SCLC's Atlanta headquarters. The assembled staff, still staggering under the oppressive weight of grief and fatigue, decided to go ahead with the campaign, as a fitting memorial to their fallen leader. According to Tom Offenburger, SCLC's director of public relations, these Atlanta sessions vacillated between group despair and renewed confidence. On April 17, the second day into the retreat, news of the successful settlement of the Memphis sanitation strike boosted staff morale. The news from Memphis was a turning point, Offenburger noted, and "we decided to go with the momentum." The only concession made to the shattering events of April was to postpone the campaign's kickoff by one week. Abernathy and his so-called Committee of One Hundred representatives of the poor delayed their mission to Washington until several days after the first caravans of the poverty pilgrims left Memphis for the nation's capital.[1]

For almost 15 years, Abernathy had labored loyally for the black freedom struggle in King's shadow. As King's chief lieutenant, Abernathy was not without his own strengths and resources. If the dynamics of their relationship eluded the general public, those close to the movement understood that Abernathy was King's indispensable alter ego. SCLC's Action Director Hosea Williams described Abernathy as "the unsung hero of the civil rights movement." King, Williams observed, "wouldn't make a decision without him. He trusted Ralph like he trusted Jesus." Andy Young, who was totally devoted to King, nevertheless was quick to point out that "at this time" Abernathy's down-home style of rhetoric and ramrod militancy might "make Ralph the better man to identify with Negroes." After April 4 Abernathy was the undisputed head of SCLC, elected unanimously by SCLC's board of directors, and the man in control of the Poor People's Campaign. The real test of his leadership, of course, was whether he could inspire and command that rich amalgam of talented, hard-driving, ambitious, and mercurial personalities that made up the SCLC's leadership circle now that King's unifying presence was gone.[2]

For the public at large and the press, comparisons between King and his 42-year-old successor were inevitable. As the caravans of the poor began to converge on Washington, national concern about Abernathy intensified. What was he really like? What would he do with 3,000 demonstrators once they reached Washington?

Despite his new and awesome responsibilities, Abernathy drew strength and took delight in his sudden emergence from relative obscurity to the national limelight. For six weeks after King's assassination, he conducted a whirlwind campaign through the Deep South, drumming up enthusiasm among black audiences for the PPC and boldly asserting his own leadership credentials. To a Selma, Alabama, crowd, he boasted, "I am a natural-born leader. Before I was conceived in my mother's womb . . . God ordained that I would lead men." The new SCLC president's parting words to a contingent of Mississippi blacks boarding a bus for Washington were: "Remember, you have a leader that's a rough boy— Ralph Abernathy." Addressing a mass rally in the nation's capital, Abernathy warned that white America would rue the day it "got rid" of King. "Under his leadership we were only going to shake America . . . until it fell into line. But under Ralph Abernathy's leadership," he trumpeted, "we're going to turn it upside down and right side up." His rough-hewn style and stand-up militancy alarmed many whites who had grown accustomed, even when they disapproved of his message, to King's disciplined eloquence and smooth intellectuality. However, Abernathy's style played well with rural southern blacks; they were his natural constituency.[3]

To a public more attuned to differences than similarities, Abernathy's quick-draw militancy grated and invited a ready interpretation that he was indulging in demagoguery and pandering to black extremists. Less obvious but more pertinent was the fact that Abernathy, suddenly faced with heading a leader-oriented movement like the SCLC, had to strike out and develop his own individual style. Any attempt to emulate King in the interest of continuity was certain to be self-defeating and foolish. Abernathy had to move quickly to fashion his own credible image as a leader if he expected to exercise authority that would move blacks. His virtual nonstop public appearances throughout the South in the early stages of the PPC was a rushed exercise in identity building.

He was effective when he stayed true to his own roots as a rural southern Baptist preacher. Abernathy projected the image of a militant, straight-talking veteran of the civil rights struggle, and his homilies were spiced with down-home wit and unvarnished political sagacity. The warm and supportive reception he received in the black South nourished and fortified his self-confidence but left little time for planning the campaign once the army of the poor was encamped in the nation's capital.[4]

Washington came down with a severe case of the jitters after learning that the SCLC planned to go ahead with the campaign despite the grievous events in Memphis. Washington had barely emerged from its ordeal by arson after King's assassination, and now new violence threatened as the first contingents of the PPC drew closer to the city. Parts of the capital city within walking distance of the White House still looked like a war zone, and preliminary damage estimates of the April rioting placed the figure at $15 million, a figure that was probably vastly underestimated. The self-flattering view shared by most Washingtonians—black and white—that their city was riotproof became just another comfortable assumption swept aside during the turbulent 1960s.

Walter E. Washington, the first elected black mayor of the District of Columbia, worried that the District's police force would be stretched too thin if riots were organized and broke out simultaneously around the city. The mayor registered his concern at the bi-weekly meetings, chaired by Special Assistant to the President Joseph Califano, to study and improve riot prevention techniques in the District of Columbia. Wrestling with the problem of enforcement needs and response time, Washington argued for prepositioning U.S. Army units in the city. Another strong advocate of prepositioning troops, Under Secretary of the Army David E. McGiffert, suggested the former Old People's Home along with other vacant city properties as ready-made staging areas. Congress responded to the perceived threat with a frenzy of preventive legislative activity. The House Subcommittee on Public Buildings and Grounds received 75 hastily drafted bills designed to prohibit or drastically reduce any large-scale demonstrations, like the PPC, in the capital. Other congressional voices, especially among the southern bloc in the House, called for immediate measures to head off "mob rule." Senator Jennings Randolph (D-W.Va.) alerted the Senate to "strong evidence of Communist planning and participation" in the PPC.[5]

Through April and early May, White House officials responsible for dealing with the PPC were on tenterhooks, uncertain about SCLC's intentions. Would the SCLC organizers submit to government regulations and request a permit to camp out on the Mall, or would waves of the poor simply bivouac in public parks, forcing the authorities to make mass arrests? One White House aide noted that racial tensions in the city "make a new outbreak of violence during the march more likely than we had originally thought."

From the Oval Office's vantage point, no desirable alternatives existed. President Johnson was appalled by the prospect of the invisible poor suddenly materializing en masse in his beloved Washington. The thought of an encampment of the nation's underclass sprawled out within the shadow of the Washington Monument, according to Johnson's attorney general, "hurt him—deeply hurt him." Johnson did not equivocate about his preferences: He wanted to deny the SCLC permission to set up an encampment in the city. The president's ruffled sensibilities were not, however, the White House's main concern. The prospect of a mass of the poor illegally camped out was the real nightmare. Confrontations between the District police and the poor would combine all the elements for a disaster in a city as racially tense as the nation's capital. The fact that the SCLC's new president was not a proven leader and was something of an enigma only heightened White House anxieties.[6]

Attorney General Ramsey Clark was the most persuasive voice in the Johnson administration for permitting the poor people to bring their message to Washington. Personally convinced that the protest movement was necessary and valid, Clark interceded with the president, arguing law and practical preventive politics. To prohibit the campaign would deny the rights of assembly and free speech, protection guaranteed under the Constitution, even for the most powerless and unrepresented. Short of declaring a national emergency, Clark argued, the White House would not have the law on its side. Moreover, the attorney general was convinced that if the demonstrators were denied legal and orderly avenues of communicating their grievances, they would resort to illegal and disruptive measures, ensuring the violence and disorder that official Washington feared. Clark's reasonable and measured response to the situation influenced some White House officials. On the eve of the PPC's Washington campaign, presidential assistant Matt Nimetz began circulating excerpts from *The Crisis of the Old Order*, by New Deal historian Arthur Schlesinger, Jr., which described how President Herbert Hoover had turned a blunder into a disaster by ordering the army under General Douglas MacArthur to evict the Bonus Army Marchers from the capital during the Great Depression. Drawing upon the lessons of history, Nimetz urged that the White House "deal with the Poor People's Campaign in a civilized manner."[7]

Under Clark's direction, the Justice Department assumed full responsibility for coordinating all dealings between executive agencies and PPC representatives. The attorney general and other Justice officials sympathetic with the protest movement worked to reduce tensions in the capital and met frequently with Abernathy and SCLC staffers to iron out mutually agreeable arrangements. Justice's number two man, Deputy Attorney General Warren Christopher, successfully opposed the recommendations of McGiffert and Mayor Washington to preposition troops in the city, arguing that it would only add to the already overheated crisis atmosphere. The attorney general was pressed relentlessly by Congress and the press, even before the first PPC marchers reached Washington, about the potential for unrest and whether his office was prepared to resort to mass arrests to preserve law and order. Clark refused to play to the galleries. He steadfastly avoided any speculation about the likelihood of rioting and denied that any additional enforcement powers were needed to prevent lawlessness and the disruption of government and private business while the poor petitioned Congress for a redress of grievances.[8]

The attorney general's moderate position was not popular in all government circles. A few members of Johnson's White House staff referred to him as "Ramsey the Marshmallow." Top FBI bureaucrats regarded Clark as a charter member of the dedicated wrong—liberals, who advocated coddling criminals and terrorists, and enemies of Hoover's law-and-order values. Nevertheless, Clark was determined to try to strike a balance between his role as chief law enforcement officer and his sworn obligation to uphold civil liberties.[9]

SCLC finally ended all the suspense when it applied for a permit for a campsite. The permit was issued on May 10 by the National Park Service. The agreed-upon site was 16 acres of West Potomac Park between the Reflecting Pool and Independence Avenue, from the Lincoln Memorial to Seventeenth Street, Northwest. The encampment was limited to a population of 3,000, and the permit was valid until June 15, with possible extensions at the government's discretion.

With the preliminaries out of the way, the SCLC leadership, contrary to the original plans, opted to make Resurrection City the focal point of the Poor People's Campaign. The idea of including some kind of tent city in the PPC originated with Stanley Levison, who drolly observed that he was the only King adviser old enough to remember the 1932 Bonus Army marchers' encampment. Levison's idea of a camp of poor squatters illegally bivouacked on the Mall was a public relations gambit, proposed largely to attract press attention to the campaign in its early stages. According to Andy Young, King turned a deaf ear to all talk about negotiating with official Washington for a permit, certain that the Johnson administration would not tolerate a shantytown on federal park grounds. More significantly, King's undivided focus was directing a massive "go for broke" nonviolent protest action and not running a tent city.

Intent on raising nonviolent protest to a new level, King vaguely favored an open-ended strategy of bringing hundreds of demonstrators to the Washington Monument grounds in the dead of night to set up camp and wait for panicked federal and District authorities to arrest them. He and his SCLC strategists envisioned this first mass arrest as only the opening phase in a repeating drama of creative nonviolent disobedience. The first arrests would be followed by wave upon wave of the army of poor descending on the Mall, setting up their makeshift camps, and preparing for arrest until the District jails were overflowing. King and his SCLC lieutenants expected to be among the first protesters hustled off to jail. King hoped that this campaign of civil disobedience would trigger an outcry of national protest, embarrass the federal government, and force the hand of Congress to address the grievances of the nation's poor.[10]

Under Abernathy's leadership the SCLC pulled back from launching the campaign with arrest-provoking tactics and settled instead on erecting a semipermanent camp, Resurrection City—a symbolic reminder to the nation that the Great Society's declared war on poverty had not produced significant tangible results. Years later, while preparing his autobiography, Abernathy recalled his vision for the city as the embodiment of hope, a model of a just society:

> We would set up a model for the rest of the nation to emulate. Everyone would live together in peace and mutual respect. . . . We would have people of all races, ethnic backgrounds, and religious beliefs. Since everyone would be poor, there would be no greed or envy. . . . [A]nd our business would be to go from government agency to government agency, representing the poor, speaking out for their interests, asking for several concrete things from our government, the richest in the world.[11]

Historically, Abernathy's model for the PPC shantytown on the Mall was quintessentially American. It was more or less a secularized version and distant heir of those first visionaries, the early Puritan fathers, who left England for the American colonies to build a city upon a hill. Like the Puritans, Abernathy placed his faith in the force of moral example, hoping that Resurrection City would galvanize the conscience of the nation and enlist its support behind the campaign's goals to roll back poverty and extend hope to the dispossessed who could not previously afford hope. In another respect, the SCLC was taking on the task of building a city from scratch and administering to its needs, an enormous undertaking without precedence in the history of American protest policies.[12]

The March 28 violence in Memphis and King's assassination were determining factors in the shift of the campaign from the politics of confrontation to the politics of persuasion. Shattered and disoriented by the nightmare of Memphis, the SCLC leaders wanted to reduce the risk of violence that was inherent in a campaign of mass civil disobedience. Unspoken but clearly understood was that Attorney General Clark was a sympathetic advocate of the PPC. All support and encouragement from the Justice Department would end if the campaign engaged in tactics that inadvertently triggered rioting, a strong likelihood in racially tense Washington.[13]

On Monday, May 13, with much fanfare and heavy press coverage, Resurrection City was declared officially open. A weary Abernathy arrived for the ceremonies about two hours late. Wearing a Levi's jacket, no shirt, and a carpenter's apron, the SCLC head drove the first nail into a 2 x 4 while the crowd chanted "Freedom!" "Freedom!" in time with the hammer blows. Abernathy iterated the campaign's intentions of staying in Washington until the federal government addressed the plight of the poor. Fighting fatigue and the noise of jet airliners overhead, he pledged that Resurrection City would be a community of love and brotherhood. All in all, Abernathy's performance was unremarkable. With the ceremonies completed, the SCLC president quickly took his leave to hold a press conference at the Pitts Motel, a black-owned, well-appointed establishment where he and most of the SCLC staff had rooms.[14]

Starting the next day and continuing for the better part of two weeks, the campsite was constructed at an impressive pace. A city of A-frame huts made of plywood and canvas took shape between the white marbled formality of the Lincoln Memorial and the Washington Monument. Aside from 300 gallons of paint, virtually all of the building materials were donated. An outpouring of volunteer labor from church and neighborhood groups helped keep construction ahead of the need, but the city's new residents pulled their own weight and then some. The delegation of poor from New York virtually hit the ground running once their buses dropped them off at the encampment. Independent, fast-paced, and no strangers to protest (such as rent strikes at home), they were accustomed to doing things their own way. Enthusiastic and well organized, they formed three-man teams and in short order were putting up shelters at the rate of about one every 15 minutes. Since the shelters belonged to their builders, enterprising residents used available materials to add second stories and sundecks to their new "homes."

The 300 gallons of paint was quickly pressed into service as residents gave vent to creative, whimsical, and proprietary impulses. Painted squares, stars, dot patterns, and faces were the most prevalent designs. Graffiti was ubiquitous, giving shelters a personal and distinctive character. "Big House of John Hickman," "Soul Sisters Shirley, Mary, Ruby, and Joyce," and "I Have Lived in Many Houses. This Is My First Home" softened a barrackslike atmosphere with the human touch. Some residents advertised their hometown, "Cleveland's Rat Patrol," "Motown," and "Beale Street Baptists, Memphis, Tennessee," while others wisecracked with "White House" and "Sugar Shack." Other huts were decorated with quotes from King and Malcolm X, and one small shack nearest the Reflecting Pool bore the legend "Vinceremos," the Spanish equivalent for "We Shall Overcome." In less than two weeks, an encampment of plywood structures covering about six city blocks was on the green lawn of the Mall. In addition to residential shelters, the city was outfitted with eating facilities, toilets, medical and child care centers, a meeting hall, and planned space for Freedom Schools. Resurrection City boasted its own flag of red and white stripes, and unlike that of the Puritans, Abernathy's "City on a Hill" had its own zip code.[15]

Despite promising beginnings, there were early indications that the SCLC was ill-suited to the task of administering a city preparing to accommodate 3,000 people. From the very outset, the PPC's relations with the Washington press corps were mismanaged. "Resurrection City, USA" promised good copy, and the editors of each of Washington's dailies assigned 8 to 10 reporters to the story on an around-the-clock vigil. Under the circumstances, mutualism, not chilly suspicion, should have characterized this relationship. The SCLC needed a sympathetic press to effectively dramatize the plight of the poor, and the press did not stint on coverage to get the PPC's story to its readers.

The trouble began the day the city opened, and the press entered the camp to take pictures and interview the residents. Camp marshals, many of them teenagers and members of Memphis and Chicago street gangs, seemed to enjoy their new authority and used it to hassle whites, making newsmen special targets of their petty harassments. This treatment was a sudden surprise to reporters who were used to an entirely different treatment when they covered King-led SCLC protest demonstrations. Most of the reporters assigned to the campaign were sympathetic to its goals and were shocked and mystified by strong-arm tactics that interfered with their efforts to get the story and meet their deadlines. Washington columnist Mary McGrory was quick to respond with a pungent column entitled "'Oppressed' Adopt Tactics of the Oppressors." "The young marshals," she chided, "some of whom probably have shouted themselves hoarse over police brutality, were pushing people around in the style to which they have become accustomed." The frustration within the news community filtered up the chain of command; SCLC staffers expressed concern, made excuses, and offered apologies but seemed unable to remedy the situation. Encounters like those described in McGrory's columns remained a constant occurrence in and around Resurrection City.[16]

SCLC bungling squandered much of the Washington press corps' initial goodwill before Resurrection City was a week old. Harassment by camp marshals, vacillation and runaround by the staff, and scheduled press conferences that were routinely one to two hours late rapidly cooled the news corps' sympathies for the campaign. By Friday, May 17, most reporters were fed up with the situation as they prepared for a one o'clock press conference called by Bernard Lafayette, the PPC's national coordinator, at the historic New York Avenue Presbyterian Church. Heavy mid-week thunderstorms halted construction on the shelters, and about 1,700 campaigners with the Midwestern and Southern caravans were due to arrive in Washington the next day. Reporters came to the church armed with questions about the building delays and SCLC's plans for accommodating the new arrivals. After waiting almost two hours, the assembled press corps was moving toward the exit when Lafayette breezed into the church. Inauspiciously launched, the press conference quickly deteriorated into a travesty.

In fielding questions about the building delays, Lafayette announced that the campaign was in deep financial straits, and about $3 million was needed to fully complete the original plans for the city. This figure landed like a bombshell, producing stunned silence followed by an explosion of questions. Reporters quoted back to the national coordinator his architect's estimates of $80 per unit for each plywood and canvas shack. Lafayette agreed with this figure and acknowledged the SCLC's original plan called for 600 units. Following the logic of this rudimentary math, reporters wanted to know why the extra millions were needed. Lafayette's figures did not stack, and reporters asked for a detailed breakdown to help them make sense of the story before going to press. Caught in the stubble of his own confusion, Lafayette tried to bluff his way through this rough patch with evasive double-talk and even implied that the press set out to ensnare him so that it could mislead the public and undermine the PPC. Lafayette broke off the questioning as pandemonium reigned. He fled from the outraged reporters, pleading he was late for another meeting while promising clarification at a later press conference.[17]

The Washington papers carried the story of the campaign's "financial crisis" and Lafayette's $3 million figure, adding that the SCLC provided no breakdown. Abernathy was in Miami at the time and only added to the confusion when he told reporters he was unaware of the extent of the SCLC's money problems. In a scarcely concealed damage control operation, Andy Young flew back to Washington over the weekend to placate the press and try to salvage some of the PPC's credibility. Young assured the press that the campaign was not facing a financial crisis and that Lafayette was under a great deal of pressure and had "just goofed." Later Young admitted that the SCLC had shot itself in the foot in the critical area of press management. Indecisive leadership and an easy tolerance for bumbling cost the campaign dearly in media support and Young knew it. "I think this is where," he lamented, "we missed Dr. King a great deal. . . . He spoke with a kind of reputation and authority that was sort of unchallengeable and we miss that."[18]

In New York Stanley Levison echoed Young's concerns, except as a private person he was free to indulge in invective. With King gone all the restraints were down, he gloomed, and the SCLC leadership was "running wild" as if they all contracted "megalomania." Abernathy was "thrill happy . . . and running around every place to lead this and that contingent." If he did not "stop addressing every fish fry" and provide leadership in Washington, Levison feared that the PPC's initial good work would be in vain. Levison blamed the botched press conference on Abernathy's absenteeism, and he was aghast when the SCLC president compounded the fiasco with his inept remarks to Miami reporters. "Then Ralph comes along and adds his own special quality to the farce," Levison quipped, sarcasm his only release, "and then you have room service on wheels." Levison's criticism was harsh but not unfair. He saw early on that the "big problem is not money, the big problem is leadership."[19]

Abernathy returned to Washington on May 19 and promptly announced that the PPC's planned central event, a day of national celebration dubbed Solidarity Day that was originally scheduled for May 30, would be postponed. The SCLC hoped that Solidarity Day would be a reprise of the historic August 1963 March on Washington and would focus the nation's attention on the basic issues of poverty and hunger. To ensure a large turnout of middle-class participants—white and black—the SCLC organizers agreed to keep the campaign subdued until Solidarity Day was behind them. In retrospect, the delay robbed the PPC of any compelling drama and reduced it to a kind of shadow play. The postponement meant that SCLC organizers' inventiveness and imagination would be taxed to the utmost in devising ways to sustain morale and interest in the campaign without resorting to civil disobedience and mass arrests.

During the next four weeks, the PPC engaged in about 40 demonstrations that consisted of orderly sallies to government agencies, the presentation of demands to officials, singing and speech-making galore, and a return to the campsite. To try to keep a militant edge on the campaign, SCLC planners resorted to peppery rhetoric. Abernathy insisted that Resurrection City was "not a plantation" and pledged that "what we're going to do is sleep at night out here, but we're going to raise hell downtown during the day." Most of these demonstrations involved less than 200 marchers, some had as many as 400, and all but one took place without incident.

Dr. George Wiley of NWRO led a march and sing-in outside of the Longworth House Office Building without SCLC's blessing. The police arrested 18 demonstrators for disorderly conduct when they refused to stop singing. All of the arrested parties were later released under their own recognizance and returned to the camp. Abernathy called the arrests "unfortunate" and asserted that they only took place "because I was not there." Despite all his bravado, Abernathy's first priority was to keep the lid on the campaign until after Solidarity Day.[20]

SCLC's strategy of low-key demonstrations met with the Justice Department's approval, allowing some key personnel to discreetly help the PPC achieve some victories. Attorney General Clark waived the requirements of march permits for demonstrations to Capitol Hill, providing they were orderly and did not interfere with traffic. Lines of communication between the Justice Department and the SCLC leadership quartered at the Pitts Motel were kept as unobtrusive as possible. Leroy Clark, a lawyer with the NAACP Legal Defense Fund, served as chief liaison between the SCLC and Clark's department. A team of CRS people was always at Resurrection City from 9:00 A.M. until midnight. Calling themselves the RC Squad, these Justice officials worked to strengthen the bonds of trust with campaigners developed during the caravan phase of the PPC and to monitor camp activities. During the early stages of the campaign, the CRS people had relatively unimpeded access to the encampment. Each team worked a five-hour shift every day, and after each tour of duty, they reported back to command central at Justice, called the Alert Room, such information as the time and place of announced demonstrations, the mood of the campaigners, and any problems that might erode morale, including personal and gang rivalries that could erupt into violence.

The RC Squad's primary responsibility was to keep a sharp eye out for any situation that might disrupt camp life or provoke violence, whether it originated from troublemakers inside the tent city or from hostile outsiders. Building rapport with the SCLC staff and camp residents to gain freer access to the camp did not relegate the CRS teams to the dubious role of double agents. The preventive intelligence they gathered was not used to embarrass or thwart the PPC. In late May, for example, the large mess tent collapsed after four days of steady rain that turned the campsite into a quagmire. John Rosenberg, one of the CRS men on the scene, took it upon himself to get Potomac Electric Power Company (PEPCO), Washington's local power company, to dispatch a repair crew to Resurrection City posthaste to restore electrical power. PEPCO's response to an emergency call from a PPC staffer would have probably meant that the camp residents would have spent most of the day sitting in the dark and eating doughnuts and cold cereal. Camp morale was not PEPCO's problem, but it was a major concern with Justice officials.[21]

Even though Clark had complete confidence in his CRS unit, he knew these dedicated professionals were overmatched by the enormity of the challenge posed by the Poor People's Campaign. One blunder or staged confrontation could ignite a chain reaction that could build quickly to tragic proportions in a city as racially volatile as Washington. The attorney general took precautionary steps when possible to minimize the danger of confrontations. Clark's waiving of march permits for PPC demonstrations was conditioned upon the size and line of march. Certain areas on Capitol Hill—such as Lafayette Park and the south side of Pennsylvania Avenue—essentially were declared off limits to keep marchers away from large concentrations of city police. Clark upgraded security at all federal agencies scheduled for visits from PPC delegations but insisted that the security guards be "unobtrusively posted" to avoid impressions of any federal show of force.

The RC Squad kept close watch on the movements of known black nationalists like Stokley Carmichael and H. Rap Brown. However, Justice was equally uneasy about some of the federal police. The U.S. Park Police, the lily-white force that had jurisdiction around Resurrection City, was a particular concern because, according to CRS's Wilkins, they "just didn't like niggers." Although the Justice Department did not have direct authority over the Park Police, Clark recommended a course of action he expected in their dealings with city residents. Furthermore, in any case of serious divergence from these guidelines, Clark made it clear he would go right up the chain of command to their ultimate superior, the Speaker of the House.[22]

Despite its compelling goals, gathered ranks of poor prepared to bear witness and face jail, and the behind-the-scenes support from the Justice Department, the PPC never got off the ground. The campaign failed to effectively focus national attention on the realities of poverty and hunger in Vietnam-era America. A combination of intermittent torrential rains and chronic mismanagement stifled almost every aspect of the six-week campaign to pressure Congress to reorder national priorities. The rains came on May 23 and for the next two weeks it rained 11 out of 14 days, turning Resurrection City into a bog. Before the spring deluge tapered off, some low-lying spots in the camp were under six inches of water.[23]

Campaigners who came to Washington prepared to confront the government instead confronted Mother Nature. Mud, food, and survival became the driving elemental concerns of the shantytown's population. The fierce downpours and the resulting mud brought most of the construction to a standstill. Work on the drainage system came to a halt, and city residents had to be bused out of the camp to bathe. Sanitation facilities were so compromised by the bad weather that Wilkins, fearing a possible epidemic, arranged for a Public Health Service team to visit the camp. Dr. Murray Grant, the District health director, reported that conditions were so appalling that the risk of typhoid and dysentery were "very high."[24]

The inexcusable failure of the camp's food committee to arrange for hot meals added to the desperate physical conditions plaguing the tent city in its early stages. The city's administrative coordinator, John C. Rutherford, complained about the demoralizing effect of "baloney and cheese, ham and cheese, and salami and cheese almost every day," but his pleas went unheeded.[25]

After five days of steady rain, morale in the camp was at a nadir. The RC Squad reported that the residents were bitter that Abernathy and most of the SCLC leaders left them in the cold and damp while they conducted the campaign from the comparatively posh quarters of the Pitts Motel. When SCLC board member Marian Logan visited the city in early June, she was disgusted with the SCLC leadership. "The staff of the SCLC is living at the Pitts Motel," she exploded, "while the poor people are up to their ass in mud." If the situation was not straightened out, she threatened to advise her friends not to contribute another dime to the campaign.[26]

The physical and organizational morass of the encampment bred serious internal unrest. Although most of the early campaigners were orderly and uncomplaining, a significant number of young "dudes," many of them members of youth gangs from urban ghettos where they held down a street corner, took advantage of the deteriorating circumstances to engage in a reign of terror inside the camp. FBI informants inside the city identified at least four major gangs by their "colors," insignias or names blazoned across their windbreakers—the "Barracudas" and "Blackstone Rangers" from Chicago, the "Commandos" from Milwaukee, and the "Invaders" from Memphis. Turf battles, drunken brawls, protection rackets, and petty theft became common occurrences. Some gang members even brought guns into the camp. Only the top SCLC leaders, when they got around to it, were able to exercise some control over the troublemakers. During the last week in May, about 200 hell-raisers, most of them from Chicago, were sent home because, according to Jim Bevel, "They went around beating up on white people . . . and were hostile to the press."[27]

Many more bravos were periodically expelled, but they were replaced by others from the Washington area attracted by the free food and shelter and the opportunity to steal everything that could be lifted. Staff members assigned to security detail, "peacekeepers" as they dubbed themselves, complained that on too many occasions they would round up problem-makers only to have them "cop a plea" with someone in higher authority, like Bevel or Rev. Jesse Jackson. Usually they would be allowed to stay in camp, where they targeted new suckers to hustle and repeated the same offenses against unsuspecting newcomers. Jackson, the shantytown's "city manager," tried to assure the press that the exodus of hundreds of campaigners was simply the "normal cycle" of departures. Jackson's assurances notwithstanding, the SCLC leadership was never able to get a firm handle on the discipline problem, and once the unrest started, it never really died down.[28]

The stress of running a city and coping with its problems gave rise to factional tensions within the SCLC leadership. Without King, the discipline he imposed on the movement's inner circle by the force of his personality crumbled. Personal antagonisms and antipathies that had simmered under the surface boiled over into a leadership crisis. During the staff meetings at the Pitts Motel at the end of May, the lid blew. Veteran staffers and long-time movement activists lashed into Jackson for undercutting Abernathy's and Young's authority with outsiders and for neglecting his administrative duties while he promoted himself to the media. Some recalled with bitterness how Jackson earlier had pressed King to abandon the idea of the Poor People's Campaign and turned on Jackson now for trying to take the campaign over.[29]

Some of King's lieutenants harbored deep resentment against Jackson for what they regarded as his tasteless, self-serving behavior at the time of the civil rights leader's assassination. Jackson engrossed the media with his fake story of reaching the stricken leader first and cradling the dying King in his arms. The morning after the assassination, Jackson appeared on the *Today* show wearing an olive turtleneck sweater stained with blood he insisted was that of the fallen leader. Later that day he showed up at a special memorial convocation of the Chicago city council in the same clothes and recited the same story—by now in the retelling it had become Jackson's own self-imagined pietà—of being the last person to speak to King as he held the head of the mortally wounded warrior for the poor. In this whole matter of what Michael Frady, Jackson's most recent biographer aptly calls "The Story of the Blood," it was understandably, given the wildness of the moment, overlooked or disremembered that it was police spy Marrell McCullough who was the first one to reach the crumpled and bloody body of Dr. King.

Some of King's staff who had been at the Lorraine Motel—Williams and Abernathy, for instance—knew that Jackson's account was a fabrication, and they could not forgive him for these cheap theatrics that verged on sacrilege, capitalizing on the violent death of a man he professed to love. According to one account, when Bevel defended Jackson at one of the stormy Pitts Motel sessions, Williams took Bevel by the collar and "literally shook him like a dog with a rat." Throughout these knock-down–drag-out internecine confrontations, Abernathy maintained his silence but "sort of beamed," one eyewitness remembered, "as we just sort of took Jesse to pieces."[30]

The internal flap over Jackson's administrative shortcomings was seized upon by a press avidly searching for dramatic copy about the shantytown in West Potomac Park. Bored with the daily round of aimless demonstrations, the press focused on these internal squabbles, dramatizing them as a power struggle that was impeding the campaign's progress. When Abernathy replaced Jackson as "city manager" with Hosea Williams, the press was quick to pick up the story. According to Abernathy the 26-year-old reverend was being reassigned to Chicago to raise recruits and funds for the campaign. However, Jackson defenders, especially the more outspoken ones among the younger SCLC staff members, complained to the press that Jackson was not being reassigned, but banished from the tent city. He was demoted, his loyal followers charged, because he wanted to pick up the campaign's tempo with more creative and militant demonstrations.[31]

By 1968 the bureaucratic machinery of the American surveillance state was humming along on all cylinders. The Interdivisional Intelligence Unit (IDIU), created by Attorney General Clark in December 1967, was fully operational by the time the PPC set up its tent city. Supervisory responsibility for managing this surveillance behemoth was assigned to Assistant Attorneys General John Doar (Civil Rights), Fred Vinson (Criminal), and J. Walter Yeagley (Internal Security) and to Roger Wilkins, director of Community Relations Service.[32]

"The RC Squad today is to be headed by John Rosenberg again. The kiosk at the Lincoln Memorial will have a phone . . . so [RC Squad] . . . can reach information Center and [Assistant Attorney General] Pollock's office." This was just one agenda item related to the ongoing surveillance of Resurrection City in a routine daily briefing in Ramsey Clark's office. Joining the RC Squad in an around-the-clock surveillance of the poor people's encampment were teams of intelligence officers from other agencies and authorities, including FBI, U.S. Army Intelligence, U.S. Border Patrol, Park Police, and an elite force from the Metropolitan Police Department (MPD) of Washington, D.C.

The Park Police converted one of its buildings adjacent to Resurrection City into a "survey lodge," which was manned 24 hours a day. A team of Border Patrol officers set up a command post at the survey lodge, from which they reported to the IDIU and directed surveillance activities from unmarked cars patrolling the immediate area around the tent city. There was virtually nothing that transpired inside the city that was not reported back to the IDIU nerve center through some intelligence channel. Each day reports poured into the IDIU's intelligence hopper—on the average of one every 30 minutes—about incidents, announced demonstrations, plans for future marches, the coming and going of residents and visitors, and the general activities inside the campsite. Government internal security bureaucrats, viewing the PPC as an army of potentially violent racial agitators instead of petitioners, enveloped Resurrection City as though it were an advance colony of some intergalactic invasion force that threatened Earth with unspeakable disaster.[33]

The FBI went through the motions of networking with the IDIU as its agents reported regularly to Justice about the city's activities and forwarded intelligence from its ghetto informers about racial activities in America's black communities. All of this was basically a sideshow performance, an overt exercise in administrative cooperation in which Hoover and the FBI hierarchy were willing to engage providing they were unimpeded in their own covert agenda.[34] Although the PPC was just one front in the FBI's secret war against the bureau-designated black menace, Hoover mobilized the FBI to penetrate the SCLC's encampment in the nation's capital.

On May 24, 1968, Hoover directed all FBI offices to prevent subversive elements from using the campaign to further their own "nefarious purposes." "To give a true picture of the situation," the directive called for meticulous reporting of the "complete facts" that "must be dug out by penetrative investigations." Nothing short of "decisive, imaginative, and aggressive investigative effort" was acceptable. To impress his bureau chiefs that the SCLC's army of the poor was at the top of the director's list for disruption programs, Hoover sent a second directive three days later instructing that "aggressive and penetrative investigation must be conducted in all phases of our coverage of the PPC."[35]

Teams of FBI agents stationed outside Resurrection City shadowed all demonstrations and worked up summary reports on meetings and exchanges between campaigners and federal agency heads. Some bureau executives, not content with this arms-length surveillance, wanted to slip FBI agents inside the camp to ensure more detailed and reliable intelligence. George C. Moore, the hard-charging chief of the Racial Intelligence Section of the DID, urged that agents be furnished press cards as a safe cover to penetrate the tent city's loose security system. Moore's superior, William C. Sullivan, supported the recommendation.

Hoover ultimately approved the use of press cards to infiltrate agents into the encampment. For the duration of the PPC, FBI agents routinely gained access to the tent city by posing as members of the fourth estate.[36] Jesse Jackson complained to CBS reporter Daniel Shorr that he suspected the government had tapped the city's phone lines.

No conclusive evidence exists to support Jackson's allegations, but some FBI intelligence on the PPC was so detailed and specific as to preclude dismissing these allegations.[37] The FBI also used black agents to do undercover work. Several of these agents (cover undisclosed) proved so adept at infiltration that they assisted at the Lost and Found counter located in the camp's headquarters tent.[38]

In addition to these surveillance techniques, the FBI carried its political warfare to a deeper level, a level of intrusion more in keeping with the aggressive tone of Hoover's May 24 and 27 directives. For a deeper penetration of Resurrection City, Hoover authorized an expensive informant coverage program responsible only to the director and the bureau's top officials.[39] Since this infiltration operation was part of the bureau's covert COINTELPRO against the PPC, the exact number of informants is impossible to ascertain. However, FBI headquarters in Washington expected at least 20 symbol informants from other field offices to join those sources already residing in the tent city. For example, the Cleveland field office alone reported that six sources who had already arrived in Washington with the Midwestern Caravan were inside the encampment. Although the numbers are sketchy, they indicate that the bureau was building its own clandestine team of "assets" inside Resurrection City, including undercover FBI agents, symbol informers, and tipsters, responsible only to their action-oriented COINTELPRO handlers.[40]

These 20 symbol informers probably were recruited from an FBI program started in the fall of 1967, when every field office was instructed to develop informers to infiltrate "militant black nationalist organizations." All informers were handpicked for this assignment through a selection process that involved the bureau chiefs of 24 field offices. The selection criteria was reliability, and the FBI's collective profile on these 20 indicated that they had in the past provided the agency "maximum benefit." To exploit their talents to the fullest, each informant was assigned a "handler," an agent attached to the WFO. Additional phone lines were installed at WFO to allow these informants to contact an agent any time of the day or night and to avoid going through the WFO switchboard, to ensure confidentiality. In view of the planning, expense, and the bureau's stated COINTELPRO goals, there is good reason to suspect that Hoover and the FBI top brass expected to employ this "fifth column" of paid informants in ways that went well beyond surveillance and data collection.[41]

By the late 1960s, military intelligence had become the single most important component, with the exception of the FBI, of the burgeoning American surveillance state. Alarmed by the exploding ghettos, black militancy, the antiwar movement, and campus unrest, the army tooled up for Armageddon. All the military snooping was influenced by the premise that local unrest and dissident demonstrations were the product of a national conspiracy, a thesis widely propagated by official circles in Johnson's Washington. A dedicated proponent of this view was the army's assistant chief for intelligence during 1967–1968, Major General William P. Yarborough, sometimes referred to as "the Big Y" because of his command presence. When the Detroit ghetto blew in 1967, General Yarborough gathered his staff in the Pentagon's war room and instructed them: "Men, get your counterinsurgency manuals. We have an insurgency on our hands." General Yarborough and other high-ranking officers of the Intelligence Command were confident that the counterinsurgency methods used to root out guerrilla cadres in the jungles of Malaya and South Vietnam could suppress and control riots in America's ghettos.[42]

By the beginning of 1968 the army had already drafted contingency plans, with the code name Garden Plot, for centralized military intervention in coordination with local and state governments to suppress large-scale civil disorders. In conjunction with Garden Plot, the army developed a massive domestic intelligence network that operated without civilian authority or control.[43] This military intelligence juggernaut complete with built-in redundancies and plenty of loose screws—like one of the Pentagon's cost-plus weapons systems—rode roughshod over the civilian body politic. In 1968 Resurrection City was the army's most challenging clandestine domestic target. An officer assigned to this operation testified before a Senate committee that "army intelligence monitored the progress of the PPC as it had never monitored anything before."[44]

In fact, army intelligence began its blanket coverage of the PPC during the caravan phase of the protest movement. Once the poverty trekkers set up their shanties, soldier-agents monitored "every march, every rally, took scores of photos, and filed hundreds of reports. This monitoring," according to one soldier-agent, "continued throughout the life of the PPC and Resurrection City."

The army's surveillance program was unlawful, redundant, and excessive. While the PPC was in Washington, military intelligence employed its Army Security Agency (ASA) units, vehicles equipped to intercept radio transmissions, to monitor civilian radio traffic as part of its surveillance operation. ASA units were used to monitor the radio network and mobile units the SCLC had in place for Solidarity Day, the one-day mammoth demonstration on June 19. Two mobile vans were stationed alternatively at the Thirteenth Street Precinct, ASA headquarters, and the Treasury Building to intercept all SCLC radio communications and disseminate them to the Secret Service. The army had no authorization from the Federal Communications Commission to engage in this electronic warfare and blatantly violated a federal statute that outlawed the interception of civilian radio traffic.[45]

For the duration of the PPC, military agents joined members of the Intelligence Division of the Metropolitan Police Department, Park Police, and FBI along French Drive overlooking the encampment and took down license plate numbers of buses and private cars transporting city residents to and from the encampment so that military intelligence command could trace their ownership. The Metropolitan Police Department used a special police van marked "Identification Division," equipped with a mugging camera to do photosurveillance. These mug shots were shared with the army and the FBI. A captain from the 116th Military Intelligence Group flew aerial reconnaissance missions in helicopters over Resurrection City and logged flight pay. Leaving no surveillance stone unturned, the army even stationed a Signal Corps unit atop the Washington Monument to photograph the tent city for imagery interpreters at the Pentagon.[46]

Most of the army's surveillance of Resurrection City was limited to snooping from outside the camp. However, the army did infiltrate the city by using phony press cards to cover PPC news conferences. One agent passed himself off as a newsman and badgered the management of the Pitts Motel to find out if Abernathy had paid his bill. A black major slated for a tour of duty in Vietnam was reassigned to penetrate Resurrection City and insinuate himself into the SCLC leadership circle. Apparently the army thought the major's counterintelligence training could be put to better use in the poor people's camp than in Southeast Asia.[47] His other less derring-do assignment was "to get information of the sanitation facilities, the depth of the mud when it rained . . . and information of that nature." The major penetrated the city about a week after it opened and continued in his undercover role until it closed. The entire time he spied on the SCLC organizers and camp residents he had access to a chauffeur and a car from the Pentagon's motor pool to drive him to and from an area close to the camp.

The army's intrusion into the PPC was symptomatic of the American surveillance state run amok in the 1960s. Even in terms of the military's own rationale for domestic snooping, its operations were mindless and wastefully redundant. General Yarborough himself inadvertently made this point clear when he admitted to a Senate committee that 85 percent of the Intelligence Command's domestic intelligence was furnished by the FBI.[48]

With the campaign drifting aimlessly, Abernathy asked Bayard Rustin to coordinate Solidarity Day, the planned demonstration on the Mall rescheduled for June 19, with which the SCLC hoped to climax its protest. As the chief architect of the 250,000-strong 1963 March on Washington, Rustin was a proven organizer of massive demonstrations. Rustin agreed to take on the task providing that he had undisputed control over the event, that there would be no disruptions or civil disobedience, and that the SCLC formulate a set of realistic demands. A desperate Abernathy agreed to Rustin's demands. On May 24 Abernathy announced Rustin's appointment as the national coordinator of the one-day mobilization.[49]

Rustin's appointment failed, however, to help the floundering PPC. His earlier opposition to the PPC and recent flippant comments that the campaign was just another "fish fry" that was long on high jinks but muddled in purpose had alienated most of the SCLC leadership. Rustin further stirred up suspicions and hostility by attempting to narrow SCLC's demands. On June 2 Rustin issued a "Call to Americans of Goodwill," which contained his own list of demands. Congress "felt trapped," he asserted "by Abernathy's nameless demands for an instant millennium." Rustin later would argue that he thought his own revised demands met with SCLC approval after running them by Andy Young; however, others in the SCLC were enraged. The "Call" made no reference to Vietnam and even fell short of the recent proposals from the president's Kerner Commission. Hosea Williams attacked Rustin's "immediate demands" as "a bunch of jazz and nonsense," telling the press that Rustin had no authority to speak for the SCLC.[50]

Away in Miami addressing a labor convention, Abernathy found himself caught in the middle of a public row. Frazzled and uncertain about how to stem the tide of revolt within his staff, he pleaded with Levison to help find a remedy for this new leadership crisis. Levison, convinced that Abernathy and his staff had frittered away the campaign's initial momentum, treated King's successor with disdain and declined to help. For Levison, the situation in Washington was beyond repair, and he expressed "no confidence" in the present SCLC leadership. "It is incredible to me," he told Abernathy, "that Bayard was brought in, and if Andy suggested it he should have his head examined." The next day over the phone with Young, Levison accused the SCLC leadership of dithering, playing house with Resurrection City, and effectively sabotaging the protest movement. A few days later, failing to obtain Abernathy's unqualified support, Rustin bowed out. Abernathy appointed Sterling Tucker, director of the Washington Bureau of the Urban League, to take over the June 19 mobilization.[51]

The Rustin affair reflected the confusion and disorganization among the PPC planners. Rustin's style may have been haughty and condescending, but his criticism of the SCLC's demands as too vague and millennial was on the mark.[52] Liberal columnists and reporters who were banking on Rustin's shorter and more focused proposals to salvage the campaign gloomed over his dismissal, fearing that now the PPC would end in a fiasco or an ugly disaster.[53] But even in the face of its many shortcomings, the PPC's central message still underscored a nagging and unsettling national paradox: Despite all the programs and money spent, the poor continued to get an unfair shake. A country that boasted a gross national product of $800 billion in 1968 still tolerated in its midst a subnation of 30 million poor.

A week before the scheduled June 19 demonstration the SCLC issued a new set of demands. The new list was scaled down to 20 priority items, four of which were identified as crucial: food, jobs, housing, and welfare. This refined list was even softer than Rustin's earlier revisionist efforts. The press attributed this turnaround to Marian Wright, a 29-year-old graduate of the Yale Law School who was in Washington on a fellowship studying government. Wright suddenly became the PPC's most sought after lobbyist. Her eloquence and incisive detailed knowledge about federal poverty programs and current legislation mesmerized reporters. The young black lawyer imposed a focus and coherence to a campaign that was languishing and demoralized.

No newcomer to civil rights activism, Wright worked for the NAACP Legal Defense Fund and was part of a 1967 team of investigators studying poverty in 12 counties in Mississippi. The survey uncovered evidence of such abject privation among the rural black population—hunger, malnutrition, and even starvation—as to defy adequate description. And Mississippi was only a microcosm for the more than one million hardcore poor blacks living in the rural backwaters of the American South in the 1960s. Intimately familiar with the Mississippi scene, Wright was the first one to suggest to King in 1967 that the SCLC take some of that state's poorest citizens to Washington to stage sit-ins with the federal government to dramatize these appalling conditions. Ultimately, King's decision to bring thousands of poor petitioners from across the nation to Washington was a logical extension of Wright's idea.[54]

The spate of press stories crediting Marian Wright with restoring the campaign's credibility unintentionally exaggerated her role. The eleventh-hour repackaging of the PPC's demands was a joint undertaking involving Wright, Roger Wilkins of the CRS, and M. Carl Holman, a Justice Department lawyer with the Civil Rights Division. Wright, representing the SCLC, joined with the others in behind-the-scenes strategy sessions to try to ensure some face-saving victories. Their frequent working sessions were intense and adhered to the attorney general's rules that insisted on low visibility to escape public notice and to avoid any impression that the Justice Department was part of the PPC.

The revised list of the PPC's priority demands corresponded closely with the congressional liberals' calendar of antipoverty measures, jobs and low-income housing, that were already in the legislative pipeline. An impressive national turnout and a peaceful demonstration on Solidarity Day might influence Congress and translate into legislative triumphs for the poor. Under the circumstances the liberal bloc in Congress and the SCLC were natural allies, partners in a holy alliance to raise hopes and remedy despair. Much of the impetus behind this coalition came from Clark and his top aides, who actively encouraged the SCLC-Justice "brains trust" to network with an informal congressional committee. The committee, chaired by Senator Edward W. Brooke (R-Mass.), was composed of about 30 House and Senate liberals who were assigned to ad hoc subcommittees on food, jobs, housing, and welfare. This liberal congressional bloc worked with the PPC to effect some positive legislative action on the most crucial needs of the poor.[55]

Always on the lookout for derogatory material to harass and drag down the bureau's enemies, Hoover anticipated that Solidarity Day would be rife with opportunities for collecting political dirt. He ordered agents to use paid informers to look for and "document such things as immorality, dishonesty, and hypocrisy" of SCLC leadership and "potential leaders" who were in Washington for the June 19 rally on the Mall. It was standard bureau practice to build a file of derogatory material on activists who showed any special talents or strengths that might elevate them into a leadership role. For example, shortly after King's death, FBI field offices were alerted to report any information on possible "immoral activities" of Abernathy and Andy Young. All of this illustrated the fundamental racist thrust of FBI thinking and effort.[56]

The bureau continued its practice of disseminating information about the PPC to the White House and other "interested" agencies. Selected information, strained through the filter of the bureau's own political biases, was furnished by teletype to the White House, secretary of state, CIA, Defense Intelligence Agency, army, and Secret Service. Copies of these teletypes were scattershot to the vice president; attorney general; secretaries of Commerce, Agriculture, Defense, and Labor; the Departments of Transportation and Interior; the U.S. Information Agency; General Services Administration; and the National Aeronautics and Space Administration.[57]

The Oval Office, of course, was the bureau's most favored client for daily intelligence summaries on the PPC and developments inside the tent city. Consequently, there was great agitation at FBI headquarters when Hoover learned that, as a result of confusion within the White House staff, these daily teletypes were not reaching the president. Assurances from Presidential Special Assistant James Jones that the snag in the routing system was corrected were not enough to appease Hoover. The director went straight to the White House staff member with easy access to the Oval Office, Mildred Stegall. From this point onward, all FBI teletypes dealing with the PPC were hand-delivered by the FBI liaison with the White House to Mildred Stegall and found their way unerringly into Johnson's daily "reading file."[58]

The bureau's rendition of Resurrection City that circulated within the higher reaches of government was an unalloyed version of a modern day Sodom and Gomorrah. According to the reports, wholesale lawlessness, violence, rape, petty theft, and interracial sex described the social order inside the PPC encampment. Accounts of interracial sex inside the tent city and interracial partying at the Pitts Motel involving SCLC staffers and white women were fixed items in these FBI briefings. One tale falsely asserted that Abernathy had lost credibility with his followers because of a "rumor" that some city residents had "caught him in bed with a white female."[59] Even when the FBI knew a story had no basis in fact, the tidbit would show up in its disseminated inventory of horrors. For instance, a rumor circulating around the camp that the "Rangers," a Chicago street gang, were planning to spray paint the Lincoln Memorial black and blow up the Washington Monument sent FBI agents scrambling. Teams of agents lost no time in tracking down the rumor and proving it groundless. Nevertheless, the bogus story that Resurrection City was harboring "black terrorists" still was circulated in the FBI intelligence reports.[60]

Tensions mounted at FBIHQ as Solidarity Day drew closer. FBI elites expected racial extremists and subversives to infiltrate the crowd of peaceful demonstrators and foment large-scale violence. The failure of the FBI to dig out any conspiracy to create mayhem during the caravan phase of the campaign only intensified the director's conviction that the June 19 rally would prove that the bureau was not crying wolf.[61]

Solidarity Day, the last large demonstration in the nation's capital during civil rights–era America, came off without a hitch. The mobilization was not marred by a riot, major incidents of violence, or a disturbance of any sort. By first light, hundreds of buses and cars arrived in Washington with the initial waves of the swelling crowd. By mid-afternoon the grounds around the Washington Monument were packed with people eating free lunches, listening to big-name entertainment at the nearby Sylvan Theatre, and generally enjoying the picniclike atmosphere. Much of the day's success could be attributed to Sterling Tucker and his small volunteer staff and to Justice Department personnel who worked closely with SCLC planners to coordinate all aspects of the demonstration.[62]

Comparisons with the 1963 March on Washington were inevitable, especially the numbers game, which became a favorite Washington pastime during this decade of monster demonstrations in the capital. Police and press estimates of the crowd ranged from 50,000 to 100,000. But the mood of the crowd was markedly different. Historian Arthur Schlesinger, Jr., summed up the mood of that 1963 afternoon in August with a felicity of expression when he wrote that the day had a "purity that no one present could ever forget." By contrast, a sympathetic participant-observer of the PPC noted that "few seemed optimistic about the rally's chances of having much impact. One got the impression they came out of a sense of duty, and once there were a little bored."[63]

During its last week of existence, Resurrection City was an unruly and dangerous place as the level of confrontations and violence reached a new intensity. Beatings and robberies were a common occurrence. Of the 567 arrests made over the entire course of the campaign, an overwhelming number took place during this final week.[64]

Unquestionably, demographics was a factor. At the end of May the city's population peaked at more than 2,000 residents. Many of these early campaigners were from the rural South, schooled in the mystique of nonviolent protests and respectful of the movement leadership. Well before the June 19 rally, according to FBI estimates, the number of residents had declined dramatically, tapering off to about 600 to 700, and a significant majority of these campers were under 25 years of age. Three-quarters of these youths were black, and many were from the hard, hostile asphalt jungles of America's inner cities. Many of these urban ghetto-dwellers viewed Resurrection City as a camp-outing away from home and an alfresco frolic. Police-baiting, or "confrontation" in the argot of the rougher camp element, became a form of amusement to vent anger, boredom, and frustration. As camp life began to spin wildly out of control, SCLC leaders and staff were helpless to stem the tide and appeared increasingly to be under siege by their own followers.[65]

"Get your feet in the street. We're marching today." Booming over Resurrection City's public address system, this was the clarion call of the PPC's newfound militancy. Abernathy had pledged that after Solidarity Day he would step up the tempo of the demonstrations and rain down "plague after plague upon the pharaohs of Congress until we get our demands." The primary target of the new direct action program was the Department of Agriculture. June 24 was designated as the day the SCLC would begin its campaign of massive civil disobedience.

After five weeks of scattershot demonstrations marked by vagueness and drift, SCLC organizers made a desperate bid to regain the initiative by focusing on hunger among America's poor. This decision was tactically shrewd and opportune, if woefully belated, for several reasons. If astutely handled, it promised to play on the conscience of well-fed Americans recently exposed to CBS's disturbing documentary "Hunger in America." Shown for the first time in May 1968, this TV special probably did more than any other event in that year to dramatize this national problem. Moreover, the SCLC had learned from trial and error that it had greater success when the injustices of American racism were personalized. The SCLC planners thought they had in Senator James Eastland a compelling symbol for why Congress needed to restructure its federal food programs. Combining a career in politics with agribusiness, the Mississippi Democrat received a monthly government check for $13,000 for not growing food; at the same time, as Abernathy tirelessly pointed out, that same government spent on "a starving child in Mississippi only nine dollars a month." The news of the campaign against the Department of Agriculture worked like a wonder drug on the sagging camp morale. Those poverty marchers still in camp who came to Washington to bear witness eagerly ratified this direct action protest, ready to "go where the spirit say go" regardless of the costs. This new élan was captured by a middle-aged black woman from Eastland's Sunflower County, Mississippi, who announced she was ready to confront Congress and "stand on Eastland's toes."[66]

The CBS documentary and the call for swift national action by food aid reformers were important, but it was still up to the PPC to create a positive impact on the Congress and the public to prepare the groundwork for legislative action. On May 31, Marian Wright arranged to bring 15 "lobbyists" from Resurrection City to speak to a Senate committee in the huge hearing room of the new Senate Office Building. Unrehearsed and without any prepared statements, the group of blacks, Chicanos, whites, and Native Americans spoke from the heart about survival in the Other America and the pathetic inadequacies of the federal food program. The session was low-key, but their stories had an impact on the assembled lawmakers. The tent city residents put a human face on the politics of hunger and deprivation, but the country was not listening. The news stories for that day focused on the angry demonstration outside the Supreme Court Building and the shattering of five windows by a small band of brick-throwing teenagers who may or may not have been from Resurrection City. Even at that, few news stories bothered to explain the reasons for the demonstration—the Court had upheld a Washington State decision prohibiting Indians from net fishing in their traditional fishing grounds.[67]

What was clear was that even as SCLC was attempting to energize its Washington campaign by concentrating on the politics of hunger, the nation had turned an unsympathetic ear to the plight of its underclass. A Lou Harris survey revealed that 61 percent of all whites polled disapproved of the Poor People's Campaign. According to the survey, fear of racial violence was the determining factor. Journalists from every point on the respectable political spectrum were calling for the poor to go home and the government to close down Resurrection City. If there had been a window of opportunity for SCLC to reach through and touch the conscience of America by spotlighting the moral issue of hunger, it was sealed shut before SCLC had come to terms with its own confusion and disarray.[68]

The decision to focus on hunger was the outcome of an SCLC strategy session in Atlanta a week before the June 19 mobilization and was programmatically consistent with the PPC's revised demands that gave priority to a war against hunger. It also underscored the fact that a direct-action group among SCLC planners was now calling the shots. Headed by Jim Bevel, this faction was determined to inject some sense of drama and momentum into the campaign by engaging in civil disobedience to close down the Department of Agriculture and fill the District's jails with wave after wave of demonstrators. Bevel's first order of business, according to one SCLC insider, was to "get Ralph's ass in jail."[69]

The PPC's action against the Agriculture Department began low-key with a handful of protesters mounting a vigil along the Twelfth Street side of the complex. Over the next five days the numbers increased to several hundred demonstrators blocking entrances to the building, occasionally stopping traffic, and taunting the onlooking police. Metropolitan Police Department units closely monitored the situation but made no arrests. On Thursday, June 21, while Abernathy was threatening a "racist Congress" with escalation unless the PPC's demands were met, a hundred marchers were approaching the Agriculture Department intent on premature escalation of their own. The police stepped in and began arresting demonstrators blocking the department's doorways. At first the arrests proceeded quietly and methodically. By 6:00 P.M. the ranks of the marchers had grown to over 500 as new protest cadres from the encampment moved into the area, and the mood of the crowd changed. Some demonstrators began to resist arrest; there were outbreaks of fist-swinging, and the police began to use their batons amidst curses and threats. The demonstration had deteriorated into a roiling melee.

Escaping from the squads of baton-wielding cops, hundreds of protesters took to the streets and began blocking homeward-bound motorists, causing a massive traffic jam. At first confused by these "mobile" tactics, the police quickly regrouped and waded into the marchers. After a week of admirable self-restraint, some Metropolitan Police Department officers assigned to the Agriculture Department took this chance to even the score with their tormentors. Before the fracas ended some police went berserk and had to be restrained by their superiors. The confrontation ended after Jesse Jackson and Hosea Williams, leading a contingent of 150 more demonstrators, arrived on the scene. After some uplifting rhetoric by the SCLC leaders, the demonstrators were persuaded to return to Resurrection City, where they could eat, bind their wounds, and prepare for Friday's action.

However, this day, a day marked by the worse eruption of violence since the campaign began, was not finished. As the campaigners filed back to the shantytown, trouble broke out at the east end of the Reflecting Pool along Seventeenth Street. Police units were called to the scene to halt the obstruction of traffic. In short order, a pitched battle lasting 45 minutes broke out between campers and the police. It was a near rerun of the scrimmage of the previous evening, except this time the police retaliated with tear gas grenades. Only the timely intervention of cool-headed camp marshals prevented a bloody riot in West Potomac Park. They rushed from the tent city and formed a human barrier between the police and the enraged rock-throwing crowd and herded the marchers back toward the encampment.[70]

During Resurrection City's last few days, life inside the camp became a nightmare. The chaos, violence, internal bickering, absentee leadership, and dispiriting anxiety about how the drama would end when authorities came to close down the camp created an atmosphere where fact and rumor were indistinguishable. Resurrection City was like a strung-out junkie—acutely vulnerable to manipulation.

All during these last days bizarre facts competed with bizarre rumors to heighten anxiety in the doomed shantytown. On Friday, June 21, a 300-pound black man wielding an axe ran amok in the camp, destroying several A-frames before being restrained by city marshals. The next evening two patients from St. Elizabeth's Hospital, the District's institution for the mentally disturbed, stole into the encampment and set a phone booth and three vacated shanties on fire before they were apprehended and returned to their caretakers.[71]

A flood of rumors kept the city's residents off balance and in a constant state of nervous excitement. Whether these camp tales were endemic to a stress-laden environment or deliberately planted, the overall effect was to make an already unstable situation even more volatile. An FBI source reported a camp rumor that Abernathy had suffered two minor heart attacks while on campaign with the poor people's army. Reportedly, the SCLC president was also drinking heavily and was seen around the campsite in an intoxicated state. This canard came from an FBI source inside the encampment. Police and federal officers monitoring Resurrection City reported at least four rumored threats against Abernathy's life from white extremists and one alleged plot by Black Panthers in New York City to have him "hit" after the June 19 rally. Whether any of these assassination rumors were bruited about the camp is uncertain, but when Abernathy moved out of the Pitts Motel to a private Washington residence, the Border Patrol attributed the move to security reasons.[72]

FBI and police informers inside the camp were the chief source of rumors that revenge-seeking hot heads and known militants were stockpiling dynamite, Molotov cocktails, rifles, and shotguns to stand off any attempt by the authorities to close the shantytown. A rumor that Black Power advocate Stokley Carmichael was shot by the police almost triggered an incident. At about 2:00 A.M. on Sunday, June 23, a man drove into the camp and began shouting that Carmichael had been shot. In a matter of minutes about 30 campers began milling around the front gate trying to incite others to violent action. Soon about 150 young people gathered at the gate, shouting threats and obscenities at the police. The police on the scene put on their riot gear and called for all available Metropolitan Police Department units to converge on the camp. A few minutes later Abernathy's voice came over the camp public address system to denounce the story as a provocation and urged the crowd to return to their shacks. Resurrection City residents settled down, and the night passed without incident.[73]

Amazingly, not until the last two days of the campaign did SCLC organizers, despairing of finding ways to enforce discipline, take steps to tighten the camp's security. Concern over security surfaced as a result of the growing suspicions that "infiltrators" and "paid agents" were responsible for the violence and disruptions. Abernathy and Williams went public with their suspicions, but they could produce no hard evidence to back their claims. Understandably, the press treated these allegations as a red herring, a lame attempt by SCLC leaders to explain their own ineptitude and failures. In any case, by this time most of the press regarded Resurrection City as some grotesque soap opera whose Washington run could not end soon enough.

As camp manager, Hosea Williams was in charge of security. Williams, Jim Orange ("The Sheriff"), and John Rutherford devised a password system for the security force that went into effect the last two days of the camp's existence. On the first night it was employed, some 15 "infiltrators" were expelled from camp. The only one identified—because he later boasted of his brush with Williams's security system—was a black reporter with the *Washington Daily News* who had spent several days inside Resurrection City gathering material for a feature story.[74]

To be sure, the city's security system was slipshod. The 65-acre campsite was surrounded by a three-foot-high snow fence, largely to separate the campaigners from curious onlookers. Security was tight at the front gate; even Abernathy had to flash identification to get past the marshals, who enjoyed playing "Checkpoint Charlie." At several points along the camp perimeter, however, the fence had gaps large enough to drive a Mack truck through.

When Abernathy and Williams raised the issue of "infiltrators" and "paid agents," they had no idea how thoroughly the camp was penetrated by operatives of the surveillance state. A muster roll of security and police bureaucracies with agents, informers, and tipsters slipping in and out of the camp is impressive: FBI agents, military intelligence, Border Patrol, and the Intelligence Division of the Metropolitan Police Department. An FBI report even mentioned that the Office of Economic Opportunity had an undercover man inside the encampment. Under these circumstances the SCLC and its security procedures were hopelessly overmatched, and no real countermeasures were possible.[75]

The FBI's intrusive operations against the PPC were not limited to monitoring and intelligence gathering. From the very outset of project POCAM, the poor people's movement was a high priority target for the bureau's action program of harassment and sabotage on every front. From the director down, the executives who ran the FBI were highly skilled, action-oriented, and dedicated adversaries. Once this formidable political elite targeted an individual, organization, or movement for a disruption campaign, the gloves came off and any rules went out the window. The operational agenda for a COINTELPRO campaign ran the gamut of action programs that included monitoring, infiltration, penetration, leaking of derogatory information, disinformation, and disruption. William Sullivan, head of the bureau's Domestic Intelligence Division, was brutally frank about these no-holds-barred action programs, characterizing this type of political warfare as "rough, tough, dirty business" subject to three controlling concerns: "will this course of action work, will it get us what we want, will it reach the objectives we desire to reach?"[76]

Since Hoover ran the FBI like his own private fiefdom within the executive branch, operationally the director was accountable to no one in the chain of command but himself. Although direct proof is lacking, it is reasonable to assume that the FBI used its paid operatives inside Resurrection City as agents provocateurs to disseminate disinformation and incite unruliness and violence to discredit the PPC and the SCLC leadership. Given the high-stakes confrontational climate in which bureau policy ends justified means in the eyes of the FBI elites, to suppose that the Hoover Bureau did not resort to this type of covert activity would be naive. Since the amending of the Freedom of Information Act (FOIA) in 1974, documents revealing FBI resourcefulness in using agents provocateurs in its domestic intelligence activities have been available. There is nothing in this record to support any conviction that the PPC was an exception, somehow exempt from FBI dirty tricks and wrecking tactics.[77]

Furthermore, during the Resurrection City phase, the FBI worked closely with the Metropolitan Police Department's Intelligence Division, sometimes even sponsoring the same informers. Operating virtually without guidelines, the District's police surveillance team, or "red squad," was free-wheeling and not shy about running its own derring-do operations against "dissident" and "subversive" groups it identified as a threat to the government. As standard practice, the Intelligence Division instructed its agents to discredit the aims of these targeted groups by sabotaging their preparations for orderly demonstrations. In the case of Resurrection City, according to one intelligence source, the Metropolitan Police Department's "red squad" did more than take mug shots of the city's residents—it ran operatives "in and out of the camp."[78]

SCLC organizers were troubled and dispirited by their lack of control over their own creation. Abernathy, playing mostly to the camp hell-raisers who were still keen on more "confrontations," insisted that the campaign would dig in and remain in Washington "until justice rolls." However, all talk about a stand in the city was ruled out. The violence in the camp and the rumors of hidden arms caches among the maze of shanties raised the fear of a bloodbath at Resurrection City if the SCLC did not voluntarily strike the camp when the permit expired. Privately, the SCLC leaders, including Abernathy, were open to any face-saving solution to end the embarrassment of Resurrection City, allowing them to negotiate a peaceful and dignified withdrawal from the nation's capital. In addition, more mundane inducements arose for striking camp. The permit, already extended once, was due to expire at 8:00 P.M. on Sunday, June 23, and any further extension was out of the question. According to prior arrangements, once the permit expired, all federal food commitments and supplementary food and aid from the Council of Churches also were scheduled to end.[79]

On Monday, June 24, Washington authorities pulled the plug on Resurrection City. The nonviolent death of the shantytown required extensive behind-the-scenes negotiations between SCLC leaders, District police, and the Justice Department. Justice's Roger Wilkins was a key player in these negotiations.

Wilkins was the right man for this potentially dangerous endgame. He had the attorney general's blessing, and SCLC leaders trusted him because in principle he supported the goals of the PPC. Sunday afternoon Wilkins hosted a hastily convened meeting at his home to discuss plans to avert bloodshed when the police attempted to close the camp the next day. He was joined by Ramsey Clark, Andy Young, and Christine Clark, legal counsel associated with the poor people's march. A specter haunted the meeting: The tensions of the past five days had built to a state of explosive hatred on both sides of the fence surrounding the encampment. Wilkins's own assessment of the situation was that any resistance to the police from inside the camp could trigger a "massacre," an American Soweto on the Mall.

The result of the discussions was a simple but effective plan that would allow those campaigners bent on protesting before striking their colors to be peacefully arrested either inside the camp or on Capitol Hill. A selected few campaigners would be permitted to participate in the dismantling of the shantytown. On the other side, Wilkins arranged for the District police, instead of the Park Police, to have the major responsibility for clearing the camp. He wisely sidestepped the Park Police because they were itching to settle scores with the rock-throwers inside the camp. Viewing all the residents as a rabble to be routed, the Park Police were part of the problem Wilkins wanted to avoid at all costs.

For the last phase of the negotiating process, Wilkins went into Resurrection City to work out the final details with the top SCLC organizers. As a rule, peacekeeping is not without its hazards, and this assignment was no exception. If any of the camp hotheads recognized an assistant attorney general "in that place at that time," Wilkins figured, "he'd likely come out dead." Andy Young furnished Wilkins with a dog-eared pass and a false identity. Wilkins completed his disguise with a pair of dirty chinos and a dashiki, entered the camp at about 1:45 A.M., and made his way to the headquarters tent without incident. The meeting went smoothly, and the SCLC officers agreed to every detail of the plan and promised their full cooperation. While Wilkins was preparing to leave, a somber Andy Young admonished, "I don't know what religion you are, Roger, but you'd better pray to some god tonight." At that moment Wilkins had his own priorities—first was to slip out of the camp and get safely back home.[80]

June 24 was a day full of apprehension for several hundred hard-core campaigners still residing in Resurrection City. The weather did little to lighten the mood inside the camp. A glowering dark-gray overcast hung over Washington, and the air was hot, heavy, and oppressive. A chronicler of the campaign recorded that it "looked like Doomsday." By 10:00 A.M. anywhere from 1,000 to 2,000 police (officials refused to reveal the exact number) already had set up a picket line completely surrounding the 65-acre campsite. After repeated warnings to clear the camp, District Police Chief John B. Layton ordered elements of the elite Civil Disturbance Unit (CDU) to begin a sweep through the camp. Moving east to west, the advancing phalanx of police, outfitted with crash helmets, flak vests, gas masks, gas guns, and billy clubs (every third man in the line carried a shotgun) proceeded to search and clear every shanty. All the A-frames were vacant, and no weapons were found, although several shacks were booby-trapped and went up in flames when the police forced them open. Williams stayed behind with a group of about 110 campaigners who were waiting to be arrested. Williams led them in freedom songs and urged calm when the heavily armed police approached. Wilkins, who accompanied the CDU officers in their search and clearing operation, observed that it was Williams's finest hour of the six-week ordeal.[81]

The entire operation took only about 90 minutes, with no violence on either side. Abernathy led a column of about 250 marchers out of the camp to Capitol Hill before the police evacuation deadline. Abernathy's last staged assault on Capitol Hill was the PPC's parting shot toward Congress, the final symbolic gesture of a protest movement that appeared to fall dead under the combined burden of its own ineptitude and congressional intransigence. The SCLC leader and the tatterdemalion remnant army of poverty marchers from the City of Hope surrendered peacefully when Chief Layton ordered their arrest for illegally demonstrating on the Capitol grounds. The encounter was largely an anticlimactic affair since both sides, the demonstrators and the police, had agreed to the terms for a peaceful evacuation of Resurrection City worked out beforehand by Wilkins, SCLC staffers, and District police officials. Abernathy and his followers spent a few days in jail before they were released.[82]

By this time the campaign had ended, except for some shouting of "Black Power" and threats of retaliation outside of SCLC's headquarters at Fourteenth and U Streets, Northwest. The emotional consensus among the SCLC planners was relief rather than crushing disappointment. A visibly drained Andy Young confessed at a press conference later that day that "in one sense, whoever ran us out of there maybe did us a real favor."[83]

Although the PPC can hardly be considered a success, it was instrumental in winning some concessions from federal agencies. Some of these "small victories" were only symbolic, agreements made by embattled government bureaucrats during the heat of the campaign that were conveniently abandoned after the army of the poor left Washington. Senator Joseph Clark's (D-Pa.) promising jobs program bill died in Congress, one of the casualties of a legislative rollback of federal expenditures for social programs, the third year in a row.

The one area in which the PPC influenced programmatic change was that of liberalizing the distribution of commodities and food stamps. Beginning in 1968, the Department of Agriculture sharply expanded the food-stamp program and increased funding for child nutrition. The revamped program now covered the nation's 1,000 neediest counties and made a critical difference for thousands of low-income families. As significant as this success was, it required only minor adjustments by federal officials, and even these improvements were not immediately forthcoming. It was indicative of the great odds stacked against the PPC that it required a massive lobbying campaign to force federal authority to ease the blight of flagrant malnutrition amongst the nation's unrepresented. Considering the magnitude of the PPC's effort, it was remarkable how few and modest the concessions were in the final accounting.[84]

Some unfinished business between the government and the SCLC remained after Resurrection City was razed. In August the National Park Service sent the SCLC an itemized bill for $71,795 for the wear and tear of the grounds in and around the former campsite. The government required immediate payment so it could close the books on the PPC. The other issue requiring attention was the 22 mules and two horses abandoned outside of Alexandria, Virginia, at the close of the campaign. Five mules were so broken down that they were placed in the custody of the Society for the Prevention of Cruelty to Animals and sent to the National Humane Education Center near Waterford, Virginia, for treatment and a prolonged rest. The other less spavined animals were rescued from an uncertain fate by a group of Washington women, headed up by Mrs. Carolyn Fortas, the wife of Supreme Court Justice Abe Fortas. The women arranged temporary quarters for the fit mules and horses at the privately owned Variety Horse Center in Columbia, Maryland, for $150 per month for each animal. Ultimately, all the animals found a permanent home on a 2,400-acre Virginia farm near Port Royal. The saga of the mules, at least, had an Edenic ending.[85]

Conclusion

THE CONVENTIONAL VIEW of the Poor People's Campaign was that it was a dismal failure. National media coverage of the poor people's movement generally concluded that the blame rested squarely on the shoulders of the Southern Christian Leadership Conference staffers who failed to fill the leadership vacuum after King's assassination. Superficially at least, this judgment has the ring of truth about it: Without King, the campaign quickly lost its focus, and the message was not conveyed.

However, even under the most favorable circumstances, the PPC probably would have floundered on its own. Had King lived to speak for the needs of the poor, had Bayard Rustin played the key role of organizer, and had the weather cooperated with sunny days, the PPC would still have had to contend with a largely uncaring Congress, a society distracted and bitterly divided by a foreign war and domestic riots, and a president who had turned his back on domestic reform and had personally grown embittered toward King and the SCLC.[1] King's opposition to the Vietnam War and the FBI's orchestrated smear campaign accounted for much of this irrational hostility. Reportedly, according to Andy Young, there were ugly scenes in the Oval Office late in the war-ruined Johnson administration when the president, in one of his Texas-sized towering rages, referred to King as that "goddamn nigger preacher." Young recalled the deceptive signals emanating from the Johnson White House: "On the surface we were being smiled at and granted grudging support; below the surface we were distrusted, resented, and undercut."[2]

As it was, the SCLC leadership did not distinguish itself by tactical acumen. Abernathy and his top lieutenants spent most of their time, energy, and resources running a city, and the basic issues they planned to dramatize became largely obscured. The most telling criticism was the striking failure of the SCLC to invest the great moral capital of the civil rights movement into transforming Resurrection City (the City of Hope) into a community of shared values and unified purpose. Instead, the public image of Resurrection City was that of an absentee-run slum afflicted with low morale, factional conflicts, and free-floating violence. Much of this criticism was legitimate. However, there was also a hidden reality, a dark counterpoint to the accepted facts.

The drama of the Poor People's Campaign ended in failure, but it was never allowed the right to collapse under the weight of its own shortcomings. Lawless elements of the American surveillance state, especially the FBI, played a major role in the campaign's bafflement and undoing.

A more accurate and balanced history of the PPC is really a story of failure and success. The SCLC's efforts to mobilize the poor and powerless ended in what was largely a self-inflicted fiasco. But if the PPC leadership went wrong, the government went wildly wrong. The Poor People's Campaign is a case study of how a lawful movement to organize the poor and powerless was targeted for disruption by a campaign rooted in racism and vicious character assassination made even more shameful because the FBI's right to engage in such a vendetta went largely unquestioned by the media and high-placed government officials. The dark underside of the PPC is a cautionary account of the triumph of repressive state power and its flagrant violation of protected freedoms that is abhorrent in a free society.

The fate of the Invaders in Memphis is a revealing footnote to the Hoover Bureau's campaign against black militancy and aggressiveness in the 1960s. Although never really more than a small and ineffective group of incipient Black-Powerites, the Invaders drew down upon themselves the full firepower of the FBI's impressive arsenal of COINTELPRO actions. The compulsive and relentless nature of this campaign against black youth was astonishing, even when judged against the overall zealotry of the FBI's war against the "Black Menace" in the 1960s. It was as if Hoover and his internal security chiefs were driven to uproot every vestige of black militancy in Memphis, the city so closely linked to King, his movement, and the Poor People's Campaign. It is not too capricious to find bureau elites guilty of lynch-mob psychology in their efforts to destroy Memphis's militant black youth.

For two years following the King assassination and the settlement of the sanitation strike, the FBI and the Memphis police worked in close cooperation to "eliminate" even as a token presence in Memphis what Director Hoover characterized as "one of the most violent black nationalist extremist groups" under bureau scrutiny. Bureau officials in Washington blocked federal grants earmarked for community action programs in Memphis employing Invaders. Any local support for the group or a patron willing, for example, to help a promising Invader leader with college ambitions prompted a quick response from the Memphis field office. The standard approach was to recruit solid citizen types, or what the FBI referred to as "trusted liaison sources," to arrange for a discreet visit to the sponsoring organization or the benefactor to poison the well.

The FBI dug deep into its bag of dirty tricks in its war against Memphis black youth: Police spy McCullough set up a drug "bust" to entrap group leaders and undercut their credibility; agents intimidated Invaders to drop out by threatening the livelihood of their parents; the bureau employed schemes to sow dissension and distrust among the Invader membership and used "cooperating" media sources with the two daily Memphis newspapers and a local black-oriented radio station to publicly discredit the Invaders. The combined impact of these tactics achieved the intended goal—the isolation of the Invaders from the larger Memphis community, both black and white. Fairness requires that it be pointed out that the Invaders contributed to their own demise by their uncanny failure to resist almost every opportunity for self-destructive behavior. By the end of 1968 most of the original BOP-Invaders members had either gone back to school, were in hiding from the law, were in jail, or were jobless and holding down a corner in the Beale Street ghetto.[3]

Despite all indications that the Invaders were organizationally defunct, FBIHQ refused to close the file on these young militants. Actually, Washington headquarters was preparing a 1969 spring offensive, with Hoover exhorting FBI Memphis to "take every opportunity" to target the Invaders with more COINTELPRO operations. The spring campaign was timed to coincide with the inauguration of the Richard M. Nixon presidency. With the "law and order" candidate of 1968 now president, the director had good reason to anticipate a sympathetic reception from the Nixon Justice Department.

Hoover marked the Invaders as a prime candidate for federal prosecution under the new federal antiriot law and other related statutes. After the Justice Department undertook its own investigation, the head of its Internal Security Division, J. Walter Yeagley, notified Hoover of the Justice Department's decision not to prosecute. The division chief agreed with the director that these militant young blacks were deplorable for their espousal of "hatred for the white race" and "hatred for all constituted authority," but they had not violated any federal laws. Furthermore, Yeagley felt constrained to point out that since the FBI's last report in December 1969 estimated only "seven active members, with no headquarters and no known bank account," his division was closing the books on the Invaders investigation. Despite Yeagley's administrative obituary, the FBI did not close its Invaders file until more than a year later.[4]

During his last year of life Dr. King was at war with war, poverty, and racism. He was convinced that these "giant triplets" threatened a holocaust-like Judgment Day unless the nation experienced a great transformation of values. Deeply distraught by the columns of smoke rising from

America's inner cities and fearing a right-wing backlash, King launched the Poor People's Campaign as a wake-up call to the nation's leaders. Certain that the nation was facing a crisis as defining as the fiery trial of the Civil War, King believed that nothing short of a fundamental reorganization of the American economy would safeguard the promise of a civil society.

Thirty years after King's last crusade the problems of racism and poverty are still not cured. This is not to say that racial politics has not profoundly transformed the way America responds to race at a personal level or in ways of collective action and at the highest level of national politics. Still, 30 years after the poor people's movement we are still a long way from morning in America. Columns of smoke are still rising from America's inner cities. King's dream was that America would live up to the promise of its creed and become a color-blind society. In today's America "color-blind" society is neoconservative coded language for the rejection of the programs of affirmative action and equal opportunity enacted in the 1970s and 1980s to compensate for the legacy of racial, sexual, and class discrimination. Reaganites trumpet the virtues of equal opportunity without guarantees of equal outcomes. Today's neoconservatives argue that interest-group or race-based projects should be shunned in favor of equal opportunity and individual attainment, when in reality interest groups more and more shape American politics as the national political parties decline in status.

As we edge toward the millennium, the jury is still out on whether our lawmakers will develop viable working programs to address the problems of racism and poverty or duck and dodge as they try to talk their way past these "giant twins." The one certainty is that the issues giving rise to the Poor People's Campaign are still with us and cannot be ignored or marginalized by semantics and political rhetoric. The question that remains open is what the shape and battle lines of mass protest movements will be like next time around.

Notes

Introduction

1. Frank Donner, *The Age of Surveillance: The Aims and Methods of America's Political Intelligence System* (New York: Alfred A. Knopf, 1980), pp. 142–143; William C. Sullivan with Bill Brown, *The Bureau: My Thirty Years in Hoover's FBI* (New York: W. W. Norton, 1979).

2. W. C. Sullivan to A. Belmont, January 8, 1964, Subversive Matters—Investigations, Headquarters file (hereafter cited as HQ file), 100-3-116.

3. Sullivan to Belmont, January 8, 1964, Subversive Matters—Investigations, HQ file, 100-3-116; *Washington Star*, June 1, 1978; *Washington Post*, May 31, 1978; *Memphis Commercial Appeal*, June 11, 1978; J. A. Sizoo to Sullivan, December 1, 1964 (an internal memo that was not filed in FBI HQ central file); Sullivan to Belmont, January 8, 1964, Subversive Matters—Investigations, HQ file, 100-3-116; *Washington Star*, June 10, 1978.

4. Sullivan, *The Bureau*, pp. 101–114.

5. William W. Keller, *The Liberals and J. Edgar Hoover: Rise and Fall of a Domestic Intelligence State* (Princeton, NJ: Princeton University Press, 1989), pp. 24–27.

6. Ibid., p. 26.

7. David J. Garrow, *The FBI and Martin Luther King, Jr.: From "Solo" to Memphis* (New York: W. W. Norton, 1981); Kenneth O'Reilly, *"Racial Matters": The FBI's Secret File on Black America, 1960–1972* (New York: Free Press, 1989); Richard G. Powers, *Secrecy and Power: The Life of J. Edgar Hoover* (New York: Free Press, 1987); Athan G. Theoharis and John Cox, *The Boss: J. Edgar Hoover and the Great American Inquisition* (Philadelphia: Temple University Press, 1988).

8. Garrow, *The FBI and Martin Luther King, Jr.*, pp. 125–126; William C. Sullivan to A. H. Belmont, January 27, 1964, FBI Documents to the House Select Committee on Assassinations (hereafter cited as FBI Docs. to HSCA), 100-106679-792. Former FBI Deputy Director Cartha D. DeLoach contends that the package was Sullivan's idea and had neither Hoover's sanction nor approval after the fact. See Cartha D. "Deke" DeLoach, *Hoover's FBI: The Inside Story of Hoover's Trusted Lieutenant* (Washington, D.C.: Regnery Publishing, 1995), p. 212. DeLoach's contention is unpersuasive. Aside from the strong feelings between Sullivan and DeLoach, none of them complimentary, it is highly unlikely that the assistant director of the bureau's crime lab and the agents working under him would engage in this project or any other COINTELPRO initiative in Hoover's FBI merely on the strength of Sullivan's word or instructions without the director's approval.

9. Early revelations about the FBI's criminal harassment of King surfaced in the U.S. Senate hearings chaired by Senator Frank Church (D-Ida.) in 1976. See *Final Report of the Senate Select Committee to Study Governmental Operations With Respect to Intelligence Activities*, Report 94-755, 94th Congress, 2nd session, 1976 (hereafter cited as the *Church Committee Report*).

10. J. Stanley Pottinger, Assistant Attorney General, to Director of the FBI, December 4, 1975, Field Office Inventories (hereafter cited as FOI), 100-106670-3967, FBI Main King file. I thank researcher and author Harold Weisberg for bringing this document to my attention.

11. U.S. Department of Justice, *Report on the Department of Justice Task Force to Review the FBI Martin Luther King, Jr., Security and Assassination Investigation* (hereafter cited as *Task Force Report*), p. 9. For example, the first FBI document submitted to the Warren Commission investigating the assassination of John F. Kennedy in 1964, Commission Document, serial 1, or CD-1, was five volumes or almost 1,000 pages. Although serials this length are not common, they are not so rare that CD-1 is a unique example.

12. Director, FBI, to All SACS (Special Agents in Charge), December 12, 1975, FOI, 100-106670-3976, FBI Main King file. For convincing evidence that FBIHQ stage-managed the process from the start see SAC, WFO (Washington Field Office) to Director, FBI, December 11, 1975, FOI, 100-106670-3390.

13. Public disclosure of King's plagiarism did not surface until November 1990. For a thorough look at this issue, see the June 1991 edition of *The Journal of American History*. In the final analysis it is not all that surprising that the FBI failed to track down King's practice of multiple authorship over the course of his academic career. What is more remarkable is that his dissertation adviser at BU failed to detect his plagiarism. The existing public record makes it clear that the Hoover Bureau did not mark King for special attention until the 1963 March on Washington, almost a decade after he completed his doctoral program. Nevertheless, the fact that the bureau missed this singular window of opportunity to destroy King diminishes the carefully cultivated image of the Hoover-era FBI—the jewel in the crown of federal agencies—as omnipotent and omniscient.

14. FBI Murkin (Murder of King) file, Memphis FO (Field Office) files, 44-1574-272 and 44-1574-284; *Washington Evening Star*, April 17, 1968; DeLoach, *Hoover's FBI*, p. 256.

Chapter One

1. For background on King's early opposition to the Vietnam War, see Adam Fairclough, "Martin Luther King, Jr., and the War in Vietnam," *Phylon* 45 (Spring 1984), pp. 19–22.

2. Fairclough, "Martin Luther King, Jr., and the War in Vietnam," pp. 23–25; Carl T. Rowan, *Breaking Barriers: A Memoir* (Boston: Little, Brown, 1991), p. 244; James Melvin Washington (ed.), *A Testament of Hope: The Essential Writings of Martin Luther King, Jr.* (San Francisco: HarperCollins, 1991), p. 373, for King's views on Goldwater in a 1965 *Playboy* interview.

3. *New York Times*, August 13, 1965; Nathan I. Huggins, "Commentary," in Peter J. Albert and Ronald Hoffman (eds.), *We Shall Overcome: Martin Luther King, Jr. and*

the Black Freedom Struggle (New York: Pantheon Books, 1991), pp. 86–87; Bayard Rustin and Tom Kahn, "Johnson So Far," *Commentary* (June 1965), pp. 43–45; David L. Lewis, *King: A Critical Biography* (Baltimore: Penguin Books, 1970), pp. 304–305; Young quoted in James Foreman, *The Making of a Black Revolutionary* (New York: Macmillan, 1972), p. 309.

4. David J. Garrow, *Bearing the Cross: Martin Luther King, Jr., and the Southern Christian Leadership Conference* (New York: William Morrow, 1986), pp. 527–546; Nancy Zaroulis and Gerald Sullivan, *Who Spoke Up?: American Protest Against the War in Vietnam, 1963–1975* (New York: Holt, Rinehart & Winston, 1984), pp. 108–109.

5. David J. Garrow, "Martin Luther King, Jr., and the Spirit of Leadership," in Peter J. Albert and Ronald Hoffman (eds.), *We Shall Overcome: Martin Luther King, Jr. and the Black Freedom Struggle* (New York: Pantheon Books, 1991), p. 25.

6. Garrow, *Bearing the Cross*, p. 533; Martin Luther King, Jr., *Why We Can't Wait* (New York: New American Library, 1964), pp. 146–147, 151–153. In this work King proposed a "Bill of Rights for the Disadvantaged," which included a guaranteed living wage for the forgotten poor, white as well as black.

7. Garrow, *Bearing the Cross*, p. 531; Rowan, *Breaking Barriers*, pp. 245–249; Fairclough, "Martin Luther King, Jr., and the War in Vietnam," p. 27.

8. Garrow, *Bearing the Cross*, pp. 539–540; Fairclough, "Martin Luther King, Jr., and the War in Vietnam," p. 27; *New York Times*, December 12, 1966, p. 33.

9. For the full text of "Beyond Vietnam," see Washington, *A Testament of Hope*, pp. 231–244.

10. Adam Fairclough, *To Redeem the Soul of America: The Southern Christian Leadership Conference and Martin Luther King, Jr.* (Athens: University of Georgia Press, 1978), p. 338; *New York Times*, April 11, 1967, p. 1; Rowan, *Breaking Barriers*, pp. 285–288.

11. For an insightful view of the role of the media during the Vietnam War, see Daniel Hallin, *The "Uncensored" War: The Media and Vietnam* (New York: Oxford University Press, 1986); *Washington Post Times Herald*, April 7, 1967 (hereafter cited as the *Washington Post*), and *New York Times*, April 7, 1967.

12. *Final Report of the Senate Select Committee to Study Governmental Operations With Respect to Intelligence Activities*, Senate Report 94-755, 94th Congress, 2nd session (1976), Vol. III, pp. 81, 173–174 (hereafter cited as the *Church Committee Report*).

13. Kenneth O'Reilly, *"Racial Matters": The FBI's Secret File on Black America, 1960–1972* (New York: Free Press, 1989), pp. 243–244; Garrow, *Bearing the Cross*, p. 570; Roger Wilkins, *A Man's Life* (New York: Simon & Schuster, 1982), pp. 230–231.

14. Liaison to Mildred Stegall, the White House, April 11, 1967, FBI Main King file, 100-106670-2882; O'Reilly, *"Racial Matters,"* pp. 262–263.

15. C. D. Brennan to Sullivan, April 6, 1967 [copy to Mildred Stegall], Main King file, 100-106670-28-illegible; Memo to Mildred Stegall, April 14, 1967, Main King file, 100-106670-2912; Liaison to Mildred Stegall, April 19, 1967, Main King file, 100-106670-289-illegible; Liaison to Mildred Stegall, July 32, 1967, Main King file, 100-106670-2897.

16. David J. Garrow, *The FBI and Martin Luther King, Jr.: From "Solo" to Memphis* (New York: W. W. Norton, 1981), pp. 40–43. This work is still the most comprehensive and balanced treatment of the FBI's interest in Stanley D. Levison.

17. Ibid., pp. 97–100; Richard G. Powers, *Secrecy and Power: The Life of J. Edgar Hoover* (New York: Free Press, 1987), p. 370; O'Reilly, *"Racial Matters,"* p. 141; G. C. Moore to Sullivan, June 3, 1968, FBI Levison Main File, 100-392452-300, for the FBI's record of authorized electronic surveillance on Levison. All the FBI "black bag jobs" against Levison were illegal. See *Church Committee Report*, Vol. II, pp. 61–62.

18. Zaroulis and Sullivan, *Who Spoke Up?*, p. 118.

19. Levison to Andy Young, May 10, 1967, 100-111180-9-1300; Young to King and Levison, May 12, 1967, 100-111180-9-1302; Fairclough, *To Redeem the Soul of America*, p. 343; Roy Levison to Levison, May 16, 1967, 100-111180-9-1306; Joan Davis to Levison, May 9, 1967, 100-111180-9-1299a.

20. King to Levison, Wachtel, and Young (conference call), July 24, 1967, 100-111180-9-1375a; Levison to King, Wachtel, Young, and (FNU [First Name Unknown]) Evans, July 25, 1967, 100-111180-9-1376a; *New York Times*, July 25, 1967, p. 20; see "Rights Leaders Appeal," *New York Times*, July 27, 1967, p. 19; King to Levison and Young, July 27, 1967, 100-111180-9-1378; *New York Times*, July 26, 1967, p. 19; *New York Times*, July 27, 1967, p. 17; (FBI memo), Martin Luther, Jr., July 21, 1967, King Main File, 100-106670-3038; FBI Liaison to Mildred Stegall, July 31, 1976, King Main File, 100-106670-3035.

21. Fairclough, *To Redeem the Soul of America*, p. 354. For King's indictment of the 90th Congress, see his "Showdown to Nonviolence," in Washington, *A Testament of Hope*, pp. 69, 70–71.

22. See the Harris opinion poll in "The Racial Crisis: A Consensus," *Newsweek* (August 21, 1967), p. 18; King to Levison, August 22, 1967, 100-111180-9-1404; Young interview with Kathy Shannon, July 7, 1968, Washington, D.C., pp. 4–5, Ralph Bunche Oral History Collection, Moorland Springarn Research Center, Howard University, Washington, D.C. (hereafter cited as the Bunche Oral History Collection).

23. Garrow, *Bearing the Cross*, pp. 577–578; King, "Showdown for Nonviolence," p. 67.

24. Quoted in Garrow, *Bearing the Cross*, p. 582; *New York Times*, December 5, 1967, p. 1; *Washington Post*, December 12, 1967; King to Levison, December 13, 1967, 100-111180-9-1517; King, "Showdown for Nonviolence," p. 65.

25. Garrow, *Bearing the Cross*, pp. 582–583; for Young's comments, see interview with James R. McGraw, "An Interview with Andrew J. Young," *Christianity and Crisis* (January 22, 1968), pp. 327–328; Levison to Wachtel, March 19, 1968, 100-111180-9-1614; Bill Rutherford to Levison, June 2, 1968, 100-111180-9-1689a; Jack Greenberg, *Crusaders in the Courts: How a Dedicated Band of Lawyers Fought for the Civil Rights Revolution* (New York: Basic Books, 1994), pp. 431–433.

26. King, "Showdown for Nonviolence," p. 65.

27. The FBI classified the POCAM file as a 157 or Extremist Matter: Civil Unrest (a security-related classification).

28. Director to SACs, January 4, 1968, POCAM, HQ file, 157-8428-1. For GIP see *Church Committee Report*, Vol. III, pp. 252–254.

29. O'Reilly, *"Racial Matters,"* pp. 267–268; Director to SAC, Philadelphia, January 31, 1968, POCAM, HQ file, 157-8428-39; Director to SAC, Louisville, January 14, 1968, POCAM, 157-8428-87; Director to SAC, Newark, January 7, 1968, POCAM, HQ file, 157-8428-104.

30. The tap on Levison's New York residence was installed on June 15, 1965, and remained operational through 1971. Moore to Sullivan, June 3, 1968, New York Main Stanley D. Levison file, 100-392452-300.

31. The FBI's Chicago field office developed a reliable source familiar with SCLC's operations in that city. See SAC, Chicago to Director, March 12, 1968, POCAM, HQ file, 157-8428-384; Director to SAC, Chicago, March 20, 1968, POCAM, HQ file, 157-8428-384; Garrow, *The FBI and Martin Luther King, Jr.*, p. 178. For Harrison's career as an FBI informer, see Garrow, ibid., pp. 173–184; Director to SACs, January 4, 1968, POCAM, HQ file, 157-8428-1; Director to SAC, Atlanta, January 17, 1968, POCAM, HQ file, 157-8428-16.

32. *Church Committee Report*, Vol. II, pp. 89–90. For example, the SAC of Jackson, Mississippi, notified Hoover that "several files have been open to all Negroes having a propensity for violence and Negroes active in the civil rights movement, who are prone to participate in civil disorders." See SAC, Jackson to Director, January 12, 1968, POCAM, Washington Field Office (hereafter cited as WFO) file, 157-1395-28.

33. For a cross section of FBI intelligence-gathering on PPC recruiters, see the following(all references are from FBI POCAM HQ file): HQ file serials 100, 193, 255, 337, 390, 485, 508, 524, 526, and 558.

34. SAC [masked] to SAC, WFO, January 6, 1968, POCAM, WFO file, 157-1395-128; SAC, Atlanta, to Director, February 9, 1968, POCAM, WFO file, 157-1395-147C; SAC, WFO, to Director, February 20, 1968, POCAM, WFO file, 157-1395-192A.

35. Director to SACs, February 29, 1968, POCAM, HQ file, 157-8428-276. For a case in point see Director to SAC, Richmond, March 4, 1968, POCAM, HQ file, 157-8428-251; SAC, Richmond, to Director, March 12, 1968, POCAM, HQ file, 157-8428-350.

36. SAC, Charlotte, to Director, April 23, 1968, POCAM, HQ file, 157-8428-693; Cincinnati, to Director, February 16, 1968, POCAM, HQ file, 157-8428-191; Letterhead Memorandum (hereafter cited as LHM), Cincinnati, February 16, 1968, POCAM, HQ file, 157-8428-238.

37. SAC, Charlotte, to Director, March 12, 1968, POCAM, HQ file, 157-8428-356; SAC, Newark, to Director, March 12, 1968, POCAM, HQ file, 157-8428-411.

38. *Washington Post*, February 8, 9, 1968; William Raspberry, "Dr. King's Reassurance Eases City's Fears," *Washington Post*, February 11, 1968, D-1; *Washington Afro-American*, February 10, 1968; *Washington Daily News*, February 9, 1968.

39. Young to Levison, March 4, 1968, 100-111180-9-1599; Fairclough, *To Redeem the Soul of America*, p. 369.

40. SAC, WFO, to Director, March 19, 1968, POCAM, HQ file, 157-8428-436; Fairclough, *To Redeem the Soul of America*, p. 361; *Washington Daily News*, February 21, 1968; William Moyer and Anthony Henry interviews with Kathy Shannon, July 7, 15, 1968, Bunche Oral History Collection.

41. LHM, Washington Spring Project, March 25, 1968, POCAM, WFO file, 157-1395-476. The source of this LHM noted that this was only a partial list and was expected to grow.

42. Levison to Wachtel, March 19, 1968, 100-111180-9-1614; *Washington Evening Star*, March 13, 16, 1968.

43. Section Chief George C. Moore to SAC, Jackson [Mississippi], March 11, 1968, HQ file, FBI Documents to the House Select Committee on Assassinations (hereafter cited as FBI Docs. to HSCA), container 21, 62-117290-851.

44. For the March 21 "urgent" teletype, see memo from Robert A. Murphy to J. Stanley Pottinger, assistant attorney general, March 21, 1975, Justice Department Office of Professional Responsibility files (or OPR files), 270-36-1980, p. 49. This document is frequently referred to as the Murphy Report. Director to SACs, March 26, 1968, POCAM, HQ file, 157-8428-438.

45. Moore to Sullivan, February 27, 1968, FBI HQ Main King file, 100-1006670-32.

46. Murphy Report, p. 49; Garrow, *The FBI and Martin Luther King, Jr.*, pp. 185–186. Sections of the March 12, 1968, King monograph can be found in FBI document entitled "Outlook for Racial Violence in Washington, D.C." See (FBI) Liaison to Mildred Stegall, March 11, 1968, New York subfile Stanley D. Levison, 157-6-53-1284; *Church Committee Hearings*, Vol. III, p. 174.

47. Moore to Sullivan, March 12, 1968, FBI HQ Main King file, 100-106670-3254.

48. SAC, Birmingham, to Director, March 3, 1968, WFO file, 157-1395-393; memo from SAC, Birmingham, to Director, May 20, 1968, POCAM, HQ file, 157-8428-1307.

49. Teletype from Savannah to Director, May 12, 1968, POCAM, HQ file, 157-8428-1253; Moore to Sullivan, May 17, 1968, COINTELPRO/BNHG [Black Nationalist Hate Groups], 100-448006-131.

50. SAC, Richmond, to Director, March 22, 1968, POCAM, HQ file, 157-8428-442; SAC, Richmond, to Director, March 27, 1968, POCAM, HQ file, 157-8428-452. For confirmation that Julia Brown was a paid FBI informant, see memo from M. A. Jones to Bishop, March 28, 1968, Southern Christian Leadership Conference file (hereafter cited as SCLC file), 100-438794-NR (not recorded).

51. For Wachtel's statement, see *Church Committee Hearings*, Vol. III, p. 184.

52. Rutherford to Levison, March 23, 1968, 100-111180-9-1618a; memo from SAC, New York, to Director, March 26, 1968, POCAM, HQ file,157-8428-422.

Chapter Two

1. For an operational definition of "security police" as it applies to the methods the FBI employed in the Memphis operation, see Otto Kirchheimer, *Political Justice: The Use of Legal Procedure for Political Ends* (Princeton, NJ: Princeton University Press, 1961), pp. 202–204.

2. William D. Miller, *Mr. Crump of Memphis* (Baton Rouge: Louisiana State University Press, 1964), pp. 102–104, 107.

3. David M. Tucker, *Black Pastors and Leaders: Memphis, 1819–1972* (Knoxville: University of Tennessee Press, 1980), pp. 128, 140; Memphis City Directory, 1967, pp. 7–8; Frank C. Holloman's speech, "Civil Disorders—Where To Now," delivered before the American Society for Industrial Security, January 23, 1968, Memphis Race Relations File, pp. 67–68, Brister Library, Memphis State University, Memphis, Tennessee; *Memphis Tri-State Defender*, September 30, 1967.

4. Rev. Samuel ("Billy") Kyles Interview, July 30, 1968, Tape 261, p. 1, the 1968 Memphis Sanitation Strike Archives, Brister Library, Memphis State University Archives (hereafter cited as MSU Archives).

5. For her correspondence with the Memphis Police Department, see folder 17, "Police Brutality Charges," Documents & Artifacts File, MSU Archives.

6. Maxine Smith Interview, June 13, 1968, Tapes 147, 148, see personal data, MSU Archives; Joan Beifuss, *At the River I Stand: Memphis, the 1968 Strike, and Martin Luther King* (Memphis: B & W Books, 1985), pp. 159–162.

7. Letterhead Memorandum (hereafter referred to as LHM), February 16, 1968, Memphis Sanitation Workers Strike file (hereafter cited as MSWS), FO file, 157-1092-21. For verification that the top NAACP executive officers were FBI informers, see FBI airtel from SAC, Memphis, to Director, February 16, 1968, MSWS, HQ file, 157-9146-X1, and FBI airtel from SAC, Memphis, to Director, February 23, 1968, MSWS, HQ file, 157-9146-X5.

8. These records have been in the public domain since 1977 in the FBI reading room at FBI Headquarters, Washington, D.C. They did not get public attention until this information appeared in David J. Garrow's 1982 work, *The FBI and Martin Luther King, Jr.* Later when Garrow appeared on a Memphis radio talk show and referred to the Smiths and Turner as FBI informers, the three black leaders denied the assertion and filed a $10 million damage suit. The suit charged that pursuant to the Garrow radio interview the plaintiffs were subjected to "public ridicule, contempt, and degradation." See story in *Memphis Commercial Appeal*, January 27, 1983. When circumstances dictated, the FBI made no bones about its steadfast responsibility to protect the confidentiality of its informers. Members of the House Select Committee on Assassinations (HSCA) investigating the King case learned this when its chairman requested that the bureau make available for review its informant files related to the King assassination. FBI Director William H. Webster denied access to these files on the grounds that this would place in jeopardy the lives of informers and their families and would severely compromise the agency's "informant development program." The FBI quite properly holds to this policy of no disclosure of informers' names unless it has political reasons of its own to break with this practice. See William H. Webster to Honorable Louis Stokes, June 13, 1978, Documents to the House Select Committee on Assassinations (hereafter referred to as FBI Docs. to HSCA), 62-117290-973.

9. Tucker, *Black Pastors and Leaders*, pp. 128, 140.

10. Quoted in David M. Tucker, *Memphis Since Crump: Bossism, Blacks, and Civil Reformers, 1948–1968* (Knoxville: University of Tennessee Press, 1980), pp. 140–141.

11. Ibid., pp. 141–142.

12. *Memphis Commercial Appeal*, February 17, 1968.

13. Robert E. Bailey, "The 1968 Memphis Sanitation Strike," (M.A. thesis, Memphis State University, 1974), pp. 18–19; Tucker, *Memphis Since Crump*, pp. 152–153.

14. Bailey, "The 1968 Memphis Sanitation Strike," pp. 20–27; *Memphis Tri-State Defender*, February 10, 1968.

15. Bailey, "The 1968 Memphis Sanitation Strike," pp. 29–34; Gerold Frank, *An American Death: The True Story of the Assassination of Martin Luther King, Jr., and the Greatest Manhunt in Our Time* (New York: Doubleday, 1972), pp. 11–12.

16. Quoted in Tucker, *Memphis Since Crump*, p. 156.

17. FBI teletype from Memphis to Director, February 16, 1968, MSWS, FO file, 157-1092-2.

18. For the duration of the strike it was the FBI's practice to circulate summaries of its intelligence-gathering throughout the regional military intelligence community by LHMs. Single copies of these LHMs were routinely sent to U.S. Army Intelligence, Third Army, Memphis and Nashville Districts; G-2 at Ft. McPherson, Georgia; Sixth Naval District, Charleston, South Carolina; and Maxwell Air Force Base, Alabama. LHMs were also routed to E. H. Arkin, Jr., of the Inspectional Bureau, Memphis Police Department.

19. FBI teletype from Memphis to Director, February 16, 1968, MSWS, FO file, 157-1092-1; see also LHMs for February 28 and 29, and March 1, 4, 5, 7, and 9, 1968, MSWS, FO file, 157-1092-30, 32, 34A, 52, 70, 72, and 74, respectively.

20. FBI teletype from Memphis to Director, March 12, 1968, MSWS, FO file, 157-1092-75A; FBI teletype from Memphis to Director, March 25, 1968, MSWS, FO file, 157-1092-147; FBI teletype from Memphis to Director.

21. *Memphis Commercial Appeal*, February 20, 1968, p. 1; Gwen Awsumb Interview, May 8, 1968, Tape 1, pp. 15–16, MSU Archives.

22. Bailey, "The 1968 Sanitation Strike," pp. 45–59; Beifuss, *At the River I Stand*, pp. 75–82.

23. Bailey, "The 1968 Sanitation Strike," p. 47; Ely H. Arkin, Jr., Report *Civil Disorders (February 12 Through April 16, 1968)*, pp. 9–10 (hereafter cited as the Arkin Report). The Arkin Report can be found in the *Report of the Office of Professional Responsibility to Review the FBI Martin Luther King, Jr., Security and Assassination Investigation* (hereafter cited as the OPR Report). Dr. King assassination researcher Harold Weisberg generously permitted the writer access to the Arkin Report and to his extensive files on the King case.

24. Bailey, "The 1968 Sanitation Strike," pp. 48–57; Beifuss, *At the River I Stand*, pp. 79–82.

25. Arkin Report, pp. 11–12.

26. Beifuss, *At the River I Stand*, pp. 75–86; Jesse Epps Interview, July 31, 1968, Tape 123, pp. 25–26, MSU Archives.

27. Rev. H. Ralph Jackson Interview, May 24, 1968, Tape 197, p. 3, MSU Archives; Rev. Richard Moon Interview, May 29, 1968, Tape 53, p. 25, MSU Archives; Gerald Fanion Interview, June 10, 1968, Tape 84, pp. 5–7, MSU Archives.

28. Ed Gillis Interview, June 2, 1968, Tape 61, p. 35, MSU Archives; Arkin Report, p. 15; Beifuss, *At the River I Stand*, pp. 88–89.

29. Rev. James M. Lawson, Jr., Interview, July 8, 1970, Tape 243, MSU Archives; Richard Moon Interview, May 29, 1968, Tape 53, pp. 25–26, MSU Archives.

30. Bailey, "The 1968 Sanitation Strike," pp. 43–59.

31. Arkin Report, pp. 16–17; Rev. James M. Lawson Interview, July 8, 1970, Tape 243, p. 4, MSU Archives; Rev. H. Ralph Jackson Interview, May 24, 1968, Tape 197, pp. 5–6, MSU Archives.

32. The use of chemical mace as a police weapon generated a great deal of media attention in 1968. Most of the reportage sided with the view that the effects of the "chemical club" were not transient but posed long-term health hazards. See

Roger Rapoport, "Mace in the Face," *The New Republic*, April 13, 1968, pp. 14–17; "Mace Questions," *Time*, May 17, 1968, p. 52; "A Case of Mace," *Newsweek*, June 10, 1968, p. 79; "A Case Against Mace," *Nation*, May 6, 1968, p. 87; "Mace in the Face," *Commonweal*, June 27, 1968, p. 141; *New York Times*, May 20, 22, 1968, pp. 95, 29, respectively.

33. Arkin Report, p. 17; LHM, February 24, 1968, MSWS, FO file, 157-1092-18.

34. Maxine Smith Interview, June 13, 1968, Tape 147, p. 4, MSU Archives; Calvin Taylor Interview, August 17, 1968, Tape 116, p. 12, MSU Archives.

35. Rev. Harold Middlebrook Interview, July 18, 1972, Tape 32, p. 19, MSU Archives; Beifuss, *At the River I Stand*, pp. 92–93; Jesse Epps Interview, July 31, 1968, Tape 123, p. 28, MSU Archives; Rev. H. Ralph Jackson Interview, May 24, 1968, pp. 4–6, MSU Archives; Tucker, *Black Pastors and Leaders*, pp. 133–134; Bailey, "The 1968 Memphis Strike," p. 64.

36. *Memphis Commercial Appeal*, March 3, 1968; *Memphis Tri-State Defender*, March 3, 1968.

37. This is a reference to the aforementioned Hoover thesis that the civil rights movement was controlled by Communists. See Frank J. Donner, *Age of Surveillance: The Aims and Methods of America's Political Intelligence System* (New York: Alfred A. Knopf, 1980), pp. 138–144.

38. For a useful account of Lawson's activist pacifist views and early involvement in "Movement" politics, see Tucker, *Black Pastors and Leaders*, especially chapter 9.

39. LHM, February 20, 1968, MSWS, FO file, 157-1092-324.

40. LHM, February 28, 1968, MSWS, FO file, 157-1092-32; LHM, February 29, 1968, MSWS, FO file, 159-1092-324. The suspicious overtones imparted to Lawson's Prague trip appeared terribly overblown when the *Memphis Tri-State Defender* reported that the popular black pastor would attend the third All-Christian Peace Assembly in Czechoslovakia at the end of the month. See *Memphis Tri-State Defender*, March 30, 1968; LHM, February 29, 1968, MSWS, FO file, 157-1092-324. For a useful summary of Lawson's political file, see FBI memo from SAC, Memphis to SAC, Cleveland, March 28, 1968, MSWS, FO file, 157-1092-180.

41. LHM, February 27, MSWS, FO file, 157-1092-324; FBI memo from SAC from William H. Lawrence to SAC [Memphis], March 25, 1968, MSWS, FO file, 157-1092-138A; LHM, February 28, 1968, MSWS, FO file, 157-1092-32.

42. The original story appears in the *Memphis Commercial Appeal*, March 8, 1968. A photocopy of the account with names underscored for indexing can be found in FBI memo, March 18, 1968, MSWS, FO file, 157-1092-110A.

43. LHM, March 16, 1968, MSWS, FO file, 157-1092-86. A spot check of just the Memphis field office reveals that at least 175 individuals and 20 organizations were indexed during the duration of the FBI's Memphis sanitation strike operation.

44. Director to SAC, Memphis, January 15, 1968, Invaders, HQ file, 157-8460-1. This serial contains a handy digest of the bureau's political surveillance of the BOP-Invaders during the period of the sanitation strike. This compendium is based on information from at least 21 different FBI informers and sources. See FBI airtel from SAC, Memphis to Director, May 6, 1968, Invaders, HQ file, 157-8460-3.

45. Arkin Report, p. 2. Arkin used the term *subversive* in an August 8, 1968, report "Summary of Militant Activities in Memphis (Subversive)," Arkin Report, fn. 7.

46. *Memphis Commercial Appeal,* July 27, 28, and 29, 1967.

47. *Memphis Commercial Appeal,* July 28, 1967; Frank Kallaher Interview, May 7, 1970, Tape 9, MSU Archives; Calvin Taylor Interview, August 17, 1968, Tape 115, p. 7, MSU Archives.

48. Police intelligence units like the DIU have historically been referred to as "red squads." See Paul G. Chevigny, "Politics and Law in the Control of Local Surveillance," *Cornell Law Review* 70 (April 1984), p. 736.

49. Deposition of Lt. Ely H. Arkin, Jr., December 14, 15, 1976, *Kendrick v. Chandler* (No. 76-449), filed September 10, 1976, W.D. Tennessee, p. 72 (hereafter cited as *Kendrick v. Chandler*); Frank Kallaher Interview, March 7, 1970, Tape 9, pp. 28–30, MSU Archives.

50. Frank C. Holloman testimony before HSCA, Vol. IV, pp. 236–237, 240, 243; Philip H. Melanson, *Murkin Conspiracy: An Investigation into the Assassination of Dr. Martin Luther King, Jr.* (New York: Praeger, 1989), p. 74; Holloman testimony before HSCA, Vol. IV, pp. 243–244.

51. Arkin Report, p. 2; Frank Kallaher Interview, March 7, 1970, Tape 9, pp. 33–34, MSU Archives; Arkin deposition, February 15, 1977, *Kendrick v. Chandler,* pp. 262–263; Deposition of George W. Hutchinson, Memphis Police Department's Deputy Chief of Operations, November 16, 1976, *Kendrick v. Chandler,* p. 25.

52. Chevigny, "Politics and Law in the Control of Local Surveillance," p. 736; Richard Harris, *Justice: The Crisis of Law, Order and Freedom in America* (New York: Avon Books, 1970), pp. 37–38; Frank Donner, "The Theory and Practice of American Political Intelligence," *The New York Review of Books* (April 22, 1971), pp. 27–38.

53. Donner, "The Theory and Practice of American Political Intelligence," p. 29; Hutchinson deposition, November 16, 1976, *Kendrick v. Chandler,* p. 12; FBI, Memphis, to Director, March 13, 1968, Murkin (Murder of King file), HQ file, 44-38861-808; Frank Kallaher Interview, March 7, 1970, Tape 9, pp. 33–34, MSU Archives; FBI memo from Lawrence to SAC, Memphis, April 3, 1968, MSWS, FO file, 157-1092-232; Lawrence to SAC, Memphis, April 13, 1968, MSWS, FO file, 157-1092-326. The Memphis field office learned about McCullough at least as early as March 27, 1968, from MPD Captain Jewell G. Ray. See Lawrence to SAC, Memphis, April 3, 1968, MSWS, FO file, 157-1092-232; Marrell McCullough police file, City of Memphis Personnel Division Office. The writer is grateful to L. Paul Barsten for sharing this document with him.

54. John T. Eliff, *The Reform of FBI Intelligence Operations* (Princeton, NJ: Princeton University Press, 1979), pp. 21–24; FBI airtel from Hoover to SAC, Albany, March 4, 1968, COINTELPRO/BNHG, 100-448006-17. Copies of this six-page directive were sent to agency field offices in 44 cities, including the bureau's Memphis office.

55. The BOP's stated goals can be found in a 13-page proposal prepared for circulation among federal government funding agencies. See LHM, May 6, 1968, Invaders, HQ file, 157-8460-3, pp. 59–71. See also LHM, June 6, 1968, Invaders, HQ file, 157-8460-(illegible). For a good account of the Johnson administration's enthusiastic support for Pride, Inc., in Washington, D.C., see Harry S. Jaffe and Tom Sherwood, *Dream City: Race, Power, and the Decline of Washington, D.C.* (New York: Simon & Schuster, 1994), pp. 63–65.

56. LHM, May 6, 1968, Invaders, HQ file, 157-8460-3, pp. 3–10.

57. FBI airtel from SAC, Memphis, to Director, May 6, 1968, Invaders, HQ file, 157-8460-3.

58. Lawrence to SAC (100-4390), March 18, 1968, MSWS, FO file, 157-1092-196; Lawrence to SAC, Memphis, April 4, 1968, MSWS, FO file, 157-1092-248; Lawrence to SAC, Memphis, March 13, 1968, MSWS, FO file, 157-1092-78; Lawrence to SAC, Memphis, March 18, 1968, MSWS, FO file, 157-1092-115. For FBI records of campus political activity related to Owen Junior College and South-western College, respectively, see Lawrence to SAC, Memphis, April 4, 1968, MSWS, FO file, 157-1092-248; and Lawrence to SAC, Memphis, April 1, 1968, MSWS, FO file, 157-1092-196.

59. Eddie Jenkins Interview, January 7, 1969, Tape 177, pp. 1–2, MSU Archives; Lawrence to SAC, Memphis, March 13, 1968, MSWS, FO file, 157-1092-78; LHM, March 1, 1968, MSWS, FO file, 157-1092-34A; LHM, March 13, 1968, MSWS, FO file, 157-1092-82.

60. Lawrence to SAC, Memphis, March 13, 1968, MSWS, FO file, 157-1092-78; Lawrence to SAC, Memphis, March 18, 1968, MSWS, FO file, 157-1092-115; Lawrence to SAC, Memphis, April 1, 1968, MSWS, FO file, 157-1092-191.

61. Bureau sources reported that barring a settlement of the strike, racial violence was a real possibility. See LHM, March 9, 1968, MSWS, FO file, 157-1092-72; Special Agent (SA) Andrew Sloan to SAC, Memphis, March 19, 1968, MSWS, FO file, 157-1092-114. For the MPD record of increased racial incidents from March 1 through March 17, see Arkin Report, pp. 23–38.

62. SAC, Memphis to Director, March 2, 1968, MSWS, HQ file, 157-9146-X20; Rev. Malcolm Blackburn Interview, May 24, 1968, Tape 76, pp. 7–8, MSU Archives; *Memphis Commercial Appeal*, March 8, 20, 1968; LHM, March 15, 1968, MSWS, FO file, 157-1092-82; LHM, March 18, 1968, MSWS, FO file, 157-1092-112A. For examples of police harassment that even the FBI characterized as "put up jobs," see LHM, March 9, 1968, MSWS, FO file, 157-1092-72; Lawrence to SAC, Memphis, March 25, 1968, MSWS, FO file, 157-1092-82; LHM, May 6, 1968, Invaders, HQ file, 157-8486-3; Gerald Fanion Interview, June 10, 1968, Tape 84, pp. 25–27, MSU Archives.

63. *Memphis Commercial Appeal*, March 15, 1968.

64. Rev. Billy Kyles Interview, July 30, 1968, Tape 260, pp. 18–19, MSU Archives; Jesse Epps Interview, July 31, 1968, Tape 123, p. 36, MSU Archives; transcript of King's March 18 speech, Tape 34, pp. 5, 7, and 8, MSU Archives; David L. Lewis, *King: A Critical Biography* (Baltimore: Penguin Books, 1971), pp. 379–381; *Memphis Commercial Appeal*, March 19, 1968, and *Memphis Tri-State Defender*, March 23, 1968.

65. For similar comments on the freak snowstorm, see Anecdotes File in the 1968 Sanitation Workers Strike Collection at MSU Archives; Bailey, "The 1968 Sanitation Strike," pp. 84–91.

Chapter Three

1. Joan T. Beifuss, *At the River I Stand: Memphis, 1968 Strike, and Martin Luther King* (Memphis: B & W Books, 1985), p. 221. For an excellent description of the

March 28 demonstration and the violence based on oral histories of Memphians who were present that day, see Chapter 10 of *At the River I Stand*.

2. Ibid., pp. 217–219; Rev. Malcolm Blackburn Interview, August 2, 1968, Tape 77, p. 12, the 1968 Memphis Sanitation Strike Archives, Brister Library, Memphis State University Archives (hereafter cited as MSU Archives); Southwestern College students Interview, June 3, 1968, Tape 113, p. 12, MSU Archives; Maxine Smith Interview, June 13, 1968, Tape 147, p. 26, MSU Archives.

3. Ely H. Arkin, Jr. Report *Civil Disorders (February 12 Through April 16, 1968)* (hereafter cited as the Arkin Report), p. 48; Letterhead Memorandum (LHM), March 21, 1968, Memphis Sanitation Workers Strike file (hereafter cited as MSWS), FO file, 157-1092-129; FBI teletype (sent 4:10 P.M.) from Memphis to Director and WFO, March 28, 1968, MSWS, FO file, 157-1092-160. For a partial log of the police radio calls from 8:30 A.M. until mid-afternoon, see *Memphis Commercial Appeal*, March 29, 1968, pp. 4–5.

4. *Memphis Press-Scimitar*, March 28, 1968; Arkin Report, pp. 48–49; Rev. Harold Middlebrook Interview, July 8, 1968, Tape 37, pp. 15–18, MSU Archives; Gerald Fanion Interview, June 10, 1968, Tape 84, p. 16, MSU Archives; Rev. H. Ralph Jackson Interview, May 24, 1968, Tape 197, p. 10, MSU Archives; Ronald Ivy Interview, May 7, 1968, Tape 170, p. 58, MSU Archives.

5. For a useful account of the March 28 riot that concentrates on the actions of rebellious teenagers see Gerold Frank, *An American Death: The True Story of the Assassination of Martin Luther King Jr., and the Greatest Manhunt in Our Time* (New York: Doubleday, 1972), pp. 22–28; ASAC (Assistant Special Agent in Charge) C. O. Halter to SAC, Memphis, March 29, 1968, MSWS, FO file, 157-1092-171.

6. For accounts of the March 28 violence that raised the issue of a "police riot," see reports by white staff writers Kay Pittman Black and Barnes Carr in the *Memphis Press-Scimitar*, March 29, 1968. Most of the coverage of that day's events in the Scripps-Howard newspapers took a monochromatic view that the rioting was an "all black affair"; *Memphis Commercial Appeal*, April 4, 1968, p. 5.

7. John Gaston Hospital records, container 5, folder 20, pp. 1–3, MSU Archives; Rev. Billy Kyles Interview, July 30, 1968, Tape 126, p. 9, MSU Archives.

8. See Joan Beifuss's notes on the February 1971 civil suit Payne's parents brought against the Memphis Police Department, Documents & Artifacts file folder 22-2, MSU Archives; *Memphis Press-Scimitar*, February 25, 1971; *Memphis Commercial Appeal*, March 29, 1968.

9. *Memphis Press-Scimitar*, February 26, 1971, March 1 and 2, 1971; *Memphis Press-Scimitar*, February 25, 1971.

10. FBI LHM, April 2, 1968, 100-4105-75, p. 3; *Memphis Tri-State Defender*, April 6, 1968, p. 12.

11. Memphis to Director, March 28, 1968, MSWS, HQ file, 157-9146-37; FBI LHM, April 2, 1968, 100-4105-75, pp. 1–3.

12. Lawrence to SAC, Memphis, April 2, 1968, MSWS, FO file, 157-1092-228; Sloan to SAC, Memphis, April 2, 1968, MSWS, FO file, 157-1092-214; LHM, March 29, 1968, MSWS, FO file, 157-1092-184.

13. Lawrence to SAC, Memphis, April 3, 1968, MSWS, FO file, 157-1092-232; Lawrence to SAC, Memphis, April 13, 1968, MSWS, FO file, 157-1092-326. The MPD regularly routed McCullough's intelligence reports to the FBI Memphis

field office, including information about the deliberations and plans of COME's strike strategy committee.

14. In response to a request for FBI records from G. R. Blakey, chief counsel and director for the House Select Committee on Assassinations, the FBI admitted having "five informers who provided coverage on the Invaders," one of whom had penetrated the Invaders. See D. Ryan to Bassett, May 19, 1978, 62-117290-926X2, FBI Documents to the House Select Committee on Assassination (hereafter cited as FBI Docs. to HSCA), container 21; J. G. Deegan to W. R. Wannall, February 24, 1976, FBI HQ file, 44-38861-NR (not recorded), p. 2, where FBI admits that one of these informers had penetrated the Invaders. See also FBI teletype (sent 4:10 P.M.) from Memphis to Director and WFO, March 28, 1968, MSWS, HQ File 157-9146-37; LHM, May 6, 1968, Invaders, HQ file, 157-8460-3, pp. 36–42. For confirmation of the point that both the FBI and MPD were aware that violence was a strong possibility, see testimony of Special Agent William H. Lawrence before HSCA, Vol. VI, pp. 545–546.

15. See House Select Committee on Assassinations (hereafter cited as HSCA), *The Final Report* (New York: Bantam Books), p. 541; FBI LHM, April 17, 1974, Murkin (Murder of King) file, HQ file, 44-38861-5935.

16. Rev. James M. Lawson, Jr., Interview, July 8, 1970, Tape 244, pp. 4–7, MSU Archives.

17. Rev. James M. Lawson, Jr., Interview, September 24, 1969, Tape 252, pp. 41–44, MSU Archives; Ron Ivy Interview, May 7, 1968, Tape 170, pp. 50–54, MSU Archives; Calvin Taylor Interview, August 7, 1968, Tape 116, p. 18, MSU Archives; Bobby Doctor Interview, June 17, 1968, Tape 146, pp. 3–10, MSU Archives.

18. Calvin Taylor Interview, August 17, 1968, Tape 116, pp. 18–19, MSU Archives; Charles L. Cabbage testimony before the HSCA Hearings, Vol. VI, p. 516; John B. Smith testimony before the HSCA Hearings, Vol. VI, p. 465; Ron Ivy Interview, May 7, 1968, Tape 170, pp. 50–51, MSU Archives.

19. Calvin Taylor Interview, August 17, 1968, Tape 116, p. 18, MSU Archives; Ron Ivy Interview, May 7, 1968, Tape 170, pp. 50–51, MSU Archives; Rev. Billy Kyles Interview, July 30, 1968, Tape 260, pp. 28, 43, MSU Archives.

20. See Eric Foner, *A Short History of Reconstruction, 1863–1988* (New York: Harper & Row, 1990), p. 117.

21. Rev. Billy Kyles Interview, July 30, 1968, Tape 260, pp. 18–25, MSU Archives; Rev. James M. Lawson, Jr., Interview, July 8, 1970, Tape 244, p. 8, MSU Archives.

22. Moore to Sullivan, March 29, 1968, COINTELPRO/BNHG, HQ file, 100-448006-93; Moore to Sullivan, March 28, 1968, MSWS, HQ file, 157-9146-38.

23. See FBI interview with Walter Lane ("Bill") Bailey, April 12, 1968, Murkin, HQ file, 44-38861-2322; ASAC C. O. Halter to SAC, Memphis, March 29, 1968, MSWS, FO file, 157-1092-171; SAC, Memphis to Director, April 17, 1974, Murkin, HQ file, 44-38861-5936; Ralph D. Abernathy, *And The Walls Came Tumbling Down* (New York: Harper & Row, 1989), pp. 418–419.

24. Moore to Sullivan, March 28, 1968, MSWS, HQ file, 157-9146-38; Moore to Sullivan, March 29, 1968, COINTELPRO/BNHG, HQ file, 100-448006-93. For the bureau's characterization of relations with the *Memphis Commercial Appeal*, see J. Edgar Hoover to (masked), June 5, 1968, POCAM, HQ file, 157-8428-1974. For the Memphis editorials, see Frank Ahlgren and Thomas BeVien in the *Commercial Ap-*

peal, March 30, 1968, and Charles Schneider in the *Press-Scimitar*, March 29, 1968. The "Chicken A La King" editorial cartoon appears in the *Commercial Appeal*, March 31, 1968, p. 8.

25. HSCA, *The Final Report*, pp. 574–578. For the *St. Louis Globe-Democrat* editorial, see HSCA, Vol. VIII, p. 107.

26. The House committee's interest was piqued by information in the FBI's St. Louis field office criminal file on a Russell G. Byers. Byers, a known St. Louis fence, had a story to tell. Sometime in either 1966 or 1967, he was approached by two intermediaries from Imperial, Missouri, who claimed to represent a group of wealthy St. Louis County businessmen who were financing a contract killing on King. Byers refused the offer, but the St. Louis FBI stumbled onto the contact through an informer; apparently they checked it out but took no action. The HSCA was intrigued because Byers's brother-in-law was serving a life sentence for murder in the Missouri State Penitentiary where James Earl Ray was incarcerated before he escaped in April 1967. This set of circumstantial connections led the House committee to posit that Ray learned of the contract on King's life and made contact with these businessmen after he escaped. About the time the Beyers story surfaced in the press, Byers was under arrest in St. Louis as a suspect in a museum burglary. See FBI Docs. to HSCA, March 20 and 24, 1978, 62-117290-576, and the *New York Times*, July 26, 1978.

27. For the House committee's case on the FBI and the *Globe-Democrat* editorial, see HSCA, *The Final Report*, pp. 574–580.

28. FBI memo from C. O. Halter to SAC (Memphis), March 29, 1968, MSWS, FO file, 157-1092-173.

29. *Washington Post*, March 30, 1968; *Memphis Commercial Appeal*, March 30, 1968.

30. Rev. Billy Kyles Interview, July 30, 1968, Tape 260, p. 42, MSU Archives; Abernathy, *And the Walls Came Tumbling Down*, pp. 419–420. For the best account of these soul-searching and agonizing days between March 28 and King's return to Memphis, see David J. Garrow, *Bearing the Cross: Martin Luther King Jr., and the Southern Christian Leadership Conference* (New York: William Morrow, 1986), pp. 611–620.

31. Abernathy, *And the Walls Came Tumbling Down*, pp. 419–420; Garrow, *Bearing the Cross*, p. 612; Levison to King, March 28 and 29, 100-111180-9-1623A; Abernathy, *And the Walls Came Tumbling Down*, p. 420.

32. Atlanta to Director and Memphis, March 28, 1968, MSWS, FO file, 157-1092-165; ASAC Halter to File (157-1092), March 28, 1968, MSWS, FO file, 157-1092-168; Garrow, *Bearing the Cross*, p. 617.

33. Beifuss, *At the River I Stand*, p. 253; Abernathy, *And the Walls Came Tumbling Down*, p. 421; Lawrence's testimony before the HSCA, Vol. VI, p. 550; Calvin Taylor Interview, August 17, 1968, Tape 115, pp. 7–8, MSU Archives.

34. Garrow, *Bearing the Cross*, p. 612; Calvin Taylor Interview, August 17, 1968, Tape 116, pp. 30–31, 49, MSU Archives.

35. That evening a distraught King spoke to Levison about the morning meeting with the three Invaders. "I talked to the fellows who organized the violence," he told his friend, but King blamed their actions on Lawson and the ministers for ignoring them. "They love me," he continued, but were "too sick to see" they were hurting King more with the violence than the preachers. See Levison to King, March 29, 1968, 100-111180-9-1623a.

36. Calvin Taylor Interview, August 17, 1968, Tape 116, pp. 43–47, MSU Archives; Garrow, *Bearing the Cross*, p. 613. SCLC top aides were clearly disenchanted with Lawson. Abernathy called him a "weak leader" and Andy Young's evaluation was even more caustic. He told Levison that "Jim Lawson has one of the most unproductive careers in the Movement." See Levison to King, March 28, 1968, 100-11118-9-1623a, for the Abernathy comment and Young to Levison, June 4, 1968, 100-111180-9-1691.

37. Calvin Taylor Interview, August 17, 1968, Tape 116, pp. 45–47, MSU Archives.

38. Garrow, *Bearing the Cross*, pp. 617–618; Jesse Epps Interview, July 31, 1968, Tape 123, pp. 37–39, MSU Archives.

39. Abernathy, *And the Walls Came Tumbling Down*, p. 428.

40. Report by Memphis Inspector G. P. Tines, July 17, 1968, "Security and surveillance of Dr. Martin Luther King from time of arrival in Memphis on April 3, 1968, until he was assassinated on the evening of April 4, 1968." Report can be found in the *Report of the Office of Professional Responsibility to Review the FBI Martin Luther King, Jr., Security and Assassination Investigation* (hereafter cited as the OPR Report). Tines's report can be found in Appendix B of the OPR Report (hereafter cited as Tines Report), p. 2.

41. Tines Report, pp. 1–2. For Inspector Smith's "Intelligence" duties, see Hutchinson deposition, October 5, 1976, *Kendrick v. Chandler*, p. 52; Arkin Report, p. 64. According to Inspector Tines, Mrs. Matthews was requested to provide a statement about waiving police protection at the airport, but she never showed up at his office. See Tines Report, p. 6.

42. Arkin Report, p. 21.

43. Arkin Report, p. 18; Beifuss, *At the River I Stand*, p. 76.

44. For the impressive record of Redditt and Richmond's surveillance activities during the strike, see Arkin Report, pp. 1–25. For threats against both men, see Arkin Report, pp. 29, 60, and Tines Report, p. 4.

45. SAC, Memphis, to Director, April 1, 1968, "Threat to American Airlines & Dr. King, Memphis, 4/1/'68," FBI HQ file, 149-121-1.

46. An FBI 10-page memo generated during the course of the bureau's investigation into King's murder itemized some 49 oral and written assassination threats against the civil rights leader that were brought to the FBI's attention. This list is incomplete because it only covers the period from 1965 to 1967. See G. L. McGowan to Rosen, April 24, 1968, Murkin, HQ file, 44-38861-2649.

47. At the time file 149-121 was closed, it contained only three serials or documents. See FBI inventory worksheet for file 149-121. I am grateful to researcher Harold Weisberg for his determined effort to wrest this file from the FBI and for bringing it to my attention. For FBI policy on subjects of threats, see Rosen to Belmont, October 1, 1964, FBI Docs. to HSCA, 62-117290-1354, container 22.

48. Arkin Report, p. 59; HSCA, Vol. IV, p. 249. The HSCA raised this issue of the April 1 threat, but in such a superficial manner that they would have been more honest not to have bothered at all. For example, Robert G. Jensen, SAC of the Memphis field office at the time, the agent designated in the FBI manual to alert the subject of a threat, was never questioned at all about this by the House committee members. A review of the FBI's released Atlanta field office Murkin file (44-2386) gives no indication that King was warned of the April 1 threat.

49. Martin Luther King, Sr., with Clayton Riley, *Daddy King: An Autobiography* (New York: William Morrow, 1980), pp. 186–187; Rev. Billy Kyles Interview, June 12, 1968, Tape 258, p. 4, MSU Archives; Rev. Harold Middlebrook Interview, July 21, 1968, Tape 38, pp. 10–11, MSU Archives.

50. From Miami to Director, February 21, 1968, Murkin, HQ file, 44-38861-X6; Rev. Billy Kyles Interview, Tape 261, p. 6, MSU Archives.

51. This theme is developed further on in the chapter.

52. The earlier request came on January 2, 1968. See Moore to Sullivan, December 29, 1967, Hoover's Confidential & Official file, 100-438794-2052 (hereafter cited as C & O file); Moore to Sullivan, March 29, 1968, Hoover's C & O file, 100-438794-2108.

53. Hoover memorandum for the Attorney General, April 2, 1968, Hoover's C & O file, 100-438794-2107; Director, FBI, to the Attorney General, May 1, 1968, Hoover's C & O file, 100-438794-NR; Attorney General Clark to Hoover, January 17, 1969, Hoover's C & O file, 100-438794-NR.

54. See Lawrence's testimony before the HSCA, Vol. VI, pp. 539–541; Arkin deposition, August 11, 1972, *Kendrick v. Chandler*, p. 365; FBI LHM, April 5, 1968, MSWS, FO file, 157-1092-273; FBI LHM, April 6, 1968, MSWS, FO file, 157-1092-275; SAC Robert G. Jensen to File (157-1092), April 3, 1968, MSWS, FO file, 157-1092-216.

55. Frank, *An American Death*, pp. 56–89.

56. Interview with Marrell McCullough, Safeway Building, Washington, D.C., July 12, 1976, OPR Records, Appendix B; FBI, Memphis, to Director, April 13, 1968, Murkin, HQ file, 44-38861-808; pp. 4–5; Abernathy, *And the Walls Came Tumbling Down*, pp. 440–441.

57. FBI teletype from Memphis to Director, April 5, 1968, MSWS, FO file, 157-1092-262; FBI teletype from Memphis to Director, April 6, 1968, MSWS, FO file, 157-1092-269; *Memphis Press-Scimitar*, April 6, 1968; Robert E. Bailey, "The 1968 Memphis Sanitation Strike" (M.A. thesis, Memphis State University, 1974), pp. 114–118; David M. Tucker, *Memphis Since Crump: Bossism, Blacks, and Civil Reformers, 1948–1968* (Knoxville: University of Tennessee Press, 1980), p. 180.

58. Bailey, "The 1968 Memphis Sanitation Strike," pp. 117–124. For the entire agreement, see *Memphis Commercial Appeal*, April 17, 1968.

59. Tines Report, p. 5; Harold Weisberg, *Martin Luther King: The Assassination* [formerly titled *Frame-Up*] (New York: Carroll & Graf, 1993), p. 345; see Judson Ghormley's affidavit, HSCA, Vol. IV, p. 285.

60. Weisberg, *Martin Luther King: The Assassination*, p. 358. Bevel elaborated on the "plot" in an interview with Claude Lewis, *Philadelphia Bulletin*, March 17, 1969. Years later, Abernathy was still convinced that either the Klan or a professional killer hired by Director Hoover was responsible for the crime. See Abernathy, *And the Walls Came Tumbling Down*, p. 453.

61. See Les Payne's "FBI Tied to King's Return to Memphis," *Newsday*, February 1, 1976, and "Cop Was Removed Before King Slaying," *Newsday*, February 15, 1976. Payne was the minority affairs specialist for *Newsday*. He was part of an investigative team that traced heroin from the poppy fields of Turkey into New York City veins. At several times during this investigation his life was in danger. Later, he went to South Africa at the height of apartheid violence to do a series on racial repression in that country. He took great risks, traveling to parts of South Africa that were prohibited to blacks. He returned to write an 11-part series on conditions in

South Africa and was recommended for a Pulitzer by one of the judging panels. When the Pulitzer advisory board overruled his nomination, the action provoked expressions of outrage and contempt by some of Payne's fellow journalists. See the Associated Press story in *Newsday*, April 22, 1978. That Redditt was able to con a veteran newsman like Payne was no small achievement.

62. J. S. Peelman to Gallagher, February 18, 1976, Murkin, HQ file, 44-38861-NR; J. G. Deegan to W. R. Wannell, February 24, 1976, Murkin, HQ file, 44-38861-NR; J. G. Deegan to T. W. Leavitt, March 2, 1976, Murkin, HQ file, 44-38861-NR; J. S. Peelman to Gallagher, August 9, 1976, Murkin, HQ file, 44-38861-NR.

63. Director Clarence Kelley to Les Payne, June 23, 1976, Murkin, HQ file, 44-38861-illegible.

64. Mark Lane and Dick Gregory, *Murder in Memphis: The FBI and the Assassination of Martin Luther King* (New York: Thunder's Mouth Press, 1993), pp. 139, 264–265. In a February 4, 1969, interview with the FBI, Lawson aired his suspicions about the transfer of Newsum "out of rotation" from the Butler Street firehouse on the evening of April 3. The impression left by the FBI account of the interview was that Newsum's removal was common and troubling knowledge within the black community. See J. S. Peelman to Gallagher, August 21, 1976, Murkin, HQ file, 44-38861-NR.

65. *Washington Post*, September 18, 1976.

66. Frank Donner, "The Theory and Practice of American Political Intelligence," *The New York Review of Books* (April 22, 1971), p. 28. See Redditt's testimony before the HSCA, Vol. IV, pp. 202–203; James F. Walker interview with John Carlisle, Chief Investigator, Attorney General's Office, State of Tennessee, September 20, 1976, OPR Records, Appendix B.

67. Arkin Report, p. 65; Tines Report, p. 4.

68. Floyd Newsum interview, July 8, 1976, OPR Report, Appendix B, pp. 1–2; see Lane's moving interview with Newsum in Lane and Gregory, *Murder in Memphis*, pp. 125–127; Newsum interview, July 8, 1976, OPR Records, Appendix B, p. 3; Memorandum of interview with James O. Barrett, former deputy chief, Memphis Fire Department, September 27, 1976, OPR Report, Appendix B; Memorandum of interview with Norvell E. Wallace, July 8, 1976, OPR Records, Appendix B, pp. 1–2; Redditt's testimony before the HSCA, Vol. IV, p. 205.

69. Redditt's testimony before the HSCA, Vol. IV, pp. 213, 218, 223, 228, 232, 230–231.

70. Philip H. Melanson in his book, *The Murkin Conspiracy: An Investigation into the Assassination of Dr. Martin Luther King, Jr.* (New York: Praeger, 1989), continued to exploit the Redditt affair à la Mark Lane as part of his grand design to persuade that King was the victim of a "federal" or "intelligence" conspiracy. Unfortunately, his reach fell far short of his grasp of the situation existing in Memphis. His allegations and construction of the events surrounding King's assassination were a sensationalized mishmash of speculation, fanciful imagination, mistakes in facts, and misrepresentation of events.

71. Tines Report, p. 5; HSCA, Vol. IV, pp. 268–269; Memorandum to the file, September 20, 1976, OPR Report, Appendix B; Memorandum of interview with Philip R, Manuel, September 28, 1976, OPR Record, Appendix B.

72. See Holloman's testimony before the HSCA, Vol. IV, pp. 333.

73. HCSA, Vol. IV, p. 255.

74. Ibid., pp. 283–284, 288.

75. See Melanson, *Murkin Conspiracy*, especially Chapter 8, "The Window of Vulnerability," in which his assertions along these lines are not buttressed with persuasive evidence. For reasons why COME and King's aides rejected police protection, see HSCA, Vol. IV, pp. 278–280, and Rev. Billy Kyles Interview, June 12, 1968, Tape 258, MSU Archives, pp. 1–3, passim.

76. HSCA, Vol. IV, p. 242.

77. For these three threats see HSCA, Vol. IV, pp. 248, 249, and 251. John Carlisle interview with Joseph C. Hester, FBI agent in charge of the King assassination in Memphis, June 23, 1976, OPR Records, Appendix B, p. 1; J. S. Peelman to Gallagher, September 21, 1976, Murkin, HQ file, 44-38861-NR, pp. 2, 8.

78. Rev. Billy Kyles Interview, July 30, 1968, Tape 260, p. 43, MSU Archives; HSCA, Vol. IV, p. 242.

79. Murtagh's testimony before the HSCA, Vol. VI, p. 109.

80. At the same time the news of King's assassination was not met with any hand-wringing regret or lament at Hoover's "Seat of Government." As early as 1964, FBI elites had tried to blackmail King into taking his own life before he was publicly disgraced by the threatened release of bureau tapes alleging King's extramarital sexual activities. In 1978 retired FBI agent Arthur L. Murtagh testified before the HSCA that one of the Atlanta field office agents, in his presence, "jumped with joy" when he heard the news from Memphis, crying out "We finally" or "They finally got the s.o.b." For more detail on this, see David J. Garrow, *The FBI and Martin Luther King, Jr.: From "Solo" to Memphis* (New York: W. W. Norton, 1981), pp. 125–126; Murphy Report, p. 44 (OPR Records); Arthur L. Murtagh testimony before the HSCA, Vol. VI, pp. 101–107.

Chapter Four

1. These demands, especially to the Departments of Housing and Urban Development (HUD), HEW, Agriculture, and Labor, were detailed and quite specific about the changes that the PPC planners wanted to see implemented. For copies of these proposals, see White House Aides file, James Gaither Papers, Presidential Task Force, "Poor People's March," Box 36, Lyndon Baines Johnson Library (hereafter cited as James Gaither Papers, Box 36, LBJ Library).

2. Ralph D. Abernathy, *And the Walls Came Tumbling Down*, (New York: Harper & Row, 1989), p. 504. For some Washington press corps reaction, see *Washington Daily News*, April 4, 29, 1968; *Washington Evening Star*, May 1, 1968, A-1; *Washington Post*, May 5, 1968, A-1; *Washington Afro-American*, April 30, 1968.

3. Abernathy to Levison, May 5, 1968, 100-111180-9-1661.

4. Rutherford to Levison, May 5, 1968, 100-111180-9-1660a; Tom Offenburger to Levison, April 19, 1968, 100-111180-9-1645; *Washington Afro-American*, April 27, 1968, pp. 1–2.

5. Andy Levison to Stanley Levison, May 10, 1968, 100-111180-9-1666; Bea Levison to Stanley Levison, May 24, 1968, 100-111180-9-1680a; Adam Fairclough, *To Redeem the Soul of America: The Southern Christian Leadership Conference and Martin*

Luther King, Jr. (Athens: University of Georgia Press, 1978), pp. 385–386; *Washington Post*, April 26, 1968.

6. Director to SAC, Albany, April 5, 1968, POCAM, HQ file, 157-8428-522; Director to SAC, WFO, April 24, 1968, POCAM, HQ file, 157-8428-663; Director to SAC, WFO, May 7, 1968, POCAM, HQ file, 157-8428-896; Director to SAC, WFO, May 8, 1968, HQ file, 157-8428-883; Director to SAC, Albany, May 8, 1968, POCAM, HQ file, 157-8428-895.

7. For Clark's characterization, see HSCA, Vol. VII, pp. 140–141; *Washington Daily News*, April 26, 1968; *Washington Evening Star*, March 29, 1968, A-1.

8. *Washington Post*, May 7, 1968, p. A-1; *Washington Post*, March 16, 1968, p. A-8.

9. Frank J. Donner, *The Age of Surveillance: The Aims and Methods of America's Political Intelligence System* (New York: Alfred A. Knopf, 1980), pp. 394–395; Kenneth O'Reilly, "The FBI and the Politics of the Riots, 1964–1968," *The Journal of American History* (June 1968), p. 110.

10. O'Reilly, "The FBI and the Politics of the Riots, 1964–1968," pp. 110–113.

11. DeLoach to Tolson, May 3, 1968, POCAM, HQ file, 157-8428-NR; Director to SACs, Knoxville and Memphis, May 3, 1968, POCAM, HQ file, 157-8428-932.

12. DeLoach to Tolson, May 6, 1968, POCAM, HQ file, 157-8428-1215.

13. For McClellan's May 7 speech, see *Congressional Record*, 90th Congress, 2nd session, 1968, pp. 1204–1208.

14. Moore to Sullivan, May 7, 1968, POCAM, HQ file, 157-8428-932; Mobile to Director, May 6, 1968, POCAM, HQ file, 157-8428-1400; Director to SAC, Mobile, May 10, 1968, POCAM, HQ file, 157-8428-925.

15. Mobile to Director, May 13, 1968, POCAM, HQ file, 157-8428-1123.

16. DeLoach to Tolson, May 10, 1968, POCAM, HQ file, 157-8428-1125; Moore to Sullivan, May 14, 1968, COINTELPRO/BNHG, 100-4480066-NR.

17. Moore to Sullivan, May 8, 1968, POCAM, HQ file, 157-8428-1125; Director to J. Walter Yeagley, Assistant Attorney General, May 15, 1968, POCAM, HQ file, 157-8428-1125.

18. Frances F. Piven and Richard A. Cloward, *Poor People's Movements: Why They Succeed, How They Fail* (New York: Pantheon Books, 1977). See their Chapter 5 on the NWRO. For this seven-page list of NWRO's proposals, see James Gaither Papers, Box 36, LBJ Library; Piven and Cloward, *Poor People's Movements*, pp. 318–319; Nick Kotz and Mary Lynn Kotz, *A Passion for Equality: George Wiley and the Movement* (New York: W. W. Norton, 1977), pp. 248–251.

19. SAC, WFO, to Director, May 6, 1968, POCAM, HQ file, 157-8428-911; SAC, WFO, to Director, May 7, 1968, POCAM, HQ file, 157-8428-926; Atlanta to Director and Washington Field (hereafter cited as WF), May 7, 1968, POCAM, HQ file, 157-8428-930; SAC, WFO, to Director, May 12, 1968, POCAM, HQ file, 1067; SAC, WFO, to Director, May 13, 1968, POCAM, HQ file, 157-8428-1234.

20. Memo from Matthew Nimetz to Warren Christopher, April 18, 1968, James Gaither Papers, Box 36, LBJ Library; Harry C. McPherson, *A Political Education* (Boston: Little, Brown, 1972), pp. 366–369.

21. McPherson, *A Political Education*, pp. 368–369. Stephen B. Oates, *Let the Trumpet Sound: The Life of Martin Luther King, Jr.* (New York: Harper & Row, 1982), pp. 466–467.

22. Allen J. Matusow, *The Unravelling of America: A History of Liberalism in the 1960s* (New York: Harper & Row, 1984), pp. 169–173.

23. McPherson, *A Political Education*, p. 252; Gaither to Califano, May 15, 16, 1968, James Gaither Papers, Box 36, LBJ Library.

24. Oates, *Let the Trumpet Sound*, p. 467; Memo from Califano to President Johnson, April 17, 1968; Minutes prepared by Matt Nimetz, "Washington, D.C. Riot and Future Planning," April 15, 1968, and May 7, 1968, all in James Gaither Papers, Box 36, LBJ Library.

25. *New York Times*, March 4, 1968; Memo entitled "Actions Taken by Army Since April 15 on Civil Disturbance Tasks Assigned by Mr. Califano," in James Gaither Papers, Box 36, LBJ Library.

26. For Califano's characterization, see *Final Report of the Senate Select Committee to Study Governmental Operations With Respect to Intelligence Activities* (hereafter cited as *Church Committee* Report), Vol. III, p. 495; McPherson, *A Political Education*, pp. 362–363; Roger Wilkins, *A Man's Life: An Autobiography* (New York: Simon & Schuster, 1982), p. 207.

27. Robert Wall, "Special Agent for the FBI," *The New York Review of Books* (January 27, 1972); William C. Sullivan with Bill Brown, *The Bureau: My Thirty Years in Hoover's FBI* (New York: W. W. Norton, 1979), p. 133. Failing to build a legal case, the FBI resorted to a COINTELPRO operation. A phone call to Carmichael's mother on the pretext of warning of a fictitious death threat from the Black Panthers convinced him to leave the country. See *Church Committee Report*, Vol. II, p. 15.

28. *Church Committee Report*, Vol. III, pp. 495–501.

29. For Doar's recommendations, see ibid., p. 496.

30. Director to SACs, May 9, 1968, POCAM, HQ file, 157-8428-965; Chicago to WFO, May 8, 1968, POCAM, HQ file, 157-8428-912; Minneapolis to Director, May 8, 1968, POCAM, HQ file, 157-8428-942; SAC, Pittsburgh, to Director, May 10, 1968, POCAM, HQ file, 157-8428-1088; Indianapolis to Director, May 14, 1968, POCAM, HQ file, 157-8428-1280.

31. SAC, Charlotte, to Director, May 14, 1968, POCAM, HQ file, 157-8428-1271; Seattle, LHM, May 14, 1968, POCAM, HQ file, 157-8428-1282; SAC, Newark, to Director, May 21, 1968, POCAM, HQ file, 157-8428-1504; SAC, San Francisco, to Director, May 14, 1968, POCAM, HQ file, 157-8428-1285.

32. For the duration of project POCAM, the FBI indexed well over 1,800 names of people associated with the PPC. SAC, Cleveland, to Director, May 24, 1968, POCAM, HQ file, 157-8428-1582; SAC, Chicago, to Director, May 20, 1968, POCAM, HQ file, 157-8428-1467; Cincinnati to Director, May 11, 1968, POCAM, HQ file, 157-8428-1156; SAC, Indianapolis, to Director, May 10, 1968, POCAM, HQ file, 157-8428-1202.

33. SAC, Chicago, to Director, May 8, 1968, POCAM, HQ file, 157-8428-941; Portland to Director, May 20, 1968, POCAM, HQ file, 157-8428-1500; SAC, Dallas, to Director, May 20, 1968, POCAM, HQ file, 157-8428-1743; SAC, Phoenix, to Director, May 20, 1968, POCAM, HQ file, 157-8428-1774.

34. SAC, Baltimore, to Director, June 19, 1968, POCAM, HQ file, 157-8428-2564; SAC, Chicago, to Director, May 21, 1968, POCAM, HQ file, 157-8428-1505; *Church Committee Report*, Vol. II, pp. 83–85; Kenneth O'Reilly, *"Racial Matters": The FBI's*

Secret File on Black America, 1960–1972 (New York: Free Press, 1989), p. 270. The Justice Department estimated that there were 3,000 or more participants in all of the caravans. See Memorandum for Attorney General, Community Relations Service, in "Poor People's Campaign—CRS Daily Log" (hereafter cited as "PPC—Daily Log"), Box 35E, Ramsey Clark Papers, LBJ Library.

35. Cincinnati to Director, May 11, 1968, POCAM, HQ file, 157-8428-1156; SAC, Portland, to Director, May 20, 1968, POCAM, HQ file, 157-8428-1500; SAC, Dallas, to Director, May 24, 1968, POCAM, HQ file, 157-8428-1743.

36. Abernathy, *And the Walls Came Tumbling Down*, pp. 412–413; SAC, Jackson, to Director, May 6, 1968, POCAM, HQ file, 157-8428-917; Moore to Sullivan, May 24, 1968, POCAM, HQ file, 157-8428-1818; SAC, Jackson, to Director, May 13, 1968, POCAM, HQ file, 157-8428-1176; Memorandum to Attorney General, May 16, 1968, "PPC—Daily Log," Ramsey Clark Papers, Box 35E, LBJ Library; SAC, Jackson, to Director, May 23, 1968, POCAM, HQ file, 157-8428-1642; SAC, Jackson, to Director, May 6, 1968, POCAM, HQ file, 157-8428-950; Abernathy, *And the Walls Come Tumbling Down*, p. 508.

37. SAC, Jackson, to Director, May 29, 1968, POCAM, HQ file, 157-8428-2279.

38. For example, see SAC, Jackson, to Director, May 7, 8, 9, and 18, 1968, all in POCAM, HQ file, serials 889, 913, 1167, and 1357.

39. SAC, Jackson, to Director, May 14, 1968, POCAM, HQ file, 157-8428-1182; SAC, Jackson, to Director, May 15, 1968, POCAM, HQ file, 157-8428-1329.

40. SAC, Jackson, to Director, May 17, 1968, POCAM, HQ file, 157-8428-1609; SAC, Jackson, to Director, May 13, 18, and 19, all in POCAM, HQ file, serials 1176, 1357, and 1379; Atlanta to Director, June 10, 1968, POCAM, HQ file, 157-8428-2277.

41. For dissemination pattern, see, for example, FBI "Treat as Yellow" summaries (TAYs) for the White House and other government officials, May 11, 1968, POCAM, HQ file, 157-8428-955. For a fair sampling of FBI reports on the caravans, see the following TAYs, May 10, 12, 13, 14, and 15, 1968, POCAM, HQ file, serials 1012, 1022, 1150, 1104, and 1204; O'Reilly, *"Racial Matters,"* pp. 272–275.

42. The daily FBI field reports on the caravans that conclude with "no incidents" or "no disorders" or words to that effect are too numerous to cite individually, but see FBI, POCAM, HQ file, for serials 824 through 932, from May 3 to May 31, 1968.

43. FBI, TAY, May 11, 1968, POCAM, HQ file, 157-8428-955; FBI, TAY, May 15, 1968, POCAM, HQ file, 157-8428-1137; FBI, TAY, May 17, 1968, POCAM, HQ file, 157-8428-1363.

44. FBI, TAY, May 10, 1968, POCAM, HQ file, 157-8428-1057; Moore to Sullivan, May 22, 1968, COINTELPRO/BNHG, 100-448006-NR.

45. Director to SAC, Albany (all FBI field offices), May 24, 1968, POCAM, HQ file, 157-8428-1524.

46. United States Code, Title 42—The Public Health and Welfare Subchapter VIII—"Community Relations Service," Washington, D.C., 1983, pp. 52–54.

47. See Ramsey Clark interview with Harri Baker, March 21, 1969, Ramsey Clark Oral History, LBJ Library, pp. 12–16.

48. CRS representatives with the caravans submitted daily summary reports to Roger Wilkins, CRS division chief. These reports are a narrative of the daily hap-

penings and are in sufficient detail to make them an invaluable source on the caravan phase of the Poor People's Campaign. The reports cover a period from May 10 to May 28, 1968. A comparison between CRS reports and FBI intelligence summaries on the caravans is instructive. See "PPC—Daily Log," Ramsey Clark Papers, LBJ Library. See also Daily Summaries of Poor People's Campaign Activities for May 15, 1968, Midwestern Caravan (IV); May 18, 1968, Western Caravan (VIII); May 21, 1968, Western Caravan (VII and VIII); and May 18, 1968, Western Caravan (VI), all in Box 35E.

49. Frank Donner, *Protectors of Privilege: Red Squads and Police Repression in Urban America* (Berkeley: University of California Press, 1990), pp. 197, 207.

50. See Daily Summaries for May 14, 1968, Eastern Caravan (V); May 15, 1968, Midwestern Caravan (IV). See the status report charts at the end of the Daily Summaries for May 18, 1968, for listings of cities where PPC marches and rallies took place, Box 35E.

51. Daily Summaries for May 11, 1968, Southern Caravan (III), and May 14, 1968, Southern Caravan (III), for favorable comments about the police in Social Circle, Swainsboro, Savannah, and Macon, Georgia; and for Charlotte, Greensboro, and Durham, North Carolina, respectively, all in Box 35E.

52. David J. Garrow, *Bearing the Cross: Martin Luther King Jr., and the Southern Christian Leadership Conference* (New York: William Morrow, 1986), pp. 397, 446. Daily Summaries for May 17, 1968, and May 13, 1968, Southern Caravan (III), all in Box 35E.

53. The precision of CRS reporting on caravan demographics varied. See Daily Summaries for May 11, 1968, Southern Caravan (III), and May 15, 1968, for Midwestern Caravan (IV), all in Box 35E. The western contingents were markedly different in demographic breakdown. For example, the caravan that made its swing through the southwestern states (Western Caravan—VIII) had about equal numbers of blacks, whites, and Mexican Americans. See Daily Summaries for May 18, 1968, Western Caravan (VIII), Box 35E.

54. Daily Summaries for May 11, 13, and 17, 1968, Midwestern Caravan (IV), Box 35E; Cincinnati to Director, May 11, 1968, POCAM, HQ file, 157-8428-1156; Charlotte to Director, May 15, 1968, POCAM, HQ file, 157-8428-1648; Moore to Sullivan, May 16, 1968, POCAM, HQ file, 157-8428-1339; SAC, Cleveland, to Director, May 11, 1968, POCAM, HQ file, 157-8428-1060; SAC, Chicago, to Director, May 11, 1968, POCAM, HQ file, 157-8428-1062; Daily Summaries, May 15, 1968, Southern Caravan (III), Box 35E; SAC, Savannah, to Director, May 12, 1968, POCAM, HQ file, 157-8428-1023.

55. Detroit to Director, May 13, 1968, POCAM, HQ file, 157-8428-1675. The basic sequence of events came from an FBI source who was caught up in the police riot. See especially Cleveland to Director, May 15, 1968, POCAM, HQ file, 157-8428-1447.

56. James A. Madison to Roger W. Wilkins, May 14, 1968, Special Report for the Director, "PPC—Daily Log," Box 35E, Ramsey Clark Papers, LBJ Library. For the FBI report on the Madison interview, see Detroit to Director, May 14, 1968, POCAM, HQ file, 157-8428-1321.

57. Seattle to Director, May 16, 1968, POCAM, HQ file, 157-8428-1462.

58. The "Detroit Incident" attracts attention because of all the caravans destined for the nation's capital, this was the only one that experienced serious vio-

lence. The major Detroit newspapers were on strike at the time of the Cobo Hall incident, making it impossible to examine coverage of the violence by nonpartisan sources. Although the HSCA was interested in examining the FBI's Detroit field office files on this matter, its requests for records ran into a stone wall. The FBI explained that although it wanted to cooperate, the Detroit file 100-34655 (COINTELPRO/BNHG) was reported missing since May 7, 1976. See Detroit to Director, June 29, 1978, HQ file, Documents to the House Select Committee on Assassinations (hereafter cited as FBI Docs. to HSCA), 62-117290-946.

59. Detroit to Director, May 14, 1968, POCAM, HQ file, 157-8428-1675; FBI, TAY, May 15, 1968, POCAM, HQ file, 157-8428-1204; Moore to Sullivan, May 16, 1968, POCAM, HQ file, 157-8428-1384; Cleveland to Director, May 15, 1968, POCAM, HQ file, 157-8428-1447; FBI, TAY, May 15, 1968, POCAM, HQ file, 157-8428-1204.

60. Madison to Wilkins, May 14, 1968, "PPC—Daily Log," Ramsey Clark Papers, Box 35E, LBJ Library.

61. *Cleveland Plain Dealer*, May 14, 1968, p. 15; *Cleveland Press*, May 14, 1968, C-6; Los Angeles to Director, May 17, 1968, POCAM, HQ file, 157-8428-1512; Albuquerque to Director, May 21, 1968, POCAM, HQ file, 157-8428-1560; St. Louis, Letterhead Memorandum (LHM), May 21, 1968, POCAM, HQ file, 157-8428-1505; SAC, Butte, to Director, May 21, 1968, POCAM, HQ file, 157-8428-1565; Milwaukee, to Director, May 21, 1968, POCAM, HQ file, 157-8428-1513; Pittsburgh, to Director, May 17, 1968, POCAM, HQ file, 157-8428-1597; Detroit to Director, May 24, 1968, POCAM, HQ file, 157-8428-1661; Pittsburgh, LHM, May 23, 1968, HQ file, 157-8428-1643.

Chapter Five

1. Ralph D. Abernathy, *And the Walls Came Tumbling Down* (New York: Harper & Row, 1989), p. 499; Tom Offenburger to Levison, April 19, 1968, 111180-9-1645, pp. 5, 8; Charles Fager, *Uncertain Resurrection: The Poor People's Washington Campaign* (Grand Rapids, MI: William B. Eerdmans, 1969), p. 19. According to Rev. Billy Kyles, naming the encampment "Resurrection City" was related to the shattering and emotion-laden events in Memphis. King's agonizing over the March 28 violence and over his decision to return to Memphis, his death, and the subsequent victory of the sanitation workers were analogized into a version of Christ's Passion by a group of ministers in Atlanta several days after the assassination. The parallels between the last days of these crusaders for the poor and powerless, Kyles recalled, were too compelling to resist: the suffering and soul-searching (Gethsemane), death (Calvary or the crucifixion), and resurrection, wherein death was not a defeat; it was a victory. See Rev. Billy Kyles Interview, July 30, 1968, Tape 261, pp. 3–4, Memphis Sanitation Strike Archives, Brister Library, Memphis State University Archives (hereafter cited to as MSU Archives).

2. Paul Good, "No Man Can Fill Dr. King's Shoes—But Abernathy Tries," *New York Times Magazine*, May 26, 1968, pp. 91, 94.

3. All the above quotes are from UPI reporters covering Abernathy during his first six weeks as the new SCLC president. See FBI, Washington Spring Project, "Newsclippings," HQ file, section 3, pp. 1–4.

4. Good, "No Man Can Fill Dr. King's Shoes—But Abernathy Tries," pp. 96–97; Offenburger to Levison, April 19, 1968, 100-111180-9-1645.

5. Kevin T. Maroney to Ramsey Clark, April 15, 1968, James Gaither Papers, Presidential Task Force, "Poor People's March," Box 36, Lyndon Baines Johnson Library (hereafter cited as James Gaither Papers, Box 36, LBJ Library); Matt Nimetz, "Minutes: Washington, D.C. Riot and Future Planning," May 9, 1968, James Gaither Papers, Box 36, LBJ Library; *Washington Post*, May 7, 1968, A–4; *New York Times*, May 7, 1968; *Washington Daily News*, May 3, 1968, p. 19; Ben W. Gilbert, *Ten Blocks from the White House: Anatomy of the Washington Riots of 1968* (New York: Praeger, 1968), pp. 1–3.

6. Nimetz to Warren Christopher, April 18, 1968, James Gaither Papers, Box 36, LBJ Library; Ramsey Clark interview with Harri Baker, June 3, 1969, Ramsey Clark Oral History Collection, LBJ Library, p. 17; Nimetz to Joseph Califano, April 24, 1968, James Gaither Papers, Box 36, LBJ Library.

7. Richard Harris, *Justice: The Crisis of Law, Order, and Freedom in America* (New York: Avon Books, 1969), pp. 15, 56; Ramsey Clark interview with Harri Baker, June 3, 1969, Ramsey Clark Oral History Collection, LBJ Library; Nimetz to Califano, May 16, 1968, White House Aides Files, James Gaither Papers: "Riots 1968—Dr. King," Box 36, LBJ Library.

8. Nimetz, "Minutes, Washington, D.C. Riot and Future Planning," May 7, 1968, James Gaither Papers, Box 36, LBJ Library; Harris, *Justice*, p. 15; for Clark's testimony before the Senate, see *Committee Conference on Problems Involved in the Poor People's March on Washington, D.C.*, Committee on Government Operations, Permanent Subcommittee on Investigations, U.S. Senate, 90th Congress, 2nd session, pp. 53–56, 60–76; *Washington Post*, May 8, 1968, A-1.

9. Kenneth O'Reilly, *"Racial Matters": The FBI's Secret File on Black America, 1960–1972* (New York: Free Press, 1989), p. 266; Cartha D. "Deke" DeLoach, *Hoover's FBI: The Inside Story by Hoover's Trusted Lieutenant* (Washington, DC: Regnery Publishing, 1995), p. 222.

10. Andrew Young interview with Kathy Shannon, July 7, 1968, Washington, D.C., Ralph Bunche Oral History Collection; Anthony Henry interview with Kathy Shannon, July 15, 1968, Washington, D.C., Ralph Bunche Oral History Collection.

11. Abernathy, *And the Walls Came Tumbling Down*, p. 502.

12. Ibid., p. 504.

13. Offenburger to Stanley Levison, April 19, 1968, 100-111180-9-645, p. 7; Anthony Henry interview with Kathy Shannon, July 15, 1968, Washington, D.C., Ralph Bunche Oral History Collection.

14. *The Washington Evening Star*, May 14, 1968; Fager, *Uncertain Resurrection*, pp. 35–36; Abernathy, *And the Walls Came Tumbling Down*, p. 504.

15. John Wiebenson, "Planner's Notebook: Planning and Using Resurrection City," *Journal of the American Institute of Planners* 35 (1968), pp. 406–407; John C. Rutherford interview with Kathy Shannon, July 4, 1968, Washington, D.C., Ralph Bunche Oral History Collection; Abernathy, *And the Walls Came Tumbling Down*, pp. 512–513; *The Worker*, May 26, 1968; Charlayne A. Hunter, "On the Case in Resurrection City," *Trans-action* 7 (October 1968), p. 49.

16. *Washington Editor and Publisher*, June 1, 1968, p. 9; Fager, *Uncertain Resurrection*, pp. 36–37; *The Washington Evening Star*, May 14, 1968, A-4.

17. *Washington Editor and Publisher*, June 1, 1968, p. 9; Fager, *Uncertain Resurrection*, pp. 42–47.

18. *Washington Daily News*, May 20, 1968, p. 5; *The Washington Evening Star*, May 20, 1968, p. 5; *The Washington Evening Star*, May 18, 1968, A-3; *Washington Post*, May 18, 19, 1968, pp. A-1, A-2; Andy Young interview with Kathy Shannon, July 7, 1968, Ralph Bunche Oral History Collection.

19. Andy Levison to Stanley and Bea Levison, May 15, 1968, 100-111180-9-1666; Andy Levison to Stanley and Bea Levison, May 10, 1968, 100-111180-9-1660.

20. Fager, *Uncertain Resurrection*, pp. 50–51; *The Washington Evening Star*, May 20 and 23, 1968, pp. A-1 and A-1; Memo for Attorney General, May 22, 1968, "PPC—Civil Rights Daily Log," Ramsey Clark Papers, Box 35D, LBJ Library; *Washington Post*, February 16, 1968, A-4; *Washington Post*, June 11, 1968; Memo for Attorney General, May 22, 1968, "PPC—Civil Rights Daily Log," Ramsey Clark Papers, Box 35D, LBJ Library; Memos to Attorney General, May 21, 27, and 28, "PPC—Civil Rights Daily Log," Ramsey Clark Papers, Box 35D, LBJ Library.

21. Ramsey Clark interview with Harri Baker, March 21, 1969, Falls Church, Virginia, Ramsey Clark Oral History Collection, LBJ Library; Memo to Attorney General, May 22, 1968, "PPC—Civil Rights Daily Log," Ramsey Clark Papers, Box 35D, LBJ Library.

22. Memo from Fred G. Folsom for the Attorney General, May 23, 1968, "PPC—Civil Rights Daily Log," Ramsey Clark Papers, Box 35D, LBJ Library; Roger Wilkins, *A Man's Life* (New York: Simon & Schuster, 1982), p. 221; Memo to Attorney General, "PPC—Civil Rights Daily Log," Ramsey Clark Papers, Box 35D, LBJ Library.

23. *Washington Daily News*, May 29 and June 17, 1968.

24. Wiebenson, "Planning and Using Resurrection City," p. 407; Wilkins, *A Man's Life*, p. 220; *Washington Daily News*, June 17, 1968, p. 7.

25. John C. Rutherford interview with Kathy Shannon, July 4, 1968, Washington, D.C., Ralph Bunche Oral History Collection. In time, the SCLC staff was able to get a handle on the food situation. See *Washington Post*, June 5, 1968, A-4, and *Washington Daily News*, June 17, 1969, p. 7. See also Nimetz to Califano, May 23, 1968, James Gaither Papers, Box 36, LBJ Library.

26. Roger Wilkins memo to Attorney General, May 28, 1968, "Poor People's Campaign—CRS Daily Log," Ramsey Clark Papers, Box 35E, LBJ Library (hereafter cited as "PPC—CRS Daily Log"); Marian Logan to Stanley Levison, 100-111180-9-1693a. According to FBI sources, as late as June 13 there were between 60 to 80 SCLC staff members and their families registered at the Pitts Motel. The SCLC booked 50 of the motel's 70 rooms for seven weeks. See SAC, WFO, to Director, June 13, 1968, HQ file, POCAM, 157-8428-2237, and *Washington Daily News*, June 17, 1968, A-2, 3.

27. SAC, WFO, to Director, May 21, 1968, HQ file, POCAM, 157-8428-1713; *Washington Post*, May 23, 1968, A-1.

28. John C. Rutherford interview with Kathy Shannon, July 4, 1968, Washington, D.C., Ralph Bunche Oral History Collection; *Washington Daily News*, May 22, 1968, p. 5; Fager, *Uncertain Resurrection*, pp. 51–53; Abernathy, *And the Walls Came Tumbling Down*, pp. 514–515.

29. Bill Rutherford to Stanley Levison, June 2, 1968, 100-111180-9-1689a; Barbara A. Reynolds, *Jesse Jackson: The Man, the Movement, the Myth* (Chicago: Nelson-Hall, 1975), pp. 86, 315.

30. Reynolds, *Jesse Jackson*, pp. 81–95; Abernathy, *And the Walls Came Tumbling Down*, pp. 448–450. Bill Rutherford to Stanley Rutherford, June 2, 1968, 100-111180-9-1689a; Marshall Frady, *Jesse: The Life and Pilgrimage of Jesse Jackson* (New York: Random House, 1996), pp. 228–239. See Chapter 4 for the circumstances accounting for Marrell McCullough's presence on the balcony at the time King was shot.

31. Fager, *Uncertain Resurrection*, p. 56; *New York Times*, June 1, 1968, p. 19.

32. Robert J. Goldstein, *Political Repression in Modern America: From 1860 to the Present* (Cambridge, MA: Schenkman, 1978), pp. 429–545; O'Reilly, "Racial Matters," pp. 261–265.

33. Memo to Attorney General, May 22, 1968, "PPC—CRS Daily Log," Ramsey Clark Papers, Box 35D, LBJ Library; Moore to Sullivan, May 16, 1968, HQ file, POCAM, 157-8428-1456; SAC, WFO, to Director, May 15, 1968, HQ file, POCAM, 157-8428-1595. For summaries and logs, the intelligence by-product of this massive stake-out, see "PPC—CRS Daily Log," Ramsey Clark Papers, Box 35E, LBJ Library.

34. The covert agenda was the FBI's COINTELPRO disruption campaign against the PPC. Hoover never reported to attorneys general any program implemented under a COINTELPRO caption, and the PPC was no exception. See *FBI Counterintelligence Programs*, Hearing, Committee on the Judiciary, House of Representatives, 93rd Congress, 2nd session (November 24, 1974), p. 12

35. Director to SAC, Albany [All Offices], May 24 and May 27, 1968, HQ file, POCAM, 157-8428-1524 and 157-8428-1851.

36. Moore to Sullivan, May 27, 1968, HQ file, POCAM, 157-8428-1752; SAC, WFO, to Director, June 3, 1968, POCAM, HQ file, 157-8428-1980; SAC, WFO, to Director, June 5, 1968, POCAM, HQ file, 157-8428-2119.

37. SAC, WFO, to Director, May 24, 1968, POCAM, HQ file, 157-8428-1742. Some FBI reports contained exact arrival time and departure time for SCLC staff using Washington's National Airport. For this and other relevant examples of what may have been intercepted phone conversations, see, SAC, WFO, to Director, May 29, 1968, POCAM, HQ file, 157-8428-1925; SAC, WFO, to Director, June 4, 1968, POCAM, HQ file, 157-8428-2065; and SAC, WFO, to Director, June 7, 1968, POCAM, HQ file, 157-8428-2190.

38. SAC, WFO, to Director, POCAM, HQ file, 157-8428-2543.

39. FBI typology makes a distinction between a human "source" and an "informant." A source is someone in a position to have logical access to information and is usually not paid, e.g., employers, landlords, bankers, college and university security heads and administrators, and so forth. An informant, or more accurately a "symbol informant," is in effect a part-time FBI employee who has passed a period of probation, usually about six months, and who is identified in FBI communications by an arbitrary symbol rather than a name. The symbol consists of the FBI's abbreviation for the field office for which the operative informs, as BH for

Birmingham, plus the arbitrary four-digit number. An FBI informant or informer supplies information on a regular basis and is usually paid.

40. Director to SAC, WFO, May 8, 1968, POCAM, HQ file, 157-8428-883; Director to SAC, WFO, May 21, 1968, POCAM, HQ file, 157-8428-1427; Cleveland to Director, May 29, 1968, POCAM, HQ file, 157-8428-1940.

41. *Final Report of the Senate Select Committee to Study Governmental Operations With Respect to Intelligence Activities* (hereafter cited as the *Church Committee Report),* Vol. III, pp. 492–493; SA [deleted] to SAC, WFO, May 16, 1968, POCAM, HQ file, 157-8428-1430; SA [deleted] to SAC, WFO, March 31, 1968, POCAM, WFO file, 157-1395-547B.

42. For a useful study of military surveillance of civilians in the 1960s, see *Church Committee Report,* Vol. III, pp. 785–834. See also Frank J. Donner, The *Age of Surveillance: The Aims and Methods of America's Political Intelligence System* (New York: Alfred A. Knopf, 1980), pp. 294–305. For the Yarborough quote, see ibid., p. 302.

43. For more on "Garden Plot," see Goldstein, *Political Repression in Modern America,* p. 459.

44. See statement of Ralph H. Stein in *Federal Data Banks, Computers, and the Bill of Rights,* Hearings, Committee on the Judiciary, U.S. Senate, 92nd Congress, 1st session, Part I, p. 272 (hereafter cited as *Federal Data Banks).*

45. *Federal Data Banks,* p. 272; *New York Times,* January 18, 1972; *Church Committee Report,* Vol. 3, pp. 807–808; Robert H. Taylor (assistant deputy director of Presidential Protection Division, U.S. Secret Service) to Jim Jones and Joseph Califano, May 29, 1968, James Gaither Papers, Box 36, LBJ Library.

46. Frank J. Donner, *Protectors of Privilege: Red Squads and Police Repression in Urban America* (Berkeley: University of California Press, 1990), p. 334; *Federal Data Banks,* pp. 197–198.

47. According to a Senate committee report, by the fall of 1968 the army had assigned more counterintelligence agents to monitor domestic targets than those covering "matters of counter-intelligence interests emanating from other areas of the world, including Southeast Asia." See Donner, *The Age of Surveillance,* p. 295.

48. *Federal Data Banks,* p. 198; Senate Committee on the Judiciary, *Military Surveillance,* 93rd Congress, 2nd session (hereafter cited as *Military Surveillance),* pp. 253, 1469, 1471; *Federal Data Banks,* p. 274; for Yarborough's testimony, see Senate Committee on Government Operations, Permanent Subcommittee on Investigations Involved in the Poor People's March on Washington, D.C., report on hearings, p. 57; DeLoach to Tolson, May 7, 1968, POCAM, HQ file, 157-8428-1586.

49. *Washington Post,* May 23, 1968; *New York Times,* June 2, 1968; Tom Kahn, "Why the Poor People's Campaign Failed," *Commentary* (September 1968), pp. 52–54.

50. *The Washington Evening Star,* May 22, 1968, A-7; *New York Times,* June 3, 1968; Andy Young to Stanley Levison, June 4, 1968, 100-11118-9-1691; *The Washington Evening Star,* June 5, 1968, C–1. For Rustin's early programmatic ideas about the PPC, see Bayard Rustin, *Down the Line: Collected Writings of Bayard Rustin* (Chicago: Quadrangle Books, 1971), pp. 202–205.

51. *The Washington Evening Star,* June 5, 1968, C-1; Abernathy to Stanley Levison, June 3, 1968, 100-111180-9-1690a; Young to Stanley Levison, June 4, 1968, 100-111180-9-1691; *The Washington Evening Star,* June 5, 1968, C-1; Kahn, "Why the Poor People's Campaign Failed," p. 54.

52. When the PPC issued its immediate and long-range demands to the federal agencies and Congress, the 90-odd demands took up two pages in Washington papers. See *Washington Post*, June 13, 1968, E-1, E-2.

53. Ben Franklin, "The Poor Campaign in Trouble," *New York Times*, June 17, 1968, E-3; William Raspberry, "Campaign Nearing Poor People's Fiasco," *Washington Post*, June 9, 1968, D-1.

54. *The Washington Evening Star*, June 16, 1968, A-1; *New York Times*, June 16, 1968; Adam Fairclough, *To Redeem the Soul of America: The Southern Christian Leadership Conference and Martin Luther King, Jr.* (Athens: University of Georgia Press, 1978), p. 356; David J. Garrow, *Bearing the Cross: Martin Luther King Jr., and the Southern Christian Leadership Conference* (New York: William Morrow, 1986), pp. 576–578.

55. Phone interview with Roger Wilkins, September 5, 1992; Wilkins, *A Man's Life*, p. 220; *New York Times*, June 14, 16, 1968; *The Washington Evening Star*, June 6, 1968, A-3; Lewis Bernstein memo to the Attorney General, May 24, 1968, Ramsey Clark Papers, Box 35D, LBJ Library; Robert B. Hummel, memo to the Attorney General, May 22, 1968, Ramsey Clark Papers, Box 35D, LBJ Library.

56. Director to SAC, WFO, June 18, 1968, POCAM, HQ file, 157-8428-2378; "Murphy Report," p. 136.

57. Moore to Sullivan, May 24, 1968, POCAM, HQ file, 157-8428-1818, is a fair representation of the bureau's dissemination pattern during project POCAM.

58. Brennan to Sullivan, May 27, 1968, POCAM, HQ file, 157-8428-1950; FBI Liaison (White House) to Stegall, May 27, 1968, POCAM, HQ file, 157-8428-1766; FBI Liaison (White House) to Stegall, June 21, 1968, POCAM, HQ file, 157-8428-2629; O'Reilly, "*Racial Matters*," pp. 262–263.

59. The heavy emphasis in the FBI reports on group and interracial sex pandered to the sort of sexual conduct that fascinated Hoover. See David J. Garrow, *The FBI and Martin Luther King, Jr.: From "Solo" to Memphis* (New York: W. W. Norton, 1981), p. 165.

60. A useful summary of the Hooverized version of Resurrection City can be found in a six-page report. See Moore to Sullivan, June 13, 1968, Hoover Confidential and Official file (hereafter cited as C & O file), 100-438794-NR. See also Moore to Sullivan, May 24, 1968, POCAM, HQ file, 157-8428-1818; Moore to Sullivan, May 25, 1968, POCAM, HQ file, 157-8428-1820; Moore to Sullivan, May 29, 1968, POCAM, HQ file, 157-8428-1859; and Moore to Sullivan, June 14, 1968, POCAM, HQ file, 157-8428-2479. For rumors about black terrorism, see Director to SACs, Chicago and Minneapolis, June 10, 1968, POCAM, HQ file, 157-8428-2037; SAC, WFO, to Director, SACs Chicago and Minneapolis, June 11, 1968, POCAM, HQ file, 8428-2213.

61. Director to SAC, Albany [All Continental Offices], May 27, 1968, POCAM, HQ file, 157-8428-1851.

62. Moore to Sullivan, June 18, 1968, POCAM, HQ file, 157-8428-2551. See Plan for Solidarity Day in "Poor People's March" (Solidarity Day), Ramsey Clark Papers, Box 96, LBJ Library.

63. *Washington Post*, June 18, 21, 1968; SAC, WFO, to Director, June 19, 1968, POCAM, HQ file, 157-8428-2619; *The Washington Evening Star*, June 19, 1968, B-1; Arthur Schlesinger, Jr., *Robert Kennedy and His Times* (New York: Ballantine Books,

1978), p. 378; Fager, *Uncertain Resurrection*, p. 76; SAC, WFO, to Director, June 19, 1968, POCAM, HQ file, 157-8428-2619.

64. "Poor People's Campaign—Arrest Statistics," Ramsey Clark Papers, Box 96, LBJ Library.

65. Hoover to James R. Jones (special assistant to the president), June 21, 1968, POCAM, HQ file, 157-8428-2629; "PPC—CRS Daily Log," June 10, 1968, Box 35E, Ramsey Clark Papers, LBJ Library, p. 4; Fager, *Uncertain Resurrection*, p. 86; *Washington Daily News*, June 24, 1968.

66. Hunter, "On the Case in Resurrection City," pp. 50, 53; *The Washington Evening Star*, June 16, 1968, A-1; Abernathy, *And the Walls Came Tumbling Down*, p. 531; Nick Kotz, *Let Them Eat Promises: The Politics of Hunger in America* (Englewood Cliffs, NJ: Prentice-Hall, 1969), pp. 115, 151–154, 168.

67. Kotz, *Let Them Eat Promises*, pp. 171–173; *The Washington Evening Star*, May 31, 1968, A-1; *Washington Post*, May 31, 1968.

68. See Harris survey, *Chicago Daily News*, June 10, 1968; James J. Kilpatrick, "Resurrection City—A Vast Amount of Sham," *The Washington Sunday Star*, June 9, 1968, E-4; Drew Pearson and Jack Anderson, "It's Time for the Poor to Go Home," *Washington Post*, June 15, 1968, D-13; William Raspberry, "Campaign Nearing Poor People's Fiasco," *Washington Post*, June 9, 1968, D-1.

69. William Rutherford to Stanley Levison, June 14, 1968, 100-111180-9-1701.

70. "PPC—CRS Daily Log," June 12–17, 1968, Box 35E, Ramsey Clark Papers, LBJ Library; Fager, *Uncertain Resurrection*, pp. 88–93; *The Washington Evening Star*, June 12, 1968, A-1.

71. "PPC—CRS Daily Log," June 21, 22, 1968, Box 35E, Ramsey Clark Papers, LBJ Library; *The Washington Evening Star*, June 8, 1968, A-1; *The Washington Evening Star*, June 9, 1968, B-1; Fager, *Uncertain Resurrection*, p. 101; *The Washington Evening Star*, June 26, 1968, B-3.

72. "PPC—CRS Daily Log," June 22, 1968, Box 35E, Ramsey Clark Papers, LBJ Library, pp. 7–8; ibid., June 8, 13, 17, and 18, 1968; Moore to Sullivan, June 19, 1968, POCAM, HQ file, 157-8428-2529; *The Washington Evening Star*, June 17, 1968, A-6.

73. "PPC—CRS Daily Log," June 21, 1968, Box 35E, Ramsey Clark Papers, LBJ Library, pp. 1, 4, and 5; ibid., June 22, 1968, pp. 7–8; ibid., pp. 2–3; Fager, *Uncertain Resurrection*, p. 107.

74. Coretta Scott King to Stanley Levison, June 21, 1968, 100-111180-9-170B; George Goodman to Stanley Levison, June 27, 1968, 100-111180-91714a; Fager, *Uncertain Resurrection*, p. 100; *Washington Daily News*, June 15, 1968, p. 3; "PPC—CRS Daily Log," June 22, 1968, Box 35E, Ramsey Clark Papers, LBJ Library, p. 6; *Washington Daily News*, June 25, 1968, p. 5.

75. For comments on security at Resurrection City, see John C. Rutherford interview with Kathy Shannon, July 4, 1968, Washington, D.C., Ralph Bunche Oral History Collection; Moore to Sullivan, June 19, 1968, POCAM, HQ file, 157-8428-2529.

76. For Sullivan's comments, see *Church Committee Hearings*: Vol. III, p. 7; Ward Churchill and Jim Vander Wall, *The COINTELPRO Papers: Documents from the FBI's War Against Dissent in the United States* (Boston: South End Press, 1990), p. 33.

77. For some examples of these studies, see Athan Theoharis, *Spying on Americans: Political Surveillance from Hoover to the Houston Plan* (Philadelphia: Temple University Press, 1978); Kenneth O'Reilly, *Hoover and the Un-Americans: The FBI,*

HUAC, and the Red Menace (Philadelphia: Temple University Press, 1983); Donner, *The Age of Surveillance*; Garrow, *The FBI and Martin Luther King, Jr.*

78. Donner, *Protectors of Privilege*, pp. 334–342. In 1974 the Intelligence Division of the Metropolitan Police Department destroyed all of its red squad records. See ibid., p. 343. "PPC—CRS Daily Logs," June 10, 1968, Box 35E, Ramsey Clark Papers, LBJ Library, p. 4.

79. Andy Young to Stanley Levison, June 15, 1968, 100-111180-9-1702a; (Unknown) to Stanley Levison, June 29, 1968, 100-111180-9-1716a; *Washington Post*, June 21, 22, 1968, D-1, D-13; Fager, *Uncertain Resurrection*, p. 113; "PPC—CRS Daily Log," Lawrence K. Bailey to Duty Office file, June 18, 1968, Box 35E, Ramsey Clark Papers, LBJ Library.

80. A useful accounting of these negotiations can be found in Carl Bernstein, "Long Discussion Preceded March's Nonviolent Arrests," *Washington Post*, June 25, 1968. Bernstein's story errs in one regard where he attributed Wilkins's role to Sterling Tucker. Phone interview with Wilkins, September 5, 1991; Wilkins, *A Man's Life*, pp. 221–223; "PPC—CRS Daily Log," June 23, 1968, Box 35E, Ramsey Clark Papers, LBJ Library, p. 4.

81. Fager, *Uncertain Resurrection*, p. 114; *New York Times*, June 25, 1968; *The Washington Evening Star*, June 24, 1968, A-1.

82. Abernathy, *And the Walls Came Tumbling Down*, pp. 533–539; phone interview with Wilkins, September 5, 1991; *The Washington Evening Star*, June 25, 1968, B-1; *New York Times*, June 25, 1968.

83. *The Washington Evening Star*, June 25, 1968, B-1; *New York Times*, June 25, 1968.

84. *Soul Force*, August 15, 1968, pp. 3, 15; *New York Times*, June 30, 1968; Abernathy, *And the Walls Came Tumbling Down*, p. 529; John E. Schwarz, *America's Hidden Success: A Reassessment of Twenty Years of Public Policy* (New York: W. W. Norton, 1987), pp. 44–46.

85. *Washington Post*, August 14, 1968; *Washington Daily News*, June 27, 1968, p. 5; *The Washington Sunday Star*, July 28, 1968, B-3; Jack Greenberg, *Crusaders in the Courts: How a Dedicated Band of Lawyers Fought for the Civil Rights Revolution* (New York: Basic Books, 1994), p. 433.

Conclusion

1. Robert Weisbrot, *Freedom Bound: A History of America's Civil Rights Movement* (New York: Penguin Books, 1990), p. 275.

2. Andrew Young, *An Easy Burden: The Civil Rights Movement and the Transformation of America* (New York: HarperCollins, 1996), p. 472.

3. "Eliminate" was the FBI's language. See SAC, Memphis, to Director, November 15, 1968, Invaders, MFO file, 157-1067-579; Director to SAC, Memphis, August 23, 1968, Invaders, HQ file, 157-8460-4. For a detailed treatment of the FBI's campaign against the Invaders, see Gerald D. McKnight, "A Harvest of Hate: The FBI's War Against Black Youth—Domestic Intelligence in Memphis, Tennessee," *The South Atlantic Quarterly* (Winter 1987).

4. Director to SAC, Memphis, March 27, 1969, Invaders, HQ file, 157-8460-20; J. Walter Yeagley to Director, FBI, March 10, 1970, Invaders, MFO, 157-1067-1795A. The last entry in the Invaders file is a one-page Letterhead Memorandum dated July 1, 1971.

Selected Bibliography

Books

Abernathy, Ralph D. *And the Walls Came Tumbling Down.* New York: Harper & Row, 1989.

Beifuss, Joan T. *At the River I Stand: Memphis, 1968 Strike, and Martin Luther King.* Memphis: B & W Books, 1985.

Bishop, Jim. *The Days of Martin Luther King, Jr.* New York: G. P. Putnam's Sons, 1971.

Branch, Taylor. *Parting the Waters: America in the King Years, 1954–1963.* New York: Simon & Schuster, 1988.

Brink, William, and Louis Harris. *Black and White: A Study of U.S. Racial Attitudes Today.* New York: Simon & Schuster, 1967.

Churchill, Ward, and Jim Vander Wall. *The COINTELPRO Papers: Documents from the FBI's War Against Dissent in the United States.* Boston: South End Press, 1990.

DeLoach, Cartha "Deke." *Hoover's FBI: The Inside Story by Hoover's Trusted Lieutenant.* Washington, DC: Regnery Publishing, 1995.

Donner, Frank J. *The Age of Surveillance: The Aims and Methods of America's Political Intelligence System.* New York: Alfred A. Knopf, 1980.

_____. *Protectors of Privilege: Red Squads and Public Repression in Urban America.* Berkeley and Los Angeles: University of California Press, 1990.

Eliff, John T. *The Reform of the FBI Intelligence Operations.* Princeton, NJ: Princeton University Press, 1979.

Fager, Charles. *Uncertain Resurrection: The Poor People's Washington Campaign.* Grand Rapids, MI: William B. Eerdmans, 1969.

Fairclough, Adam. *To Redeem the Soul of America: The Southern Christian Leadership Conference and Martin Luther King, Jr.* Athens: University of Georgia Press, 1978.

Foner, Eric. *A Short History of Reconstruction, 1863–1888.* New York: Harper & Row, 1980

Foreman, James. *The Making of a Black Revolutionary.* New York: Macmillan, 1972.

Frady, Michael. *Jesse: The Life and Pilgrimage of Jesse Jackson.* New York: Random House, 1996.

Frank, Gerold. *An American Death: The True Story of the Assassination of Martin Luther King Jr., and the Greatest Manhunt in Our Time.* New York: Doubleday, 1972.

Garrow, David J. *The FBI and Martin Luther King, Jr.: From "Solo" to Memphis.* New York: W. W. Norton, 1981.

_____. *Bearing the Cross: Martin Luther King Jr., and the Southern Christian Leadership Conference.* New York: William Morrow, 1986.

_____. "Martin Luther King, Jr., and the Spirit of Leadership." In Peter J. Albert and Ronald Hoffman, eds., *We Shall Overcome: Martin Luther King, Jr., and the Black Freedom Struggle.* New York: Pantheon Books, 1990.

Gilbert, Ben. *Ten Blocks from the White House: Anatomy of the Washington Riots of 1968.* New York: Praeger, 1968.

Goldstein, Robert J. *Political Repression in Modern America: From 1860 to the Present.* Cambridge, MA: Schenkman, 1978.

Greenberg, Jack. *Crusaders in the Courts: How a Dedicated Band of Lawyers Fought for the Civil Rights Revolution.* New York: Basic Books, 1994.

Hallin, Daniel. *The "Uncensored" War: The Media and Vietnam.* New York: Oxford University Press, 1986.

Harris, Richard. *Justice: The Crisis of Law, Order, and Freedom in America.* New York: Avon Books, 1969.

Huggins, Nathan I. "Commentary." In Peter J. Albert and Ronald Hoffman, eds., *We Shall Overcome: Martin Luther King, Jr., and the Black Freedom Struggle.* New York: Pantheon Books, 1990.

Jaffe, Harry S., and Tom Sherwood. *Dream City: Race, Power, and the Decline of Washington, D.C.* New York: Simon & Schuster, 1994.

Keller, William W. *The Liberals and J. Edgar Hoover: Rise and Fall of a Domestic Intelligence State.* Princeton, NJ: Princeton University Press, 1989.

King, Martin Luther, Jr. *Why We Can't Wait.* New York: New American Library, 1964.

King, Martin Luther, Sr., with Clayton Riley. *Daddy King: An Autobiography.* New York: William Morrow, 1980.

Kirchheimer, Otto. *Political Justice: The Use of Legal Procedure for Political Ends.* Princeton, NJ: Princeton University Press, 1961.

Kotz, Nick. *Let Them Eat Promises: The Politics of Hunger in America.* Englewood Cliffs, NJ: Prentice-Hall, 1969.

Kotz, Nick, and Mary Lynn Kotz. *A Passion for Equality: George Wiley and the Movement.* New York: W. W. Norton, 1977.

Lane, Mark, and Dick Gregory. *Murder in Memphis: The FBI and the Assassination of Martin Luther King.* New York: Thunder's Mouth Press, 1993.

Lipset, Seymour M., and Philip G. Altback, eds. *Students in Revolt.* Boston: Houghton Mifflin, 1969.

Manchester, William. *The Death of a President: November 20–November 25, 1963.* New York: Harper & Row, 1967.

Matusow, Allen J. *The Unravelling of America: A History of Liberalism in the 1960s.* New York: Harper & Row, 1984.

McPherson, Harry C. *A Political Education.* Boston: Little, Brown, 1972.

Melanson, Philip H. *The Murkin Conspiracy: An Investigation into the Assassination of Dr. Martin Luther King, Jr.* New York: Praeger, 1989.

Miller, William D. *Mr. Crump of Memphis.* Baton Rouge: Louisiana State University Press, 1964.

Neier, Aryeh. "Dissemination of Derogatory Information: A Weapon Against Crime or Part of the Problem?" In Pat Watters and Stephen Gillers, eds., *Investigating the FBI.* New York: Ballantine Books, 1973.

Oates, Stephen B. *Let the Trumpet Sound: The Life of Martin Luther King, Jr.* New York: Harper & Row, 1982.

O'Reilly, Kenneth. *Hoover and the Un-Americans; The FBI, HUAC, the Red Menace.* Philadelphia: Temple University Press, 1983.

_____. *"Racial Matters:" The FBI's Secret File on Black America, 1960–1972.* New York: Free Press, 1989.

Piven, Frances F., and Richard Cloward. *Poor People's Movements: Why They Succeed, How They Fail.* New York: Pantheon Books, 1979.

Powers, Richard G. *Secrecy and Power: The Life of J. Edgar Hoover.* New York: Free Press, 1987.

Reynolds, Barbara A. *Jesse Jackson: The Man, the Movement, the Myth.* Chicago: Nelson-Hall, 1975.

Rowan, Carl. *Breaking Barriers: A Memoir.* Boston: Little, Brown, 1991.

Rustin, Bayard. *Down the Line: Collected Writings of Bayard Rustin.* Chicago: Quadrangle Books, 1971.

Schlesinger, Arthur, Jr. *Robert Kennedy and His Times.* New York: Ballantine Books, 1978.

Schwarz, John E. *America's Hidden Success: A Reassessment of Twenty Years of Public Policy.* New York: W. W. Norton, 1983.

Sullivan, William C., with Bill Brown. *The Bureau: My Thirty Years in Hoover's FBI.* New York: W. W. Norton, 1979.

Theoharis, Athan G. *Spying on Americans: Political Surveillance from Hoover to the Huston Plan.* Philadelphia: Temple University Press, 1978.

Theoharis, Athan G., and John Cox. *The Boss: J. Edgar Hoover and the Great American Inquisition.* Philadelphia: Temple University Press, 1988.

Tucker, David M. *Black Pastors and Leaders: Memphis, 1819–1972.* Knoxville: University of Tennessee Press, 1980.

_____. *Memphis Since Crump: Bossism, Blacks, and Civil Reformers, 1948–1968.* Knoxville: University of Tennessee Press, 1980.

Washington, James M., ed. *A Testament of Hope: The Essential Writings of Martin Luther King, Jr.* San Francisco: HarperCollins, 1991.

Weisberg, Harold. *Whitewash IV: JFK Assassination Transcript.* Frederick, MD: Harold Weisberg Publishers, 1974.

Weisbrot, Robert. *Freedom Bound: A History of America's Civil Rights Movement.* New York: Penguin Press, 1990.

_____. *Martin Luther King: The Assassination.* New York: Carroll & Graf, 1993.

Wilkins, Roger. *A Man's Life.* New York: Simon & Schuster, 1982.

Young, Andrew. *An Easy Burden: The Civil Rights Movement and the Transformation of America.* New York: HarperCollins, 1996.

Zaroulis, Nancy, and Gerald Sullivan. *Who Spoke Up?: American Protest Against the War in Vietnam, 1963–1975.* New York: Holt, Rinehart, & Winston, 1984.

Articles

Abramovitz, Robert, et al. "Psychiatric Services to a Sustained Social Protest Campaign: An On-site Walk-in Clinic at Resurrection City." *The American Journal of Psychiatry* 125 (May 11, 1969).

Dinnerstein, Harvey. "The Face of Protest/1968." *Esquire* (December 1968).

"Domestic Intelligence Reform: A Court Order Against a Red Squad." *First Principles* 4 (October 1978).

Donner, Frank. "The Theory and Practice of American Political Intelligence." *The New York Review of Books* (April 22, 1971).

Fairclough, Adam. "Martin Luther King, Jr., and the War in Vietnam." *Phylon* 45 (Spring 1984).

Good, Paul. "No Man Can Fill Dr. King's Shoes—But Abernathy Tries." *New York Times Magazine* (May 26, 1968).

Halberstam, David. "The Second Coming of Martin Luther King." *Harper's* (December 1968).

_____. "The Man Who Ran Against Lyndon Johnson." *Harper's* (December 1968).

Harris, Lou. "The Racial Crisis: A Consensus." *Newsweek* (August 21, 1967).

Hunter, Charlayne A. "On the Case in Resurrection City." *Trans-action* 7 (October 1968).

Kahn, Tom. "Why the Poor People's Campaign Failed." *Commentary* (September 1968).

O'Reilly, Kenneth. "The FBI and the Politics of the Riots, 1964–1968." *Journal of American History* (June 1968).

Ridgeway, James. "Freak-out in Chicago." *The New Republic* (September 16, 1967).

Rothman, Robert. "Congress Clears King Holiday After Heated Debate." *Congressional Quarterly Weekly Report* 41(October–December 1983).

Wall, Robert. "Special Agent for the FBI." *New York Review of Books* (January 27, 1972).

Wiebenson, John. "Planner's Notebook: Planning and Using Resurrection City." *Journal of the American Institute of Planners* 35 (1968).

Government Documents and Reports

Congressional Record. 90th Cong., 2nd sess., 1968.

Congressional Record (Senate). 93rd Cong., 2nd sess., 1974.

U.S. Congress. Committee on the Judiciary. *Senate Hearings on Federal Data Banks, Computers, and the Bill of Rights.* 92nd Cong., 1st sess., 1971.

U.S. Congress. House Select Committee on Assassinations. *Investigation of the Assassination of Martin Luther King, Jr.* 95th Cong., 2nd sess., 1979.

U.S. Congress. Senate. Committee on Government Operations. Permanent Subcommittee on Investigations Involved in the Poor People's March on Washington, D.C. 90th Cong., 2nd sess., 1968.

U.S. Congress. Senate. Committee on the Judiciary. Subcommittee on Constitutional Rights. *FBI Counterintelligence Programs.* 93rd Cong., 2nd sess., 1974.

U.S. Congress. Senate. Select Committee to Study Government Operations with Respect to Intelligence Activities. *Final Report—Book II, Intelligence Activities and the Rights of Americans.* 94th Cong., 2nd sess., 1976.

U.S. Department of Justice. *Report of the Department of Justice Task Force to Review the FBI Martin Luther King, Jr., and Assassination Investigations.* January 11, 1977.

Files of the Federal Bureau of Investigation, U.S. Department of Justice

44-1574	Memphis Murkin FO file
44-2386	Atlanta Murkin FO File
44-38861	Main FBI HQ Murkin File (Murder of King)
62-117290	FBI Documents to the HSCA
89-43	JFK Main Assassination File, Dallas FO file
100-106670	Main FBI HQ Martin Luther King, Jr., File (including the Field Office Inventories)
100-11180-9	Stanley D. Levison (New York FO file including subfile 157–6–53)
100-158790	Main Bayard Rustin File
100-392452	Main Stanley D. Levison File
100-438794	Southern Christian Leadership Conference File
100-448006	COINTELPRO "Black Nationalist Hate Groups" File
105-82555	Main FBI HQ Oswald File
149-121	Threat to American Airlines and Dr. King Memphis, 4/1/68
157-1067	Invaders, Memphis FO File
157-1092	Memphis Sanitation Workers' Strike, FO File (including Marrell McCullough subfile)
157-1395	POCAM, Washington FO File
157-4689	Vista File
157-8428	POCAM, Washington HQ File
157-8460	Invaders, Washington HQ File
157-9146	Memphis Sanitation Workers' Strike, Washington HQ File
270-36-1980	U.S. Department of Justice File Report of the Office of Professional Responsibility to Review the FBI Martin Luther King, Jr., Security and Assassination Investigation (OPR Report).

Court Cases

Kendrick v. Chandler (No. 76-449), W. D. Tennessee, 1976.

Manuscripts

Clark, Ramsey. Papers. LBJ Library, Austin, Texas.
Gaither, James. Papers. Presidential Task Force, "Poor People's March." LBJ Library, Austin, Texas.

Oral Histories, Interviews, Other Documents

Bunche, Ralph. Oral History Collection. Moorland-Springarn Research Center, Howard University, Washington, DC.
Clark, Ramsey. Oral History Collection. LBJ Library, Austin, Texas.
McCullough, Marrell. Police file, City of Memphis Personnel Division Office, Memphis, Tennessee.

Memphis Sanitation Strike Archives. Brister Library, Memphis State University, Memphis, Tennessee.
Wilkins, Roger. Telephone conversation with author, September 5, 1992.

Newspapers

Birmingham News
Cleveland Plain Dealer
Cleveland Press
Los Angeles Herald-Examiner
Memphis Commercial Appeal
Memphis Press-Scimitar
Memphis Tri-State Defender
Miami Herald
Nashville Banner
New York Times
Soul Force
Washington Afro-American
Washington Daily News
Washington Evening Star
Washington Post
Washington (Sunday) Star
The Worker

Index

Abernathy, Ralph D., 66, 67, 92, 131
  arrest of, 138
  Committee of One Hundred and,
    108
  criticism of, 87
  demonstrations and, 64, 130, 132
  FBI and, 99, 129
  infiltrators/paid agents and, 134
  on Invaders, 65
  King and, 72, 109, 160(n60)
  on Lawson, 159(n36)
  leadership by, 73, 108–109, 113, 120,
    141
  Mule Train Caravan and, 97
  PPC and, 83–84, 101, 107, 108, 109
  press and, 116
  Resurrection City and, 112–113, 114,
    117, 119, 133, 136, 137
  SCLC and, 108–109
  Solidarity Day and, 125
  surveillance on, 125, 128
  threats against, 133
ADA, 18
Adams, John P., 105
AFDC. See Aid to Families with
  Dependent Children
Affirmative action, rejection of,
  144
AFL-CIO. See American Federation of
  Labor-Congress of Industrial
  Organizations
Afro-American Brotherhood, 46
AFSC. See American Friends Service
  Committee
AFSCME. See American Federation
  of State, County, and Municipal
  Employees

Agriculture Department
  campaign against, 130, 131, 132
  food stamps/child nutrition and,
    138
Aid to Families with Dependent
  Children (AFDC), 89
All-Christian Peace Assembly, Lawson
  at, 153(n40)
American Communist party (CPUSA)
  Levison and, 17
  W.E.B. DuBois Clubs of America
    and, 43
American Federation of Labor-
  Congress of Industrial
  Organizations
  (AFL-CIO), 33, 53
American Federation of State, County,
  and Municipal Employees
  (AFSCME), 41
  sanitation strike and, 33, 34, 36, 39
American Friends Service Committee
  (AFSC), 25
Antiwar movement, 12, 16, 19, 43
Arkin, Ely H., Jr., 40, 46, 51, 70, 76
  red squad and, 68, 71, 75
Armour, Claude A., 45, 80
Armour Center, training school at, 46
Army Security Agency (ASA), 124
Awsumb, Gwen, 36

Bailey, Walter "Bill," 81
Baptist Ministers Council, PPC and, 25
Belafonte, Harry, 84
Belafonte, Mrs. Harry, Mother's Day
  march and, 90
Bell, Ezekiel, 43
  strike and, 36–37

Printed in the United States
113203LV00004B/290/A